TALK ABOUT WRITING

Talk about Writing: The Tutoring Strategies of Experienced Writing Center Tutors offers a book-length empirical study of the discourse between experienced tutors and student writers in satisfactory conferences. The study uses a research-driven, iteratively tested framework to help writing center directors, tutors, writing program administrators, rhetoric and composition researchers, first-year composition instructors, and others interested in talk about writing to systematically analyze tutors' talk and to use that analysis to train new tutors.

The book strives toward two main goals: to provide an analytical research and assessment tool—the coding scheme—that other researchers can use to understand writing center tutor talk and to provide a close, empirical analysis of experienced tutor talk that can facilitate tutor training. The study details tutors' use of three categories of tutoring strategies—instruction, cognitive scaffolding, and motivational scaffolding—at macro- and microlevels and results in practical recommendations for improving tutor training.

Jo Mackiewicz is an associate professor of rhetoric and professional communication at Iowa State University.

Isabelle Kramer Thompson is emerita professor of technical and professional communication and former director of the writing center at Auburn University.

TALK ABOUT WRITING

The Tutoring Strategies of Experienced Writing Center Tutors

Jo Mackiewicz and
Isabelle Kramer Thompson

 Routledge
Taylor & Francis Group

NEW YORK AND LONDON

First published 2015
by Routledge
711 Third Avenue, New York, NY 10017

and by Routledge
2 Park Square, Milton Park, Abingdon, Oxon, OX14 4RN

Routledge is an imprint of the Taylor & Francis Group, an informa business

© 2015 Taylor & Francis

Library of Congress Cataloging in Publication Data
A catalog record has been requested for this book

ISBN: 978–1–138–78206–8 (hbk)
ISBN: 978–1–138–78207–5 (pbk)
ISBN: 978–1–315–76859–5 (ebk)

Typeset in Bembo
by Florence Production Ltd, Stoodleigh, Devon, UK

Printed and bound in the United States of America by Publishers Graphics,
LLC on sustainably sourced paper.

CONTENTS

ACKNOWLEDGMENTS

From Both of Us

Even before we started to develop this book, we received support from our friends/colleagues, as they read and commented upon the articles that preceded the project. For their help and encouragement, we thank Kevin Roozen, Derek Ross, Trish Serviss, Michelle Sidler, Stewart Whittemore, Chad Wickman, and Susan Youngblood. We also thank Anna Gramberg, former dean of the College of Liberal Arts, who supported Jo Mackiewicz with a summer research grant in 2013. Thank you to Linda Bathgate at Routledge, who kindly helped us through, from proposal to printing. Thank you to Melissa Flowers Shaddix, Robyn Weaver Wilborn, and Joel Kobzeff, who helped us code tutoring strategies. And, finally, thank you to the tutors and student writers who participated in the project.

From Isabelle Kramer Thompson

First, I would like to thank all of the tutors who worked in the writing center under my direction. I learned a lot from them all and totally enjoyed the 17-year learning process.

Second, thank you to my smart sister and my kind son, who let me brag about him so that I wouldn't bore my friends by talking endlessly about this book.

Finally, most importantly, I want to thank Jo Mackiewicz, who has made my early retirement very interesting and who, during the writing process for this book, never once told me to hurry up. She has led me to the best research of my career.

From Jo Mackiewicz

First, a big thank you to the ladies on the morning shift at Panera Bread in Auburn, Alabama, who provided me with fuel (coffee) to work on the book: Mary Westfall, Jen Dorman, and Adrianna Tapscott.

Thank you Linda Christensen, Andrea Nelson, and Linda Shook, for providing needed diversion in the way of road biking, running, and chatting. Thanks also to my wonderful friend Barb Wild, for swim and support and M (Michael Sharman) for everything.

Thank you to my mentor, Tony Bukoski, for years of encouragement and conversation.

Thank you to my coauthor, Isabelle Thompson, for her friendship and her endless patience with me. Every day, working with her is a joy.

Finally, I dedicate my work on this book to my family. Thank you to my mom and dad, Sherry Mackiewicz and Joe Mackiewicz, whose care—particularly in the summer of 2013—helped me find confidence and peace to research and write. Thanks also to my most amazing sister, Lisa Hughes, for listening to me go on and on about work and all else and for inspiring me to be a better person.

PREFACE

In *Talk about Writing: The Tutoring Strategies of Experienced Writing Center Tutors* (*TAW*), we respond to a relative lack of empirical research on the one-to-one discourse that unfolds during writing center conferences. That little research on tutor–student writer discourse exists is somewhat surprising, given the ubiquity of writing centers across the United States and Canada and, increasingly, in Europe, the Middle East, and Asia as well. Many two- and four-year colleges, universities, and, more and more, secondary schools as well see the value in supporting spaces where student writers (and often other writers, such as faculty and staff) can meet one-to-one with a trained writing tutor. But what actually goes on in tutor–student writer conferences? What do experienced writing center tutors say in order to help student writers? *TAW* answers this question in part by examining tutors' talk—their tutoring strategies—in satisfactory conferences with student writers.

Our empirical study of experienced tutors' strategies employs quantitative and qualitative analysis. We developed, iteratively tested, and used a 16-code scheme to identify and subsequently analyze tutoring strategies that fell into three categories: instruction, cognitive scaffolding, and motivational scaffolding. We have two main goals for our analysis: (1) to describe and exemplify the coding scheme so that others can use it to analyze writing center tutors' talk (a goal that promotes replicability in writing center research) and (2) to empirically analyze experienced tutors' talk in order to facilitate tutor training.

Given these goals for *TAW*, our book will likely most interest and benefit writing center directors and tutors, but it will also be useful to others concerned with one-to-one talk about writing, especially rhetoric and composition researchers and students (particularly graduate students), writing program administrators, and first-year composition and world literature instructors. Because *TAW* includes a rich case study of an experienced tutor (turned writing fellow) working with one undergraduate business student, at two points during a semester in a purchasing (business) course, a second audience includes business communication researchers, instructors, writing fellows, and writing tutors. It also includes writing-across-the-curriculum and writing-in-the-disciplines administrators, as well as other administrators who have an interest in writing tutoring, perhaps because of Association to Advance Collegiate Schools of Business (and other) accreditation requirements for communication-related learning outcomes. In addition, because we discuss in detail our development, testing, and application of the coding scheme, *TAW* may interest researchers in applied linguistics and education who analyze natural-language data.

We begin in Chapter 2 by reviewing theoretical and practical discussions of scaffolding and the zone of proximal development. This constructivist research, along with prior studies of tutoring and teaching and writing center discourse, reflects our views about the learning process and has influenced our development of our coding scheme. After explaining our methods (Chapter 3), we apply the coding scheme to the 10 satisfactory conferences. In Chapters 4–7, we analyze those conferences at the macrolevel—in conference opening stages, teaching stages (including the chain of topic episodes that comprise the teaching stage), and closing stages—in order to determine the role that tutoring strategies play at a global level. We also analyze conferences at the microlevel—the utterance level—to discuss the role of tutoring strategies in the moment-to-moment progression of conferences. Chapter 4 holistically describes findings about all three categories of tutoring strategies. Chapters 5–7 focus on the three categories of tutoring strategies individually, using quantitative and qualitative analysis to examine instruction strategies (Chapter 5), cognitive scaffolding strategies (Chapter 6), and motivational scaffolding strategies (Chapter 7). Finally, in Chapter 8, we switch gears to present a case study. We analyze four conferences, conducted by one individual working in two pedagogical situations: as an undergraduate tutor in a writing center, tutoring a variety of different students from first-year composition and world literature courses and, later, as a graduate student working as a writing fellow in a writing-in-the-disciplines program. To conclude, we discuss our main findings and the implications of those findings for tutor training in relation to each of the three categories of tutoring strategies, and we explore some possibilities for future research on writing center tutors' talk.

Writing studies research has largely overlooked *TAW*'s subject matter, even though many claims about the efficacy of writing centers hinge on the nature of the talk that takes place during conferences. As the only book-length empirical study about writing center tutors' talk, *TAW* helps close this gap in writing center research, even as it provides a tool—the coding scheme—that other researchers can subsequently use to further this scholarly effort.

Jo Mackiewicz and Isabelle Kramer Thompson

1

TALK ABOUT WRITING

An Introduction to Our Empirical Study

Reflecting back on the importance of Davis et al.'s (1988) article, "The Function of Talk in the Writing Conference: A Study of Tutorial Conversation," 18 years after its publication, Pemberton (2010) laments that, in the interim, "a few writing center researchers . . . have analyzed transcripts of tutor–student conversations . . . but the number and frequency of such studies are too few and too far between, I believe" (24). We strongly agree with Pemberton that writing center researchers have barely begun the much-needed systematic, empirical analysis of the ways writing center tutors talk to student writers during writing conferences. Given that writing center practice critically hinges on one-to-one talk, we too find it odd that so few studies, particularly ones employing quantitative analysis, have found their way into publication. Indeed, Pemberton goes on to say that, as researchers of writing, we need to use "every technique in our methodological tool kit" to study writing center praxis and pedagogy (24). The main benefits of employing quantitative as well as qualitative techniques lie in implications for tutor training, and considering such implications certainly is one of our goals for this book, *Talk about Writing: The Tutoring Strategies of Experienced Writing Center Tutors* (*TAW*). In this book, we present a theory- and research-driven, recursively tested scheme for analyzing talk in writing center conferences and use that scheme to analyze the tutoring strategies that experienced tutors used in conferences with student writers.

Our Goals for *Talk about Writing*

We have two main goals for *TAW*: (1) to present an analytical research tool that others outside our locality can use to examine writing center talk, specifically writing center tutors' talk, and (2) to provide a close, empirical analysis of experienced tutor talk that can facilitate tutor training.

Toward accomplishing the first goal, we explain the theory, research, and iterative testing that contributed to the analytical tool—the coding scheme—that we present. And throughout *TAW*, we exemplify the detailed coding scheme so that other writing center researchers working on their own discourse data can readily employ it themselves. Toward accomplishing our second goal, we argue that a close, empirical analysis of experienced tutor talk can facilitate tutor training. What tutors say has been found to make a difference in students' learning. Take, for example, Chi, VanLehn, and Litman's (2010) study of tutors' "microlevel" decisions. They found that microlevel decisions such as asking a student for justification (or not) had a significant impact on students' learning outcomes. But, more important, they point out that, "the fine-grained interaction (microsteps) of human tutoring are a potential source of pedagogical power, but human tutors may not be particularly skilled at choosing the right microsteps" (233). In other words, tutoring strategies that can make a difference in students' learning do not necessarily come naturally.

For the analysis that composes the majority of *TAW* (Chapters 4–7), we selected arguably the 10 best writing center conferences from our corpus of 51 conferences. The tutors and student writers who participated in these 10 conferences evaluated them as highly satisfactory (five or six on a six-point scale). Our analysis of these conferences is detailed, examining both macrolevel and microlevel conference features and reporting quantitative and qualitative data. In Chapter 8, we focus on one of the 10 tutors (T9). We examine four of her conferences: one is a first-time meeting with a student writer, a conference that we also examine in Chapters 4–7. To that conference, we add three more: one, a writing center conference with a repeat student visitor, and two with a student writer whom T9 tutored as a writing fellow in a writing-in-the-disciplines (WID) program. Comparing T9's talk in these four conferences allowed us to consider effects of tutoring familiar versus unfamiliar student writers and tutoring as a writing center tutor versus as a writing fellow embedded in a particular class.

We acknowledge that some might question why they should invest time and energy into picking apart and digging into the details of writing center discourse. Indeed, we realize that most who administer writing centers develop an innate sense of the kinds of talk that facilitate satisfactory conferences, a sense that comes from hundreds of hours enveloped in the rhythms of tutoring discourse. In *TAW*, we try to show how a research-driven framework can help even experienced directors and tutors systematically analyze tutors' talk and use that analysis to train new tutors.

Our Theoretical Framework and Coding Scheme for Analyzing Tutor Talk

In *TAW*, we describe and employ a framework for quantitative and qualitative analysis of writing center talk at the macro- and microlevels. We developed our coding scheme from research and theory derived from tutoring and teaching in areas other than writing. Research about scaffolding, led by Wood, Bruner, and Ross's 1976 study (where the term "scaffolding" originated) and informed by Vygotsky's definition of the zone of proximal development (ZPD) (1978, 1987), provides the primary theoretical framework for our study. This groundbreaking research portrays learning as developing from a collaborative, context-dependent relationship between a student (a less expert member of a community) and a teacher or tutor (a more expert member of a community). The process of teaching begins with what the student currently knows or can do and moves forward toward mastery, the tutor's support decreasing until the student can perform the task independently. Adapted to writing center conferencing, this cultural psychological or social constructivist theory of learning requires the following:

- Tutors are more knowledgeable about writing than students.
- Tutors understand how people learn, particularly in terms of writing performance.
- Tutors know how to work collaboratively with student writers by building rapport and trust, and they encourage student writers' active participation in conferences.
- Tutors know how to diagnose what a student writer currently knows and how to determine when a student writer is floundering.
- Tutors know how to help students achieve their practical goals and, at the same time, increase their writing competence.
- Although student writers dominate agenda setting, tutors try to ensure that the conference achieves that agenda, and, therefore, tutors typically control most of the topics introduced.

Because of the complexity of writing, student writers will not likely improve their writing competence much in a single conference. However, with tutors' support, they can gain answers to the questions that brought them to the writing center (unless they came to please a teacher) and possibly newly consider their writing practice, so that their writing competence continues to evolve. Further, when tutors help student writers set goals to pursue later, postconference, the teaching process can continue after the conference ends.

Macrolevel Analysis

Mehan's (1979) observations of teaching in an elementary school classroom influenced our coding at the macrolevel. Mehan, along with later researchers such as Nassaji and Wells (2000), discusses a three-part (*not* a three-step or three-turn) sequence beginning with initiation, a teacher's question, possibly revised and restated several times until students can respond appropriately. Responses from students follow. Finally, the teacher's feedback (or follow up) addresses students' responses, and this feedback often does more than simply evaluate students' responses for correctness. In his work, published shortly after Wood, Bruner, and Ross introduced scaffolding and a little before Vygotsky became well known in the United States, Mehan does not reference Bruner or Vygotsky. Finally, socio-cognitive research about motivation (Bandura 1997), politeness research (Brown and Levinson 1987), and other linguistic research also inform our theoretical framework.

At the macrolevel, we identified three conference stages—opening, teaching, and closing. Tutor training manuals (for example, Gillespie and Lerner 2008; Ryan and Zimmerelli 2010) often discuss the opening and closing stages, and we derived our definitions from those sources, as well as from discussions of tutoring in other contexts. The teaching stage comprises a chain of topic episodes, defined as talk focused on a single topic. In examining topic episodes, we consider who begins them, how they begin, and, if more than one turn occurs, how the dialogue is sequenced. This macrolevel analysis in the teaching stage allows us to examine conference control, as well as sequences of individual tutoring strategies.

Microlevel Analysis

Research about tutoring in math (Putnam 1987) and science (Chi 1996), both problem-solving disciplines, influenced our coding at the microlevel. Such research aims to identify the strategies of expert tutors in order to develop effective instructional software. We based our coding scheme on the one that Cromley and Azevedo (2005) developed to examine one-to-one adult literacy instruction, specifically, tutors' strategies to teach decoding. Cromley and Azevedo, in turn, based their scheme on prior studies examining tutor discourse "moves" (a unit of discourse serving a communicative function) associated with student learning (for example, Juel 1996; Pinnell et al. 1994). Like those in problem-solving tasks for math and science, the tasks in decoding are often well defined, and mistakes are often easy to identify. The tutor discourse moves that Cromley and Azevedo found in literacy tutoring corresponded with those revealed in studies of tutoring in problem-solving disciplines, leading the researchers to conclude that the moves they coded are "powerful teaching strategies" (2005, 91). We chose to develop our framework from one specifically designed for fine-grained analysis of tutors' discourse, one built on previous research about expert tutoring, and one comprising tutoring moves associated with learning.

At the microlevel, we examine in detail three categories of tutoring strategies—instruction, cognitive scaffolding, and motivational scaffolding. These three categories contain a total of 16 individual tutoring strategies. Instruction refers to the directive aspects of teaching and tutoring—supplying solutions or options, rather than supporting or making room for student writers to generate solutions themselves. The category comprises three codes: telling, suggesting, and explaining. Although they share the same directive goal, telling and suggesting differ in tutors' use of mitigation to soften their directiveness. In telling, tutors do not mitigate their directiveness: "Before you turn in your essay, be sure to proofread it." In suggesting, tutors mitigate their directiveness: "So what you might do, then, is go back to that topic sentence and think about how this topic sentence can kind of forecast what's about to come in the paragraph." Explanations may accompany telling and suggesting, aiding implementation and perhaps justifying advice. Instruction strategies do not probe student writers' thinking but rather tell, suggest, or explain what to do. We examine instruction strategies in depth in Chapter 5.

Defined generally, scaffolding metaphorically refers to teaching a student to determine an answer to a question, to correct an error, or to perform a task, without telling the student the answer or doing the work for him or her. All cognitive scaffolding strategies require students, as polite conversationalists, to engage in dialogue of some sort with tutors. In an ideal writing center conference, the dialogue of cognitive scaffolding allows the tutor to assess the student writer's level of understanding and then adapt his or her next moves according to what the student writer already knows. Cognitive scaffolding includes a range of strategies that prod students to think and then help them to push their thinking further. For example, a tutor might ask a pumping question such as this: "Since um, smoking is already banned in you know, some restaurants, or um, whatever, uh, would you say anything that Hollywood should do as far as smoking?" Eight tutoring strategies composed our cognitive scaffolding category: pumping, reading aloud, responding as a reader or a listener, referring to a previous topic, forcing a choice, and three strategies that rarely appeared in our corpus—prompting, hinting, and demonstrating. We examine cognitive scaffolding closely in Chapter 6.

Motivational scaffolding strategies focus on student writers' affect. These strategies provide encouragement through praise, assurances of caring, and statements reinforcing student writers' ownership of their writing. They assist tutors in building rapport, solidarity, and trust during conferences, helping to construct a safe space that encourages student writers' active participation. Thus, talk attending to student writers' motivation is critically important, as it can direct attention toward particular tasks and increase effort and persistence, thereby likely leading to improved performance. We coded five motivational scaffolding strategies: showing concern, praising, reinforcing student writers' ownership and control, being optimistic or using humor, and giving sympathy or empathy. We examine motivational scaffolding in depth in Chapter 7.

The coding scheme that we developed allows us first to describe and analyze writing center conferences according to stages, so that we can look closely at how conferences begin and end and how progress toward achieving goals set in an agenda occurs (in chains of topic episodes). Then we shift to individual tutoring strategies, so that we can analyze how tutoring gives student writers direction (through instruction), helps them progress in their thinking (through cognitive scaffolding), and encourages them to continue their efforts (through motivational scaffolding).

Two Examples

Using this framework and employing both quantitative and qualitative analysis, we move beyond general, ad hoc descriptions of tutor talk. To illustrate, consider for a moment the following turn at talk from a tutor (T2) working with a student writer (S2) on an essay for her first-year composition (FYC) class. In this conference, T2 and S2 discussed a paper that describes two important changes in the student's life—but the assignment requires students to focus only on one change. T2 suggested choosing one life-changing experience and then exploring that change and its repercussions through the entire paper. Without a detailed, tested scheme for analysis, observers of this conference would be able to say that, in the comment below, T2 delivered a criticism ("a little unfocused"), gave advice based on what she would do, and asked a question about S2's preference for revising:

T2: And I think that talking about those transitions [changes in S2's life] is making your paper seem a little unfocused. And so I think what I would think about is which of these you would like to focus on. Do you want to focus on what you learned from this change, or do you want to focus on what you learned from that change?

Our coding scheme pushes these analyses further. With a theory- and research-based scheme for analyzing tutors' talk, observers can dissect the ways in which experienced tutors such as T2 employed strategies. For example, they can examine T2's advice more closely to identify it as suggesting rather than telling, the latter of which conveys more obligation to comply: "And so I think what I would think about is which of these you would like to focus on." Further, they can categorize the question that follows the suggestion as one that helps S2 determine the focus of her essay by forcing her to choose between two alternatives: "Do you want to focus on what you learned from this change, or do you want to focus on what you learned from that change?" Observers can also count the frequency with which tutors used certain microlevel tutoring strategies and identify patterns and clusters of their use. With a theory- and research-based, tested scheme, others can replicate our work and, more importantly, reuse the scheme on their own data, hence broadening implications of the research beyond the local.

The next excerpt comes from a conference in which the student writer (S1) and tutor (T1) discussed a paper intended to make a claim about a space, in this case, the university library, and to support that claim with observational details and explanation of those details. S1 chose to argue that the library is a calm, relaxing space and, at the start of the excerpt, was working on coherence as a means for focusing in on his claim. In the opening stage of the conference, S1 began the agenda setting with the common request for grammar help, as well as a request for help with making the paragraphs "flow." In her postconference interview, T1 said that, by the time she got to the end of the first paragraph, she realized that S1 needed help with more than grammar. So, she said, she "helped with grammar, but also looked for larger concerns."

The excerpt contains two topic episodes, topic episode (TE)22 and TE26; in these topic episodes, then, T1 and S1 were well into the conference. Based on the position of the topic episodes in the chain of episodes that composes the teaching stage of the conference, we would expect that T1 and S1 have developed rapport, and the relaxed quality of the dialogue and S1's active participation support that prediction. S1 relies on T1's expertise and support, as is shown by his introduction of TE26.

As it stood, S1's paper took the reader from space to space, room to room, spatially throughout the library, starting at the entryway. T1 and S1 read through some of the paper together. As they did, T1 identified a spot between paragraphs that needed transition. At the start of TE22, T1 had identified yet another point between paragraphs that needed transition. She began with cognitive scaffolding— specifically, a pumping question ("And then what are you doing in this paragraph here?")—to get S1 talking about a paragraph's topic, so that he could determine the paragraph's connection to the one that preceded it:

T1: And then what are you doing in this paragraph here?
S1: This one is the paragraph noticing the weird coffee lounge.
T1: O.K.
S1: And I think my goal with this one is to point out that the atmosphere is down here totally different from the one upstairs, where I like to study.
T1: Right.
S1: So—
T1: Are you—What I would suggest is looking at each sentence in [here, each
S1:   [Uh-huh
T1: detail you provide and making sure that relates. That—that you're showing the contrast.
S1: O.K.
T1: So, some of the sentences do that better than [other sentences
S1:   [O.K. But some of them might not even need to be there.

S1 responded by articulating his goal for that paragraph: to point out that the atmosphere downstairs is completely different from the more relaxing atmosphere upstairs. After agreeing, T1, using instruction, suggested that S1 carefully consider each sentence he had written so far, presumably so he could edit out those that lacked relevance. Some sentences, T1 pointed out, did not support the contrast of the coffee shop with his preferred spots for studying in the library. The sequence of turns in TE22 is as follows: T1 initiates (I) with a pump question; S1 responds (R); T1 evaluates the response as appropriate and adds instruction as a follow up (F); S1 responds again, accepting S1's advice (R).

A little later, S1 introduced TE26. He had noticed that some sentences—ones about the coffee shop's décor—did not connect to his claim (at least, not at this point). T1 agreed that the sentences did not relate to S1's thesis. S1 pointed to a single sentence, and T1 read the sentence aloud (a cognitive scaffolding strategy). Then, she suggested some editing and refocusing to make a transition.

S1: Um. This—these last sentences don't necessarily relate to the atmosphere. But—

T1: Right.

S1: I don't know.

T1: I think you're correct.

S1: I don't even really see that this, now that I look at it, needs to be there. But it's, um—

T1: Well you say here, this—It's not a—it's not a very appealing area. [Reading aloud.] "I wouldn't consider myself be an interior designer, but even so this place is bad." Maybe instead of taking this last sentence here that talks about, you know, the décor, [and you are not appreciating the décor. "I don't find

S1:   [Yeah.

T1: this a very appealing area." And then you could just provide us a sentence about, "O.K. I decided to go back upstairs."

S1: Yeah.

T1: And then, that's enough of a transition so that this [would not be necessary.

S1:   [I don't need a whole paragraph. O.K. So I'm just going to get rid of this one.

After T1 suggested a transition sentence, a sentence that explicitly maps his movement through the library, S1 accepted the tutor's suggestion to delete other, unnecessary details.

TE26 then continued with T1 further explaining her instruction, but at this point she used motivational scaffolding, praise, to soften her suggestion that he delete sentences:

T1: [It's—I like that you're doing transitions between the paragraphs, but

S1: [It's great design—

T1: sometimes like, I think it's important here for an entire paragraph. But maybe here we just need a sentence.
S1: O.K. So I'm just going to get rid of this   [and replace it with a transitional
T1:   [O.K.
S1: sentence. [Let me see the other paragraph—
T1:   [Right. Does that make sense?
S1: Yeah. And this—this is possible to, uh—

T1 used the motivational scaffolding strategy of showing concern when she asked S1 if he understood her suggestion: "Does that make sense?" He clearly did, and, in the end, S1 accepted T1's suggested solution. The problem that led S1 to introduce TE26 appeared to be solved, and S1 likely learned something about revision.

We present these excerpts and our brief analyses early on to give a sense of the benefits of empirically, systematically, and exactly analyzing tutor talk. Through careful coding with a tested scheme, we can identify the strategies that tutors used alone, paired, and in strings, as they co-constructed satisfactory conferences with students. In the excerpt above, for example, T1 read S1's words back to him ("I wouldn't consider myself be an interior designer, but even so this place is bad."), a cognitive scaffolding strategy that reminded the student of what he had written, gave him an opportunity to hear how someone else interpreted his words, and gave him time to think about the extent to which his words actually conveyed his intended meaning and his purpose. T1 paired that strategy with a suggestion for writing a sentence ("And then you could just provide us a sentence about, 'O.K. I decided to go back upstairs.'"), one that conveys his movement through the library from one space to another, without belaboring an explanation about the coffee shop's décor.

An Overview of *TAW*: Chapters and Contribution

As we mentioned above, in *TAW*, we aim to carry out two main objectives:

- to provide a framework, a coding scheme, that others can use to analyze and to understand writing center tutors' talk; and
- to use the theory- and research-driven framework to analyze experienced tutors' talk in satisfactory conferences in order to consider ways to improve current tutor-training practices.

We attempt to carry out these goals throughout the chapters that make up *TAW*.

In Chapter 2, we discuss Wood, Bruner, and Ross's (1976) notion of scaffolding and Vygotsky's definition of the ZPD (1978, 1987), and more contemporary treatments of each. We also discuss Mehan's (1979) research and research in linguistics that informed our definition of topic episodes. Then we examine prior research on instruction, cognitive scaffolding, and motivational scaffolding in detail in order to situate our own study. In doing so, we review research on one-to-one tutoring in problem-solving domains, as well as writing center research.

We not only explain the development and iterative testing of our coding scheme in Chapter 3, but we also widen our scope to discuss some of the challenges of coding natural-language data for writing studies research. We describe our research methods, discussing our decision making as we formulated codes and categories, tested those codes through iterations of testing, assessed inter-rater reliability, and came to consensus. We also argue for more transparent coding practices and more detailed reporting in scholarly publications.

In our Chapter 4, we provide a quantitative overview of the 10 satisfactory writing center conferences. We begin by looking closely at the opening, teaching, and closing stages of the conferences and provide quantitative data about topic episodes. Then we move to a quantitative analysis of the three categories of tutoring strategies.

In Chapter 5, we use quantitative and qualitative analysis to closely examine experienced tutors' instruction strategies. Specifically, we examine how tutors use telling strategies to show engagement. We also examine how tutors use suggestions to convey politeness and to convey the optionality of their advice, such as when a student writer could address an issue in multiple—though all potentially effective—ways. Finally, we examine how tutors used instruction in conference closings.

In Chapter 6, we examine tutors' cognitive scaffolding strategies, again employing both quantitative and qualitative analysis. We examine how tutors use pumping strategies to guide student writers' thinking and to generate responses (and thus more active participation) from them. We discuss how pumps make room for student writers to think out loud and take some control over the direction of the conversation. We examine tutors' use of the reading-aloud strategy, showing how tutors used it with discretion to focus a student writer's attention on a particular section or line of text. We also examine how tutors responded as readers or listeners, paraphrasing student writers' words and conveying their understanding and engagement. We finish by looking at how tutors used cognitive scaffolding strategies in conference closings.

In Chapter 7, we focus our quantitative and qualitative analysis on motivational scaffolding strategies. We show how, much of the time, tutors' demonstrations of concern and their praise—the two most common motivational scaffolds—follow semantic and syntactic formulae. We discuss their use of motivational scaffolds in conference opening and closing stages, paying particular attention to tutors' salient use of demonstrations of concern in the conference closings to signal that they must soon finish up the conference.

In Chapter 8, we provide a unique analysis: we compare the strategies that one tutor, T9, used when she worked as a tutor in the writing center and later when she worked as a writing fellow in a WID program. We also compare the strategies that she used when she tutored familiar and unfamiliar student writers. We discuss the differences in the frequencies and types of the strategies that she used. For example, among other differences, T9 employed more demonstrations of concern in conferences with unfamiliar student writers; she followed up on her advice—her telling and suggesting—with questions aimed at checking the student writer's comprehension.

In Chapter 9, we return to our two main goals for *TAW*: to present a framework—our coding scheme—that others can use to analyze and understand their own discourse data and to present an empirical analysis of experienced tutors' talk that can facilitate tutor training. We tie together our analysis of tutors' talk in the writing center that we studied—the macrolevel analysis of opening and closing stages, the macrolevel analysis of the chains of topic episodes that constitute teaching stages, and the microlevel analysis of the ways that tutors used and integrated the three categories of strategies as they co-constructed satisfactory conferences with student writers. We also use our findings to consider current tutor-training practices and discuss how writing center directors and others who work with new tutors might use our findings to improve the tutor training that they provide.

Throughout the chapters summarized above, *TAW* contributes to the field in that it does the following:

- demonstrates a coding scheme for analyzing writing center talk at the macrolevel and the microlevel;
- empirically studies the strategies that experienced tutors used in 10 satisfactory conferences and considers the ways such analysis can help in reexamining and improving tutor training;
- uniquely compares the tutoring strategies of one experienced tutor working with unfamiliar and familiar student writers in the writing center and in a college of business WID program (as a writing fellow in a purchasing class);
- uses the opportunity of reporting research methods in Chapter 3 to discuss challenges in coding practices and, thus, to help other researchers as they carry out similar work, as well as to report on our own methods.

A Final Thought before We Begin

In their conclusion to *A Synthesis of Qualitative Studies of Writing Center Tutoring, 1983–2006*, Babcock, Manning, and Rogers (2012) write, "Where research must move in the future is toward articulating new methods of tutoring that use complementary features from the ways of the old grammarians and the techniques of writing teachers who want their students to focus on self-expression" (123). Understanding how experienced tutors achieve this "middle way" on a moment-to-moment basis as they meet student writers' expectations and adhere to writing center policies demands, we believe, systematic and empirical analysis of their discourse. In *TAW*, we provide a tested framework that others can use to examine the building blocks of successful conferences and analysis using that framework that undergirds our recommendations for tutor training. In trying to achieve our goals for *TAW*, we hope that we, in the words of Babcock, Manning, and Rogers, "begin to reach toward a more definitive understanding of what occurs in writing center tutorial sessions" (124).

2

LITERATURE REVIEW

- The Macrolevel: Conference Stages and Topic Episodes
- Scaffolding and the Zone of Proximal Development
- Operationalizing Scaffolding and the ZPD
- Conclusion

According to fairly well-known research in cultural psychology (Bruner 1996), learning occurs incrementally as students, with the assistance of more expert collaborators, move from what they currently know to what they are able to understand at that moment. This process continues as students move toward mastery, which, in the case of writing, never happens. This view of learning from cultural psychology, embraced also by adherents to social constructivism, seems particularly appropriate for writing center tutoring, with its opportunity to individualize teaching and its emphasis on collaboration. In this chapter, we discuss the theoretical framework that informs our study. We review learning theory associated with cultural psychology, but we also discuss research informing the development of our coding scheme, for example, linguistic analyses examining everyday conversation, large-scale studies from education describing teacher behavior during lessons, and research about tutoring in math and science. We pull together ideas from divergent sources to coherently explain the theory behind our arguments in *TAW*.

We begin by reviewing research that informed our macrolevel coding and analysis of conference stages and topic episodes within the teaching stage. Then, we discuss the theories of teaching and learning that led to and informed our microlevel analysis of tutoring strategies and, a little less directly, our macrolevel analysis as well. We review Bruner and his associates' discussions of scaffolding and make connections with Vygotsky's ZPD. Afterwards, we discuss how

Cromley and Azevedo (2005), in their study of adult literacy tutoring, operationalized the three categories of tutoring strategies that we examine—instruction, cognitive scaffolding, and motivational scaffolding. As we point out, we augmented Cromley and Azevedo's definitions of the three categories by drawing upon research about politeness and motivation, as well as research about writing center tutoring. We describe in detail each tutoring strategy within each of the three categories.

The Macrolevel: Conference Stages and Topic Episodes

In this section, we discuss prior research with relevance to our macrolevel analysis—our analysis of the ways tutoring strategies compose and operate within the more global analytical units of conference stage, topic-episode chain, and topic episode.

Conference Stages

We examined tutoring strategies within three stages of writing center conferences: stage 1, the opening stage; stage 2, the teaching stage (also called the tutor-assistance stage); and stage 3, the closing stage. Although we agree with Thonus (1999a, 1999b, 2002) that writing center tutoring is institutional discourse, the stages of conferences she adapted from Agar's (1985) phases of diagnosis, directive, and report writing seem, in their language, to restrict analysis of tutors' discourse, not fully capturing the variety of discourse moves that tutors make. The analytical limitations of Agar's framework factored into our decision to develop our macrolevel framework based on current discussions of writing center conferences in tutor training materials and on research about tutoring in other disciplines (for example, Fox 1993).

In "The Concept of the Writing Center," a statement that the National Council of the Teaching of English originally published and that the International Writing Centers Association maintains on its website, the opening stage, often called the agenda-setting stage, is that period of time at the beginning of a conference during which the tutor and the student writer collaborate to determine the student writer's needs and the focus for the conference (Harris [1988] 2006). During the opening stage, tutors welcome student writers to the writing center, introduce themselves, begin developing rapport, and collaboratively set an agenda. Describing tutoring with undergraduates in science, computer science, and math courses, Fox (1993) refers to agenda setting as a negotiation that begins with the student's input on how to focus the conference. Then, the agenda-setting process moves, if necessary, to the tutor's suggestions for modifying the student's suggested focus and concludes, finally, with the student's agreement or disagreement with those suggested modifications and, perhaps, with further modifications (35). These negotiations can end with the student's first input, or they can continue with even further modifications. To aid in agenda setting, writing center researchers suggest that tutors pose questions to determine when the paper is due, what constraints on the paper the instructor has imposed, what comments, if any, the instructor has already provided for the draft, and how much time the student writer will invest in writing or revising (Gillespie and Lerner 2008; Ryan and Zimmerelli 2010). Hence, from the opening stage of a writing center conference, tutors assume the roles of discourse facilitators and conference managers, in addition to their role of writing experts.

As Henning (2001) points out, negotiating an agenda that meets the student writer's expectations critically contributes to the student writer's perception of the conference's success, and neglecting to negotiate the agenda can lead to a conference that fails to meet the student writer's expectations. As Sloan (2013) explains, "Students and tutors often enter a tutorial with drastically different priorities"; thus, "they rarely view 'need' in the same way" (para. 3). In addition, the agenda often changes as the conference proceeds and as the tutor and the student writer identify more serious problems in the draft. In some cases, they can move from revising sentences back to brainstorming content. In sum, the opening stage prepares tutors to make the diagnoses necessary to achieve student writers' goals and to begin collaborations that will produce good writing outcomes.

Stage 2, what Fox calls the "tutor assistance" stage (52) and what we call the teaching stage, was by far the longest stage in the conferences that we examined. In the teaching stage, tutors and student writers work together to achieve the goals set forth in the agenda. Tutors want to ensure that student writers get their questions answered and to prepare them to move forward with their writing assignments when they leave the writing center. The teaching stage consists of a chain of topic episodes. We describe topic episodes in detail below and discuss the sequences that compose them and their connection in chains across the teaching stage.

Stage 3, the closing stage, ends conferences. In this stage, the tutor and the student determine whether they have met the goals for which they set the agenda. As Fox (1993) points out, completing the agenda does not mean that the student is now an expert or even that he or she can independently perform the tasks practiced during the conference (85). Students' achievement depends on the particular agenda and on their capabilities at a particular time. Tutoring guidebooks for writing centers recommend that, before student writers leave, tutors ask whether they have any further questions, help them summarize what they have accomplished during the conference, set goals for the next steps in the writing process, and, if warranted, make an appointment for a future conference (Gillespie and Lerner 2008; Murphy and Sherwood 2011; Ryan and Zimmerelli 2010).

As a last step in their conferencing work and in keeping with their institutional representative role (Agar 1985), writing center tutors often write up reports of their work. The tutors in our study wrote up a short report for each student writer's instructor. Although these reports became part of the writing center's records, their writing was not included in our recorded conferences.

Topic Episodes

To identify and analyze topic episodes within the teaching stage, we adapted definitions and descriptions used in research about educational discourse and multiparty conversations. The studies we drew from included analyses of oral responses during work with instructional software (Johnson et al. 2003) and using the help function on computers (Novick, Andrade, and Bean 2009). In these studies, an episode consists of a single turn or a string of turns focused on a single topic. Analyzing multiparty conversation, Korolija and Linell (1996) clarify the concept of the topic episode further. In their research, "episodes" consist of "boundaried" sequences at a structurally intermediate level: they lie above the utterance and turn levels but below the "major phases" of the interaction (for example, stages) and the whole of the interaction (799). Chafe's (2001) clear definition influenced our coding as well; he defines a topic as a "coherent aggregate of thoughts introduced by some participant in conversation, developed either by that participant or another or by several participants jointly, and then either explicitly closed or allowed to peter out" (674). Topic episodes, then, are monologic or dialogic strings of conversation that coherently address one subject. They can consist of a single turn or a string of turns. They can also begin and end within a single turn, as when a tutor or student finishes with one topic and, without ceding the conversational floor, moves immediately to another. Finally, even though (like other researchers) we identified topic episodes by content, we verified our coding by attending to discourse markers (for example, "O.K." and "now") that often signaled the beginnings and endings of topic episodes. (See Chapter 4 for further explanation of discourse markers.)

To help identify and understand topic episodes, we also analyzed the sequences of collaborative exchange that comprise them. We looked to classroom research on turn taking in lessons. Mehan (1979) explains that, in what he calls the "instructional phase" of a classroom lesson (36), instructor–student dialogue tends to proceed in a three-part sequence of initiation, response, and evaluation (IRE). In most instances, an instructor initiates the sequence, often with a pump question; the student responds; and the instructor evaluates the student's response. Mehan points out that sequences can be elaborated when students cannot respond to teachers' questions, and his three-part sequence is not necessarily confined to three steps.

According to Mehan (1979), when evaluating, the instructor aims for "the cooperative completion of an activity by the participants involved" (63). Positive evaluation indicates that a student has provided a "mutually acceptable reply," and the sequence ends (64). If the student provides an incorrect or incomplete answer (or cannot respond at all), the sequence continues until the instructor and student establish "symmetry between initiation and reply acts" (65). In a later study, Nassaji and Wells (2000) expand the idea of an evaluation discourse step into what they call follow up (F)—also called feedback. They identify four follow-up choices: (1) accept or reject students' responses; (2) evaluate students' responses; (3) comment on, exemplify, expand, and justify students' responses; (4) ask another question. In our analyses, we use Nassaji and Wells's (2000) idea of feedback/follow up rather than evaluation.

Finally, we also analyzed the chain of topic episodes that comprised a conference's teaching stage. Through such analysis, we could see the extent to which the topic episodes revealed a straightforward, linear progression chronologically through the teaching stage and the extent to which they revealed an indirect, circuitous progression—particularly when the negotiated conference agenda did not supply the assistance the student writer needed.

In conclusion, at the macrolevel, we identified and analyzed the opening, teaching, and closing conference stages. We also identified and analyzed topic episodes within the teaching stages, attending in particular to sequences of tutoring strategies and student writers' responses.

Scaffolding and the Zone of Proximal Development

A term first used in Wood, Bruner, and Ross's 1976 article, "The Role of Tutoring in Problem Solving," scaffolding is a metaphor for an instruction process in which the tutor enables a student to achieve a goal beyond his or her current capabilities. Wood, Bruner, and Ross describe the interactions of an expert adult tutor (Ross) working individually with three-, four-, and five-year-olds to build a three-dimensional block structure. They define scaffolding as follows:

> More often than not, [a tutor's intervention] involves a kind of "scaffolding" process that enables a child or novice to solve a problem, carry out a task, or achieve a goal which would be beyond his unassisted efforts. This scaffolding consists essentially of the adult "controlling" those elements of the task that are initially beyond the learner's capacity, thus permitting him to concentrate upon and complete only those elements that are within this range of competence. The task thus proceeds to a successful conclusion. We assume, however, that the process can potentially achieve much more for the learner than an assisted completion of the task. It may result, eventually, in development of task competence by the learner at a pace that would far outstrip his unassisted efforts. (90)

Wood, Bruner, and Ross believe that, in order for scaffolding to be successful, the tutor has to be very proficient in the task and has to compensate for children's difficulties in completing the task. In other words, the tutor has to know how to demonstrate and correct students' errors and how to motivate the children to persist in the task performance. Also, the children have to actively participate and attempt to learn strategies and principles, as opposed to passively observing.

In another important study conducted around the same time, Wood and Middleton (1975) observed mothers teaching their children how to construct the same block structure and identified four possible approaches. Wood, Wood, and Middleton (1978) followed up, assessing the effectiveness of each of the four tutoring approaches according to the child's ability to complete the building task independently. Both of these studies indicated the importance of the contingency rule in tutoring: "If the child succeeds, when next intervening offer less help. If the child fails, when next intervening take over more control" (Wood, Wood, and Middleton 1978, 133). In other words, contingency requires that tutors stay as close to the upper level of students' current knowledge and performance ability as possible. If tutors pose questions or assign tasks that appear to be beyond what students are currently able to comprehend, they should circle back. If they pose questions or assign tasks that students can easily answer or complete, they should ask more difficult questions and assign more difficult tasks on the next round.

Contingency is a consideration in the "region of sensitivity to instruction—a hypothetical measure of a child's current task ability and his 'readiness' for different topics" (Wood and Middleton 1975, 181). This region is a "recognition–production gap" (Wood, Wood, and Middleton 1978, 132); that is, in the process of learning, children are able to identify the intended outcome before they can perform the task. If children can identify goals, they can likely learn to achieve them. Together, these three studies showed that repetition, directiveness, and an increase in instruction failed to facilitate learning outside of the region of sensitivity to instruction. Further, instruction aimed generally at the region of sensitivity to instruction, without considerations of contingency, was equally ineffective. This research points to what most writing center tutors already know: learning is an individually different process for each student.

One-to-one scaffolding relates to Bruner's (1963) development of the spiral curriculum. Its development paid for with federal and private endowment funding after the Sputnik scare, the spiral curriculum advocated instruction that "spiraled"—reconsidering topics with increases in complexity. The premise was that, as Bruner (1996) repeats later, "Any subject can be taught to any child at any age in some form that is honest" (119). Teaching begins with what a student knows about a topic—his or her current "recognition"—and moves forward, circling back as necessary, through more formal versions or highly developed mental functions. The tutor or teacher acts "as a vicarious form of consciousness until such a time as the [student] is able to master his own action through his own consciousness and control" (Bruner 1986, 24). Further, learning occurs in a "topic–comment" (or "given–new") fashion, with the topic shared between the teacher or tutor and the student and the comment the new information or skill to be learned (Bruner 1986). Individuals construct knowledge with assistance and through appropriation of socially determined concepts, and, in the process, those concepts are recreated, personalized, and reenvisioned. Although Bruner does not dismiss Piagetian theories of development, he argues that teachers often do not need to wait for students to be ready to learn (Bruner 1996).

Over the past 40 years, the scaffolding metaphor has expanded. Even though, sometimes, this expansion can lead to misappropriation (Pea 2004; Puntambekar and Hübscher 2005; Stone 1993, 1998; Yelland and Masters 2007), the metaphor remains a useful means for discussing tutoring. Current discussions of scaffolding agree that its goals are to assist students in completing specific tasks important to them at that moment and, at the same time, to help them develop the skills and knowledge to independently complete similar tasks in the future (Applebee and Langer 1983; Clark and Graves 2005; Gaskins et al. 1997; Hogan and Pressley, 1997; Langer and Applebee, 1986; Puntambekar and Hübscher 2005; Stone 1998). Holton and Clark (2006) push this common definition further. They discuss self-scaffolding, where the learner forms a bridge between the teacher's support and control of his or her learning process, and they argue that self-scaffolding equates to metacognition (128). Hence, according to Holton and Clark, teachers can support students not only in completing particular tasks and in extending that knowledge to other tasks but also in learning how to control their own scaffolding processes.

Puntambekar and Hübscher (2005) provide a four-element framework for discussing the scaffolding process and for contextualizing other researchers' discussions. Taking into account the importance of beginning with a student's current understanding and of developing rapport with a student, this framework— or at least some of its elements—likely dominates in successful writing center conferences. First, intersubjectivity is a collaborative, shared understanding and ownership of the task (2; see also Roehler and Cantlon 1997). It begins with the topic that the tutor and student share. When intersubjectivity is achieved, the tutor and student understand the goal of the tutoring, and the tutor understands the student's investment in the task and develops ways of maintaining the student's motivation (see also Daniels 2001). Although it begins in the opening stage, the development of intersubjectivity likely continues throughout the conference. In discussing the interpersonal dimensions of scaffolding, Stone (1993) reinforces the need for a common understanding of the task and adds that, rather than being "faceless functionaries," tutors and students need respect for each other so that their repeated interactions in the scaffolding process will allow "the range of perceived 'fair' inferences and context to be incorporated as ground for the inferences" (178).

The second element is the tutor's ongoing diagnosis of the student's under-standing as the scaffolding proceeds. The ongoing diagnosis allows the tutor to provide calibrated support (Puntambekar and Hübscher 2005, 2; see also Lajoie 2005). It satisfies Wood and Middleton's (1975) need for contingent instruction in that it allows a tutor to work on the edge of a student's current knowledge and willingness to learn. Wood and Wood (1996) define two types of contingency: (1) domain contingency, the content or skill the tutor should teach next, based on the learner's current responses, and (2) temporal contingency, the tutor's awareness of the learner's motivation, including the level of frustration.

Puntambekar and Hübscher's (2005) third element is scaffolding's dialogic and interactive nature (3). This interactivity can be verbal or nonverbal, and it allows tutors to make their ongoing diagnoses (Holton and Clark 2006; Stone 1993, 1998). Further, the resulting "communicational tension and resolution" leads students to construct personal meaning by inferring what tutors mean and by drawing on the interaction thus far (Stone 1998, 354). As the scaffolding proceeds, the student comes to share the tutor's perspective and mastery of the task.

The fourth element is fading (Puntambekar and Hübscher 2005, 3). When the learner can complete the task alone and clearly understands the process, the tutor hands over responsibility and leaves the teaching role.

Essential to successful scaffolding is the tutor's awareness of the upper and lower boundaries that define a student's target area for teaching. As previously stated, learning—defined as a connection and reconstruction of previously mastered knowledge and skills (topic) and new knowledge and skills (comment)—occurs as students are challenged just beyond their current level of understanding. Wood and Middleton (1975) referred to that area as the "region of sensitivity to instruction" (181). However, before 1985, Wood and Middleton's designation, "the region of sensitivity to instruction," had been changed to the "zone of proximal development," or ZPD, in accordance with the growing popularity of, and acquaintance with, the works of Lev Vygotsky. The research about scaffolding overlays with theoretical neatness the earlier research about the ZPD. In fact, Bruner and his colleagues were certainly familiar with Vygotsky's work when their 1976 article was published. As Stone (1998) points out, Bruner wrote the introduction to the first English translation (1962) of Vygotsky's *Thought and Language* and, in his later works, Bruner acknowledges Vygotsky's influence on his thinking (for example, Bruner 1986).

Vygotsky discusses the ZPD in two distinct situations (Daniels 2001; Wells 1999). First, in *Mind in Society*, Vygotsky (1978) argues for dynamic assessment of intellectual abilities based on potential rather than a static measure of IQ. He provides this definition of the ZPD: "*It is the distance between the actual developmental level as determined by independent problem solving and the level of potential development as determined through problem solving under adult guidance or in collaboration with more capable peers*" (86; italics in original). Before he states this definition, Vygotsky (1978) compares the achievement of two 12-year-olds, both 8 years old in terms of mental development:

> These children seem to be capable of handling problems up to an eight-year-old's level, but not beyond that. Suppose that I show them various ways of dealing with the problem . . . Under these circumstances it turns out that the first child can deal with problems up to a twelve-year-old's

level, the second up to a nine-year-old's. Now are the two children mentally the same? (86)

Second, in *Thinking and Speech*, Vygotsky's last major work, he discusses the ZPD in terms of instruction:

> We have seen that instruction and development do not coincide. They are two different processes with very complex interrelationships. *Instruction is only useful when it moves ahead of development.* When it does, *it impells* [sic] *or awakens a whole series of functions that are in a stage of maturation lying in the zone of proximal development.* This is the major role of instruction in development. This is what distinguishes the instruction of the child from the training of animals. This is also what distinguishes instruction of the child which is directed toward his full development from instruction in specialized, technical skills such as typing or riding a bicycle. The formal aspect of each school subject is that in which the influence of instruction on development is realized. Instruction would be completely unnecessary if it merely utilized what had already matured in the developmental process, if it were not itself a source of development. (1987, 212; italics in original)

In other words, Vygotsky views interaction with teachers, tutors, and other more expert members of society, or even educational material as vital in assisting not only learning but also development and readiness for learning. Bounded on its low side by a student's current mastery and on its upper boundary by what the student can identify independently and achieve with assistance, the ZPD provides an area for student growth pushed along by external assistance of some kind.

Contemporary definitions of the ZPD focus on its potential as a social space for individuals to learn through the influence of others, often through other people in communities of practice (Wells 1999). Wells (1999) suggests four "salient features" of contemporary views of the ZPD in education (330–31). First, the ZPD is a space where individuals learn though social participation, and, although it exists at a particular moment, the upper boundary of ZPD moves through time. The ZPD "emerges in the activity" as participants collaborate (330), and, in the process of joint focused activity, "the potential for further learning is expanded as new possibilities open up that were initially unforeseen" (331). Second, all participants in the collaboration are learners, and, regardless of age or expertise, learning occurs through the ZPD across an individual's lifespan. Third, through memories, mental echoes of previously given advice, or artifacts, such as books or online materials, learning can occur when individuals are alone. Fourth, learning in the ZPD affects all mental aspects of the participants—cognition, motivation, emotion, even their personal identities. Therefore, in writing center conferences, collaboration established through rapport and a shared commitment to the intellectual exploration required to achieve an agenda can theoretically push forward a student writer's writing ability. After he or she leaves the writing center, the writing growth can continue by way of the student writer's notes and by recall of a tutor's advice. In addition, the process of teaching stimulates growth for tutors as well as for student writers.

Learning occurs through the mediation of external support and leads to internal conscious control of performance, also called internalization, a metaphor for the processes through which individuals move, typically through inner speech, to control of their own understanding and performance at a certain level (see Cazden 2001). With its power to develop higher mental processes, internalization is not a passive process; it requires individuals to be active agents in their own learning (Daniels 2001). In addition, it involves more than the mastery of a single task, but instead generalizes to similar tasks (Litowitz 1993). It is important to note, however, that, even though Vygotsky perceived internalization as a process of construction, he did not believe that students needed to rediscover well-established concepts and skills—an idea associated with discovery learning, which also views learning constructively. Instead, to save time and possibly wasted energy, Vygotsky advocated instruction, telling students definitions and providing explanations of known cultural principles (Daniels 2001; Karpov and Haywood 1998).

Even though Wood, Bruner, and Ross and Vygotsky developed their theories by observing the development of children, the concepts of scaffolding and ZPD, as Wells (1999) argues, are equally appropriate for adult learners. Wells calls Vygotsky's assisted learning within a definable intellectual and interpersonal region a "general developmental law" (25). The theoretical framework associated with scaffolding and the ZPD is relevant for writing center tutoring. The emphasis on teaching as a means for the cultivation of intelligence, rather than viewing intelligence as an absolute genetic trait, and the notion of teaching as the moving forward of development reflect an optimism about students' abilities to grow as learners that many writing center tutors share. Intersubjectivity and contingency support the well-known advice for writing center tutors to start where students are and to teach each student as an individual. In addition, intersubjectivity, as discussed by Puntambekar and Hübscher (2005), requires collaboration between tutors and students in agenda setting and all other aspects of conferencing. Through the interactive and dialogic element of scaffolding, tutors control the progress of the conference with a constant diagnosis of what the student currently knows and his or her level of motivation and frustration. The conversation in scaffolding requires students' attention and participation and connects with writing centers' commitment to active learning. Unfortunately, a single writing center conference is not likely to culminate in internalization, and tutors typically stop their support of student writers' learning because conferences have time limits or students appear unable to benefit from further tutoring. However, through summarizing and collaboratively setting new goals, tutors hope that student writers will move forward in developing writing competence on their own, perhaps using the notes generated during the conference or with the tutors' advice echoing in their thoughts.

Our understanding of writing center tutoring has been strongly influenced by Bruner's notion of scaffolding paired with Vygotsky's discussion of the ZPD. In the section that follows, we will review research about tutoring in problem-solving disciplines and in writing centers. This operationalization of scaffolding and the ZPD, along with research about politeness and motivation, is evident in the three categories of tutoring strategies we describe: instruction, cognitive scaffolding, and motivational scaffolding.

Operationalizing Scaffolding and the ZPD

In the conclusion of *A Synthesis of Qualitative Studies of Writing Center Tutoring: 1983–2006*, Babcock, Manning, and Rogers (2012) argue that, "much of what we have found to occur in writing center tutorials is a Vygotskian scaffolding event" (114). Even so, other than our own research, we were able to locate only one other empirical study of scaffolding in writing center conferences. Williams (2004), studying writing center conferences with second-language (L2) speakers of American English, found that scaffolding stimulated revision but, in her study, the revisions made did not improve the quality of the drafts. Given scant precedent on which to base our framework, we turned to research in math and science tutoring, where educators, psychologists, and computer scientists have been working since the late 1980s to provide "an Aristotle at every desk" as a tutor for students (Lepper et al. 1993, 76).

To develop instructional software for tutoring in math and science, researchers conducted large studies of expert human tutoring with students of all ages. Many tasks in math and science disciplines require predictably structured problem-solving procedures, often resulting in single answers. Based on this tendency toward invariability—in their entry-level courses at least—researchers have referred to these disciplines as "closed-world domains" (Person et al. 1995, 185). In the tasks of closed-world domains, questions and answers—processes and products—are usually well defined. The tasks in open-world domains are not so predictably structured and often do not result in single, objectively correct products. Writing is an open-world-domain task. Its processes are difficult to replicate or generalize. Its products are highly variable and typically evaluated in terms of effectiveness—rather than simply correctness—based on rhetorical considerations such as audience (and its unpredictable response) and purpose.

To develop a coding scheme that could fully accommodate most tutoring strategies, we looked beyond the scaffolding research of the 1970s to the more detailed and operationalized discussions of tutoring in closed-world domains. We found that coding in these studies incorporated and augmented the tutor scaffolding that Wood, Bruner, and Ross (1976) describe. The following list delineates the functions of tutor scaffolding moves according to Wood, Bruner, and Ross as the functions relate to our coding scheme's three categories of strategies:

- *Recruitment* (motivational scaffolding): Enlists students' interest in tasks and in meeting the requirements of those tasks.
- *Reduction in degrees of freedom* (instruction): Simplifies tasks by "reducing the number of constituent acts required to reach solution" (98). Working with young children in a laboratory rather than a classroom, the tutor in Wood, Bruner, and Ross's (1976) study performed the parts of the building task that the children could not. Although writing center tutors do not complete writing tasks for students, they can simplify tasks by leading students to focus on one aspect of composing at a time or on a particular section of the draft. For example, a tutor can lead a student to revise organization before beginning to proofread.
- *Direction maintenance* (motivational scaffolding): Keeps students on task. With college students, this function likely means recruiting and maintaining their active participation in conferences.
- *Marking critical features* (cognitive scaffolding): Leads students to identify and correct errors, revise for effectiveness, or formulate ideas for drafts. Tutors do not do these tasks for students, but rather create boundaried situations in which students can successfully do these tasks themselves.
- *Frustration control* (motivational scaffolding): Helps students develop and maintain confidence about completing the writing task.
- *Demonstration* (cognitive scaffolding): Models ways of performing tasks that students do not know how to begin or to complete on their own. Wood, Bruner, and Ross point out that demonstrating requires an "idealization" of the task (98). The tutor "imitates" the idealization, so that the student can imitate it as well (98).

Except for reducing the degrees of freedom to allow students to better focus on one aspect of the composing task at the time, all of these scaffolding functions can be classified as either cognitive or motivational scaffolding in our coding scheme. Further, the instruction used to focus student writers' attention on single aspects of the writing task does not tell or suggest answers for them. In this instance, tutors provide instruction about process rather than about product; they are directive, but do not reduce student writers' responsibility for and ownership of writing tasks.

Specifically, for our coding scheme, we looked to Cromley and Azevedo's (2005) study of adults learning the decoding skills required for reading. Although decoding is not problem solving, unlike reading comprehension, it represents "a well-defined, even mechanical, domain" (Cromley and Azevedo 2005, 85). Like those for many math problems, students' responses are easily identifiable as correct or not. We chose their scheme as the base of our framework for its detail and for its consistency with Wood, Bruner, and Ross's (1976) discussion of scaffolding strategies. Also, Cromley and Azevedo specifically compared the tutoring strategies of experienced (arguably more expert) tutors with those of inexperienced (arguably less expert) tutors.

In the sections that follow, we discuss the coding scheme we developed to describe and analyze experienced tutors' strategies. Like Cromley and Azevedo, we ground our scheme in motivation theory (for example, Lepper, Drake, and O'Donnell-Johnson 1997) and in discourse processing theory (for example, Person et al. 1995). In addition, our coding scheme incorporates some tenets of Bandura's (1986, 1997) social cognitive psychology, which does not fully accept the social constructivist view of knowledge, but holds that learning occurs in a social context. Particularly relevant for our study, social cognitive psychology has inspired extensive research in motivation. Studies of human-to-human tutoring often use Bandura's work to situate discussions of motivation in terms of self-efficacy and self-regulation (for example, Boyer et al. 2008). Also, our scheme employs Brown and Levinson's (1987) politeness theory, a theory that Person et al. (1995) use as well. Besides modifying our coding scheme, based on relevant theoretical frameworks, we piloted our scheme by recursively testing it on data from our corpus of conferences, adding and dropping strategies as we saw tutors use them and discuss them in postconference interviews.

Instruction Strategies

With instruction strategies, tutors attempt to convey information to students—giving advice and explaining and exemplifying their advice. In reviewing research that informed their study, Cromley and Azevedo (2005) wrote that tutors instruct by explaining concepts, rules, facts, and procedures; giving an answer; summarizing; using analogies; and planning for students. Instruction strategies do not focus on helping students pull forth what they already know, but rather they tell, suggest, or explain new concepts to supplement students' current understanding. They do not always require substantive responses from students and can diminish students' participation in learning opportunities, possibly because they can negate students' needs to arrive at and explain ideas for themselves (Chi 1996; Chi et al. 1994). Instruction strategies are intentionally directive, but tutors can mitigate the imposition through politeness (Brown and Levinson 1987). In our scheme, telling strategies incorporate little or no mitigation, whereas suggesting strategies soften directiveness with mitigation.

Instruction and Negative Politeness

As previously stated, the germinal work of Brown and Levinson (1987) influenced the modifications we made to Cromley and Acevedo's (2005) coding scheme. Brown and Levinson's linguistic theory of politeness is based primarily on

Goffman's (1967) concept of face, or self-image. Their theory accounts for the ways people attend to others' negative and positive face. Brown and Levinson define negative face as "the want of every 'competent adult member' that his actions be unimpeded by others" (62) and positive face as "the want of every member that his wants be desirable to at least some others" (62). Face-threatening acts (FTAs), such as giving advice or criticizing, disrupt negative and positive face and, hence, can alienate students from tutors (and all other conversation participants), harming chances for effective communication. To avoid FTAs, tutors in writing center conferences can use negative-politeness strategies, which help maintain negative face, and positive-politeness strategies, which help maintain positive face. Negative-politeness strategies are "avoidance-based" and allow hearers to "maintain claims of territory and self-determination" (Brown and Levinson 1987, 70). Positive-politeness strategies are "approach-based" and convey that speakers share hearers' wants and understand and value hearers (70). Discussing politeness theory, Scollon, Scollon, and Jones (2012) refer to negative politeness as "deference politeness," emphasizing independence (49), and positive politeness as "solidarity politeness," emphasizing involvement (48).

Differences between the speaker and hearer in terms of power, social distance, and the gravity of the FTA (such as a request) influence the use of politeness strategies (Brown and Levinson 1987). Often, in typically asymmetrical teaching relationships, the power and distance between teachers and students are great; although the power difference between tutors and students is less, it is still substantial—even when tutors are called "peers." Therefore, in the asymmetrical relationship of writing center conferences, tutors might be direct with student writers and not particularly concerned with politeness.

Indirectness in conveying advice, as when tutors make suggestions rather than tell student writers what to do, can create problems for student writers trying to understand and apply tutors' advice. On the one hand, directness as in telling can offend students and diminish their motivation to actively participate in writing center conferences. On the other hand, concern for politeness can cause tutors to miss opportunities for effective instruction and cause them to generate unclear feedback. Studying the effects of direct and indirect written teacher comments on the speed and accuracy with which first-language (L1) and L2 American English speakers revised, Baker and Bricker (2010) found that both groups responded to positive comments more quickly and accurately, regardless of the comments' level of directness. They also found that both groups were quickest but least accurate when making corrections based on indirect comments, and they were slowest but most accurate at making corrections based on direct comments.

Instruction in Closed-World-Domain Tutoring

Research has shown variable results about the effectiveness of instruction for learning. Along with linguistic descriptions and empirical research about politeness, our category of instruction strategies stems from research in education and psychology about the nature and value of explaining. Although some studies of tutoring in closed-world domains yielded different results (Cromley and Azevedo 2005; Lepper et al. 1990, 1993; Lepper, Drake, and O'Donnell-Johnson 1997), in a study of math, science, and computer science tutoring for undergraduates, Fox (1993) found that tutors used explanations and examples frequently. According to Merrill and his associates and VanLehn and his associates, tutors can most profitably use explanations when students reach an impasse and cannot move forward in their thinking without tutors' intervention (Merrill et al. 1992, 1995; VanLehn et al. 2003). Further, tutors may be more likely to use explanations when they perceive that students are anxious as opposed to frustrated. Attributing anxiety to a lack of knowledge, tutors may try to fill in students' knowledge deficits to reduce their anxiety and avoid calling attention to these knowledge deficits (Lehman et al. 2008).

However, that explanations from tutors do not require students' active participation might be problematic; they might not support learning as much as co-constructed explanations that come from cognitive scaffolding. Testing the notion that scaffolding is more effective than instruction for tutoring students in solving math problems, Lepper et al. (1990) compared the responses of three groups of elementary school students. The first group was taught through scaffolding, what Lepper et al. (1990) call the "indirect style" (231). The second group was taught through instruction, what Lepper et al. call the "direct style" (231). The third group—the control condition—worked on an unrelated task. The researchers found no significant differences in independent performance between the group that was taught through scaffolding and the group that was taught through instruction. However, in selecting future problems to solve, the members of the first group chose more difficult problems than the members of the second group. In another study with a similar goal, Chi et al. (2001) found similar results. The researchers compared science learning as measured by pre- and posttest scores for two groups of eighth-grade students. The first group received tutors' explanations, and the second group was taught through scaffolding. The members of the second group learned as much as the first group, but were more willing to take control of their learning processes. Two conclusions are important here: first, instruction and cognitive scaffolding led to equivalent knowledge and performance gains, but, second, cognitive scaffolding increased students' motivation for future learning, as well as their self-confidence.

To make sense of these and other results, Wittwer and Renkl (2008) reviewed research and developed guidelines for effective instructional explanations. First, they suggest that explaining should adapt to students' prior knowledge and individual learning characteristics. Hence, tutors have to make quick and accurate diagnoses of what students are capable of learning or doing and then determine what to teach. Second, explanations should help students move beyond singular, immediate tasks to tasks requiring higher performance levels. In a writing center conference, that could mean, for example, a student writer's move from evaluating potential ideas for a particular essay to brainstorming independently. Third, once tutors have provided explanations, students should quickly apply what they have learned so that they can begin to internalize the skills, strategies, and concepts. If possible, they should also practice self-explanation as they apply what they have learned. Fourth, tutors should use instructional explanations in concert with cognitive and motivational scaffolding. In addition, Wittwer and Renkl believe that preliminary instructional explanations may help students reduce errors in co-constructed explanations developed through scaffolding.

Wittwer and Renkl's (2008) guidelines may decrease some of the angst from using instruction tutoring strategies. In fact, with their incorporation of Puntambekar and Hübscher's (2005) features of scaffolding, they seem to embody some best practices of writing center tutoring. Tutors have to make quick diagnoses of student writers' prior knowledge and needs, to use a variety of tutoring strategies to foster and maintain active participation, to provide opportunities for practice, to promote and sustain student writers' motivation, and to keep student writers from becoming frustrated. They also have to summarize the issues discussed during the conferences and to ensure that student writers have goals for working on their assignments and for practicing what has been done during the conference. Finally, Wittwer and Renkl's second guideline echoes the writing center ideal that tutors should help students become better writers, rather than simply help them improve a particular draft.

Instruction and Directiveness in Writing Centers

Because of the association with directiveness, many writing center scholars have considered telling and suggesting the strategies of last resort. In the 1970s, as writing centers proliferated to offset the challenges of open admissions (Boquet 1999; Carino 1996), the proscription against direct instruction dominated advice about effective tutoring practice. Writing center lore said tutors should ensure student writers do most of the talking and maintain ownership of their writing, and tutors should assist student writers in finding their own answers without being told (Harris 1992), should avoid editing and proofreading for students (Brooks 1991), and should refuse to write on draft papers (Brooks 1991)—possibly should not even hold a pen. These admonitions grew out of a concern with differentiating writing center tutoring from classroom teaching and supporting a preference for peer tutors—similar to student writers in age, experience, and expertise (Bruffee 1984). To further reduce the possibility that tutors would direct student writers in what to do, writing center lore favored generalist tutors over tutors who had subject-matter expertise relevant to student writers' papers (Hubbuch 1988). The mandate to avoid directiveness, says Boquet (1999), "succeeds in securing the space of the writing lab as sacrosanct, as distinct from the classroom, a space where students should feel secure in their expression of thoughts and ideas, as they should in a therapist's office" (470). The resistance to instruction, therefore, created a culture that led to hiring tutors lacking subject-matter knowledge and, particularly with peer tutors, lacking writing experience, and to silencing some of tutors' attempts at teaching.

Since the 1980s, researchers and practitioners have questioned these admonitions. Of particular concern is the tutor's role as a peer. As Trimbur (1987) points out, tutors have difficulty perceiving themselves as peers and tutors at the same time. Harris (1992) suggests that, by receiving training in the conventions of academic discourse, tutors become removed from peer status, to become what Trimbur (1987) calls "apprentice" writing teachers (26). Clark (1990) reminds writing center practitioners of their commitment to good writing, concerned that the urgency for peerness will interfere with tutors' effectiveness. In essence, if tutors have more expertise as writers and more knowledge about the characteristics of good writing, they are no longer peers with the students they tutor; however, if they are not trained and experienced in writing, they are likely to mislead students, and writing center tutoring takes on the lack of effectiveness associated with classroom peer review (see Conroy, Lerner, and Siska 1998). Finally, regarding the preference for peers as tutors, in part to avoid an imbalance of power in writing center conferences, Latterell (2000) argues that writing center scholars have wrongly conceived the notion of power as property, implicit in the concerns that tutors maintain students' ownership of their writing and in the advice that tutors give their power and authority to students. Instead of a commodity, power and authority occur through activity, and shifts in power and authority between tutors and student writers happen all the time, on a moment-to-moment basis, during conferences.

Empirical research about the influence of tutors' directiveness and expertise on perceptions of conference success and on student writers' satisfaction with conferences has led to further questions about the lore associated with directiveness. In a questionnaire study of tutors' and student writers' attitudes about directiveness, Clark (2001) found differences in student writers' perceptions of the amount of tutor telling and suggesting. Those who believed themselves to be good writers perceived less influence from tutors than those who perceived themselves as poor or adequate writers, but perceptions of directiveness did not affect student writers' overall satisfaction with their conferences. These results indicate that notions of directiveness compose a continuum rather than absolutes, and they emphasize the benefits of individualized, one-to-one tutoring. Using a questionnaire to identify conference attributes that affect tutors' and student writers' satisfaction, Thompson et al. (2009) found that student writers' perceptions of tutors' expertise and having their questions answered correlated positively and strongly with their satisfaction, but perceptions that they rather than tutors talked the most and that tutors behaved more like peers than instructors did not influence student writers' satisfaction. Tutors' perceptions of having answered student writers' questions—likely through instruction—correlated strongly with their satisfaction, although their satisfaction correlated only slightly with how well they perceived themselves as acting as peers rather than as teachers. In addition, nondirectiveness appeared to be a concern only for inexperienced tutors.

Writing center researchers have also used discourse analysis to investigate the effects of tutors' talk, including the extent of their directiveness. Studying dominance in terms of the frequency of directives, directive type, and the use of mitigation strategies, Thonus (1999a) says that directives are interesting because they make the "perceived status and dominance of participants" particularly salient (233). Analyzing 2,763 suggestions according to the presence or absence of mitigation, she found that, possibly owing to time pressures, some of the shortest conferences contained the most suggestions. Further, the effect of repeated conferences on measures of dominance was negligible. After finding that L1 males received the most suggestions, Thonus says that, "the offering of suggestions may be an expression of solidarity rather than dominance, if [L1] males are considered more powerful (and thus more deserving of assistance) than [L2] males, or [L1 or L2] females" (241). Hence, telling strategies may signal tutors' interest in creating rapport with certain student writers.

In another study, Thonus (2002) continued her discussion of directiveness and instruction in developing a profile of a successful conference based on linguistic features and conference attributes. She found that tutors' mitigation of directives positively influenced perceptions of conference success. However, she also found that tutors were frequently directive, often using little mitigation. In this study, Thonus carefully distinguished between interaction-internal directives, those that relate to work done during the conference, and interaction-external directives (which she calls suggestions), those that relate to work to be done after the conference ends (118). Like Clark (2001) and Thompson et al. (2009), Thonus found that directiveness, especially mitigated directiveness, had little detrimental effect on student writers' conference satisfaction.

Along with the frequency of directiveness or attitudes toward this conference characteristic, researchers have considered its relationship to perceptions of tutors' roles. For example, Thonus (2001) conducted interviews, collected assignment sheets and drafts, and gathered the tutors' records of the conferences, and she analyzed recorded conferences for the tutors' and student writers' use of directiveness, pronouns, and off-task talk—what Thonus refers to as "linguistic exponents of role perception" (63). Based on her interviews with faculty, tutors, and student writers, she found that some instructors perceived tutors as their surrogates; however, tutors viewed themselves as "*colleague* pedagogues" (68; italics in original). They saw instructors rather than student writers as their peers, but at the same time they worried about being too directive. She also found that student writers viewed tutors "as distinct and less authoritative" than instructors, and that they did not feel they had to enact tutors' suggestions (71). Further, Wolcott (1989) and Davis et al. (1988) analyzed tutors' roles in terms of their control (or lack of it) over conferences. Both studies found that tutors sometimes were directive like classroom teachers, but sometimes took on the nondirective style that writing center lore prescribes.

Writing center research has also examined tutors' and student writers' roles as collaborators in writing center conferences. Ede and Lunsford's (1990) distinctions between hierarchical and dialogic collaboration have been applied to tutors' and student writers' roles in writing center conferences. In hierarchical collaboration, the tutor assumes the role of an expert and likely favors instruction strategies, and, in dialogic collaboration, the tutor and student writer share control of the conference. Analyzing two conferences involving one student writer working with two tutors, Severino (1992) labeled one, characterized by closed questions and directives, as hierarchical, and she labeled the other, characterized by a lack of directives, as dialogic (54–55). Severino does not explicitly say one is better than the other, but she clearly favors the dialogic one. Further, although she does not discuss this matter in much detail, the tutor with the most expertise in writing—a former high school teacher and a current PhD candidate—led the hierarchical conference; in contrast, an undergraduate with far less expertise in writing tutored in the dialogic conference. Finally, Blau, Hall, and Strauss (1998) identified tutoring strategies that suggested dialogic collaboration and examined their effect on student writers' satisfaction with their conferences. They equated dialogic collaboration, which they refer to as "collaboration" (22), with a nondirective tutoring style and hierarchical collaboration, which they refer to as "hierarchy" (22), with a directive tutoring style. In accordance with Ede and Lunsford's work, they say that dialogic collaboration emphasizes "creating solidarity in relationships often between two people who feel equal in status," whereas hierarchical collaboration "suggests a relationship based on one person having more power than the other" (22). Blau, Hall, and Strauss identified three "recurring rhetorical strategies" that they see as indicators of the tutor–student relationship: questions (open-ended versus closed), echoing (repeating another person's words), and qualifiers (usually some type of FTA mitigation). They concluded that, although "true" collaboration usually meets student writers' needs effectively, sometimes "an undue—or misdirected—emphasis on [dialogic collaboration] resulted in tutorials that seemed to waste time and lack clear direction" (38).

Some writing center scholars have also questioned the lore of the generalist tutor—a tutor lacking subject-matter expertise and perhaps expertise in relevant disciplinary genres as well. Studying four conferences about engineering writing, Mackiewicz (2004) found that the three tutors without subject-matter knowledge or familiarity with conventions of engineering writing often misled student writers; in contrast, the tutor who had spent 20 years as a technical writer—though she lacked expertise in engineering—understood the student engineer's writing task as a "real" rather than an academic assignment, mitigated her advice according to the necessity of following it, and generated rapport. In a study examining the effects of subject-matter expertise in writing center tutoring, Kiedaisch and Dinitz (1993) recorded conferences about literary essays that either generalist tutors or tutors who were literature majors conducted. They played the recordings back to literature instructors. The literature instructors rated the conferences involving tutors who were literature majors higher than they did those involving generalist tutors. Like Mackiewicz (2004), Kiedaisch and Dinitz note that the generalist tutors focused on local-level rather than global-level concerns (see also Dinitz and Harrington 2014). Such studies call into question the purported benefits of tutors lacking knowledge about relevant subject matter and disciplinary genres.

Student writers, however, can reject tutors' advice and thus refuse to ratify tutors' expertise. Waring (2005) describes a series of conferences between an L1 graduate-student tutor and an L2 graduate student in which the student writer resists the tutor's advice in part because the tutor lacks relevant subject-matter knowledge. Investigating how classroom discourse differs from writing center discourse and how tutors and student writers modify conference agendas as they go along, Porter (1991) analyzed IRE sequences between a "non-traditional" student (an undergraduate student older than 22) and an experienced graduate-student tutor. During their third conference about the same essay, the tutor told the student writer that her thesis was too broad and advised rewriting the essay. The student writer, however, had already invested a lot of time and wanted to avoid a cumbersome revision. In the end, the student writer accepted some of the tutor's advice, but she did not completely revise her essay. These two studies show that student writers—certainly student writers who are somewhat older and likely a bit more confident than traditional undergraduates—can enact power at their discretion.

Since the late 1980s, writing center researchers have forcefully questioned the efficacy of prescribing nondirective tutoring strategies, and their research has provided evidence for their doubts. Researchers advocate choosing tutoring strategies based on the needs of individual students (for example, Conroy, Lerner, and Siska 1998; Hawthorne 1999; Henning 2001, 2005; Shamoon and Burns 1995). Blau, Hall, and Strauss (1998), write that such "informed flexibility has always been the hallmark of good teaching and tutoring" (38). They suggest a nondirective approach when tutors want "to help students figure out for them-selves what they are trying to say and how best to say it" (38), such as during brainstorming, and when tutors and student writers are dealing with global-level issues such as organization and voice. On the other hand, a more directive approach may better facilitate proofreading. Henning (2005) says that, when student writers need "objective" knowledge, tutors should use directive tutoring strategies, and when they need "subjective" knowledge—defined as "residing in the writer"—tutors should use nondirective tutoring strategies. Finally, when student writers need "intersubjective knowledge"—defined as "created through interaction" and "dependent on rhetorical context"—tutors should work collaboratively with students to develop these ideas (5). Writing center research has moved on from blanket prescriptions for nondirective tutoring and against directive tutoring, taking instead a more nuanced, individualized approach to choosing tutoring strategies.

Instruction Strategies in our Coding Scheme

In our study, instruction comprised these three tutoring strategies:

- *Telling*: Tutors used little to no mitigation to direct students in revising or brainstorming ideas and in pointing out errors or problems: "Put it in there, at the beginning of that one." Tutors also used little to no mitigation to direct students in improving their composing processes: "Make sure they all relate back to that thesis as well." In some instances, tutors also used telling to move to a new topic in a conference or to plan what a student should do after the conference ended.
- *Suggesting*: Tutors used more mitigation, thus lowering the face threat of their advice. They often used negative politeness: "But since the focus of the paper is law enforcement, you probably want to bring it back to law enforcement here." As directive instruction strategies, suggesting and telling have similar goals; the difference is in the tutor's use of mitigation.
- *Explaining and exemplifying*: Tutors offered reasons for, and illustrated, their advice: "Because you're saying, you know, they cause their life to be or feel meaningless. And it seems like from what we talked about here you're going to say, like, however, in *Notes from the Underground*, the author does show that there's hope for a better life."

Cognitive Scaffolding Strategies

Cognitive scaffolding includes a range of tutoring strategies to prod thinking and lead to "the development of conceptual and procedural understandings" (Yelland and Masters 2007, 367). Rather than telling, suggesting, or explaining, cognitive scaffolding leads students to find their own solutions to composing or content problems. Cognitive scaffolding strategies create opportunities for a student writer to construct his or her own meaning with a tutor's assistance, and they guide a tutor's use of strategies by exposing a student writer's lack of understanding. They vary in the extent to which they set boundaries around and constrain student writers' possible responses. They also are interactive to varying degrees, but they require student writers to respond substantially, although perhaps briefly, to tutors' comments or questions, in a "*cooperative execution* or *coordination*" that gradually increases student writers' control (Chi et al. 2001, 490; italics in original).

Studying the task of decoding in the closed-world domain of literacy tutoring, Cromley and Azevedo (2005) found that experienced tutors use cognitive scaffolding strategies more often than instruction or motivational scaffolding strategies. Cognitive scaffolding composed 58% of their recorded strategies, with experienced tutors providing more cognitive scaffolding than inexperienced tutors (66% of experienced tutors' tutoring moves versus 46% of inexperienced tutors' tutoring moves). In observations of elementary school at-risk children receiving math help from experienced (expert) tutors, Lepper and his associates (Lepper et al. 1990; Lepper et al. 1993; Lepper, Drake, and O'Donnell-Johnson 1997) also assessed motivational and cognitive gains. As previously stated, they found that tutors seldom intervened directly to point out errors or tell or suggest corrections to students immediately. Instead, they ignored errors that seemed inconsequential, attempted to forestall errors often through leading questions, or helped students debug their incorrect responses, sometimes through step-by-step questioning. These tutors usually reserved instruction until after the students had arrived at correct answers to particular problems, as a review and as a demonstration about solving problems efficiently as well as correctly.

Cognitive Scaffolding, Pump Questions, and Other Questions

Questioning is one of the most frequently used classroom teaching techniques, with elementary and high school teachers asking as many as 400 questions per day (Tienken, Goldberg, and DiRocco 2010). Questions play a critical role in pedagogical conversations. They can direct students' knowledge construction through self-explanation or, with tutors, co-explanation of concepts (Chi 1996; Chi et al. 1989; Chi, DeLeeuw, and LaVancher 1994; Graesser, Baggett and Williams 1996; Rosé et al. 2003). They can also provide models for students' subsequent self-questioning, a process important for self-regulation of learning (Graesser and Person 1994).

Research on questions in classroom teaching posits two question types defined in terms of expected responses from students (Nassaji and Wells 2000; Piazza 2002; Smith and Higgins 2006). Teachers ask the first type, open-ended questions, when they do not have an answer in mind and cannot (and do not intend to) judge the appropriateness of students' potential responses, for example, when they ask for students' opinions. Many researchers see open-ended questions as very important for stimulating and respecting students' thinking, and writing center scholars especially value them as the gold standard of tutoring discourse. Teachers ask the second type, closed questions, when they have an answer in mind or intend to evaluate a range of responses according to their appropriateness. Researchers have criticized closed questions because they associate them with instructors' demands for students to "display" what they know (Lee 2008) and with instructors' need to "test" students' knowledge (Lee 2008; Nystrand, Wielmelt, and Greene 1993). Although their display and test functions are clearly useful in informing tutors' diagnoses of students' understanding, we argue that closed questions can do more pedagogical work.

Examining closed questions in tutoring conversations reveals their usefulness in promoting students' discovery and, with tutors, their co-construction of meaning and, thus, their learning. In her analysis of questions occurring in writing conferences involving instructors and L2 student writers, Koshik (2010) points out that instructors can use closed questions to address local- and global-level problems and, hence, help student writers to identify and rectify those problems. She suggests that, with such questions, instructors can scaffold student writers' performance.

Further, closed questions can allow students a range of responses. Cognitive scaffolding questions fall along a continuum of potential responses. At one end are cognitive scaffolding questions that allow just a single correct response. Such questions are the most severely constraining of all cognitive scaffolding questions. At the other end of the continuum are cognitive scaffolding questions that allow a wide range of appropriate responses. Such minimally constraining questions allow students a wide range of options. In practical terms, then, open-ended and closed questions may differ little in the amount of talk they solicit from student writers; rather, they differ in a tutor's ability and willingness to evaluate the appropriateness and quality of student writers' responses.

In a study of questions in writing center conferences, we examined questions from a different perspective (Thompson and Mackiewicz 2014). We adapted our coding scheme for questions from Graesser and his co-researchers' description of four "question-generation mechanisms" (Graesser, Person, and Huber 1992; Graesser and Person 1994; Person et al. 1994): (1) knowledge-deficit questions, asked when the questioner needs information about a topic (see also Koshik 2010; Lee 2008); (2) common-ground questions, asked when the questioner wants to ensure shared knowledge and mutual understanding; (3) social-coordination questions, asked when the questioner attempts to get the hearer to perform some action, such as when the questioner wants to guide the conversation in a particular way; (4) conversation-control questions, used to greet, to gripe, and to question rhetorically. These four question-generation mechanisms do not include cognitive scaffolding questions, but they do inform our analysis of cognitive scaffolding questions in subsequent chapters.

In our study, we added cognitive scaffolding questions as a fifth category in our coding scheme. Of the 690 questions we coded from 11 writing center conferences, tutors asked 562 (83%), whereas student writers asked only 128 (19%). Tutors' questions mainly established common ground, for example, questions that assessed student writers' understanding ("Do you see what I mean?") and thus were motivational scaffolds. Tutors also frequently used cognitive scaffolding questions to move student writers' thinking forward. Tutors used the two types together in sequences similar to the IRF sequences discussed earlier in this chapter. We found that, even though early mandates for writing center tutors prescribed open-ended questions, closed questions can benefit student writers too. They can simplify immediate responses, lessen confusion, and allow tutors to lead student writers in appropriate and efficacious directions. Tutors in our study used closed questions to move student writers from highly constrained responses to slightly constrained responses. We also saw the reverse occur: tutors started with minimally constraining questions that student writers could not answer and then used more constraining questions to move student writers' thinking forward with less frustration. Despite writing center lore's proscription against closed questions, our own and other research suggests that they have value in writing center conferences.

Cognitive Scaffolding Strategies in our Coding Scheme

Eight tutoring strategies composed the cognitive scaffolding category:

- *Pumping*: Tutors withheld their advice or part of the answer. Pumping could be highly constraining: "Where does the comma go in this sentence?" Or, it could be minimally constraining: "How can you incorporate those ideas into your draft?" We included leading questions in this category because they can act as pumps for thinking and require at least minimal responses from students: "Isn't this change in topic a good spot for a paragraph break?"
- *Reading aloud*: Tutors read sections of student writers' drafts aloud so that student writers could hear what they had written. In addition, tutors read instructors' assignment sheets aloud to help student writers understand the writing requirements better and to model the sort of word-by-word attention to detail required for understanding assignments. For example, a tutor read aloud the gist of the assignment from the instructor's explanatory handout: "'You must state your position on an issue and convince your reader that your position is correct.'" Tutors also asked student writers to read their drafts aloud to identify errors and passages that needed revision and to teach student writers a strategy they might use after they left the writing center.
- *Responding as a reader or a listener*: Tutors read a section from a draft, either aloud or silently, and then told student writers what they took away as readers: "You say that, you know, this is the way I like it because it's suitable to my needs in getting things done." They also paraphrased what student writers had said orally to allow the same kind of comparison between what student writers believed they were saying and what listeners heard.
- *Referring to a previous topic*: When tutors saw that student writers were making the same error or having the same problem in several places in a draft, they referred the student writers back to the earlier occurrence to help them identify the problem and practice the previously discussed revision or correction strategy: "And then, T-O-O, 'too good.' Again, like we talked about in the beginning."
- *Forcing a choice*: Tutors presented student writers with several alternatives and expected them to choose one. Forcing a choice constrained, and therefore directed, student writers' responses to increase their chances of success: "Now, 'the boys tell their friends,' or 'the boys tells their friends'?"
- *Prompting*: Tutors set up responses from student writers by providing partial responses or by leaving a blank for them to fill in, narrowing the possible

answers: "So if you were to, you know, if you were to say '*Cosmo Girl* targets . . .' what?"

- *Hinting*: Tutors used "nonconventional indirectness"; that is, they relied on context to refer to or raise an issue (Blum-Kulka, House, and Kasper 1989; Mackiewicz and Riley 2003, 85): "So it also demonstrates punishment. Just punishment in general": the tutor used this hint to get the student writer to see that there is more to "punishment." The student writer elaborated afterwards with "Oh, like, right and wrong."
- *Demonstrating*: Tutors showed student writers how to do something: "Like this. They give you like 'You should have a cover page that does this.' That we don't want you to pay attention to": a tutor used this strategy while showing a website that exemplified APA citations.

Prompting, hinting, and demonstrating tutoring strategies rarely occurred in the 10 writing center conferences described in Chapters 5–7. However, we did find incidences of two of them in the conferences that we examine in Chapter 8.

Cognitive scaffolding begins with what students currently know, and tutors co-construct meaning with students, helping them to move their thinking forward toward new understanding. This assisted connection between what a student can do and a next, more sophisticated step anchors all eight cognitive scaffolding strategies.

Motivational Scaffolding Strategies

With motivational scaffolding strategies, tutors encourage student writers by building and maintaining a sense of rapport and feelings of solidarity and thus can increase student writers' motivation—the "desire to achieve a goal and the willingness to engage and persist in specific subjects and activities" (Margolis 2005, 223). Motivation is rooted in both cognition and affect, which reciprocally influence each other. It influences and reacts to learning-relevant affective states, such as confusion, frustration, anxiety, contempt, feelings of eureka, and curiosity, as well as emotions such as anger, fear, sadness, disgust, surprise, and happiness (Bye, Pushkar, and Conway 2007; Lehman et al. 2008). In educational settings, motivation includes the drive to invest time and energy in learning and possibly to transfer learning from one task to another (Bransford, Brown, and Cocking 2003).

According to Bruning and Horn (2000), four "clusters of conditions" are critical to enhancing student writers' motivation: convincing them of good writing's usefulness, assigning authentic writing tasks, providing support, and creating "a positive emotional environment" (25). Writing center tutors do not influence the writing tasks that student writers bring to the writing center, but they can play a role in the other three conditions for motivation. For example, when tutors scaffold student writers' learning, tasks can seem "less dangerous or stressful," possibly less frustrating and anxiety provoking than those undertaken alone (Wood, Bruner, and Ross 1976, 98). Just as cognitive scaffolding can lead to the co-construction of meaning, motivational scaffolding, through "mutual reciprocity," can lead to the co-construction of motivation (Meyer and Turner 2002, 112). Writing center conferences, therefore, can create conditions that can enhance student writers' motivation.

As we noted above, our description and analysis of motivational scaffolding strategies draw from Bandura's (1997) discussion of self-efficacy, Hidi's, Boscolo's, and Pajares's reviews of research about writing and motivation (Boscolo and Hidi 2007; Hidi and Boscolo 2006; Pajares and Valiente 2006), and Brown and Levinson's (1987) politeness theory, particularly in relation to positive politeness.

According to recent discussions of writing and motivation, motivation involves three major components: student writers' interest in writing tasks, their self-efficacy about successfully completing the tasks, and their abilities to self-regulate their performances (Boscolo and Hidi 2007; Hidi and Boscolo 2006; Pajares and Valiente 2006; Zimmerman and Kitsantas 2007). Interest impacts attention, concentration, and affect (Boscolo and Hidi 2007; Hidi and Boscolo 2006). It can be individual or situational. Individual interest is "a relatively enduring predisposition to attend to events and objects, as well as reengage in activities," and situational interest arises "suddenly," from "something in the environment that focuses attention" (Hidi and Boscolo 2006, 146). Situational interest "may or may not have a long-term effect on individuals' knowledge and value systems" (Hidi and Boscolo 2006, 146). Situational interest likely plays an important role in learning, particularly when student writers receive assignments that interest them, when they work with people they enjoy, or when they get good grades. If a student writer maintains situational interest in a task, it may turn into individual interest.

Because collaboration can influence interest, tutoring offers a promising environment for triggering situational interest (Hidi and Harackiewicz 2000). Research that Hidi and Boscolo (2006) reviewed showed that students with little interest in a writing task tried to complete it as soon as possible; those with situational interest wanted to do a good job so that they would get good grades; and students with individual interest willingly invested time and effort, because they wanted to feel good about their writing.

Interest helps generate intrinsic motivation, defined as "the degree to which students perceive themselves to be participating in a learning task for reasons such as challenge, curiosity, and mastery" (Bye, Pushkar, and Conway 2007, 143). When they are intrinsically motivated, students see completing the task effectively as an end in itself, and rewards are internal. Intrinsic motivation likely increases persistence in a task. In contrast, extrinsic motivation leads students to complete tasks to achieve external rewards, including approval, a good grade, winning a competition, or avoiding punishment. Extrinsically motivated students are likely to focus their efforts on the "instrumental," or (in their view) the most practical, aspects of task performance (Lepper 1988, 299). Both extrinsic and intrinsic motivation are important for learning (Bye, Pushkar, and Conway 2007; Hidi and Boscolo 2006; Hidi and Harackiewicz 2000). When a student lacks interest in a task, an external reward and its concomitant extrinsic motivation can spur task completion.

Self-efficacy and self-regulation mutually depend on each other, and interest influences both (Bandura 1997). Self-efficacy is "a cognitive construct that represents individuals' beliefs and personal judgments about their ability to perform at a certain level and affects choice of activities, effort, and performance" (Hidi and Boscolo 2006, 148; see also Boscolo and Hidi 2007). As an internal self-portrait of capabilities, self-efficacy predicts what students will do with the knowledge and skills they currently have and how much effort they will invest in learning new knowledge and skills (Pajares 2003; Pajares and Valiante 2006). People form self-efficacy beliefs by interpreting their previous performances, by observing others perform tasks, by interpreting assurances and persuasions from trusted others, and by feeling emotions such as anxiety (Margolis 2005; Pajares 2003; Pajares and Valiante 2006). Low self-efficacy can lead students to think that tasks are more difficult than they are.

Self-regulation consists of "the self-directive processes and self-beliefs that enable learners to transform their mental abilities, such as verbal aptitude, into an academic performance skill, such as writing" (Zimmerman 2008, 166; see also Zimmerman 2001). Self-regulatory processes include the abilities to set goals, to self-improve learning through controlling metacognitive and motivational strategies, to structure effective learning and task-completion environments, and to request help (Zimmerman 1998, 2008). However, developing self-regulating skills alone is difficult. Zimmerman and Kitsantas (1999) suggest that less-proficient writers can benefit from focusing initially on writing procedures and processes that more expert writers model. When those processes and procedures become automatic and self-regulation is possible, student writers can attend to outcomes— the writing product—instead of processes.

Motivational Scaffolding and Positive Politeness

We also used Brown and Levinson's (1987) politeness theory to develop our codes for motivational scaffolds. Earlier, we discussed the relevance of negative politeness to instruction strategies, particularly the relationship between conveying an FTA directly (telling) or mitigating that FTA with negative politeness, such as a low-value modal verb (suggesting). Here, we discuss the relationship between positive politeness—politeness that conveys understanding and appreciation—and motivational scaffolding.

Positive-politeness strategies relevant to writing center conferences fall into three broad categories. First, tutors can give understanding and sympathy. They can do so by articulating their understanding of a student writer's situation and by acknowledging that they wish a challenging situation were otherwise (thus conveying sympathy). Second, they can notice or attend to student writers' accomplishments or conditions, as when they employ the strategy of noticing by offering praise ("That's a good change"). However, they may also claim common ground when they demonstrate concern that a shared understanding of the task at hand exists, as when they ask "Do you see what I mean?" to ensure that a student writer understands and, therefore, to ensure that the two are on "common ground." Joking also suggests common ground. Jokes rely on shared knowledge and values (Brown and Levinson 1987, 124). Thus, as a kind of shibboleth, jokes convey solidarity and generate rapport. Third, tutors can convey that they and the student writers are cooperators. Brown and Levinson (1987) explain this broad category of showing cooperation, which appears to be a critical one for writing center tutors, this way: if two people are conversationally cooperating, "then they share goals in some domain" (125). This category includes being optimistic and reinforcing the student writer's ownership and control.

Motivation in the Tutoring of Closed-World Domains

In interviews with experienced tutors, Lepper et al. (1993) found that the best tutors seemed to "devote at least as much time and attention to issues of motivation and affect" as to "issues of information and cognition" (77). Although meeting students' cognitive needs may be entirely congruent with meeting their affective needs, at times these needs appear to require contradictory actions from tutors. Lepper et al. identified four major motivational goals that math tutors attended to when working with at-risk elementary school students. First, tutors attended to students' confidence by commenting on the difficulty of the math problems before them, by emphasizing the students' role in solving the problems, by commiserating about errors, by providing indirect feedback rather than immediately labeling an answer as incorrect, and by praising students' successes. Second, tutors challenged students by selecting problems of appropriate difficulty and by using cognitive scaffolding strategies to help students solve them. Third, tutors stimulated students' curiosity, an influence on interest and therefore on intrinsic motivation, by using Socratic questioning when possible and by discussing the solution's usefulness. Fourth, tutors promoted students' feelings of control, thus attending to self-efficacy and self-regulation (Lepper et al. 1993).

However, in studies of tutoring adults or college students in similar closed-world domains, results did not substantiate the conclusion that tutors should consciously attend to students' motivation. Comparing experienced and less experienced literacy tutors' moves, Cromley and Azevedo (2005) found that tutors used fewer motivational scaffolding strategies than cognitive scaffolding or instruction strategies and that experienced tutors used fewer motivational scaffolding strategies than inexperienced tutors did (11% versus 20% of total strategies). A slightly later study of 43 tutor–student conferences about computer software supported these results. Comparing two categories of corrective feedback, Boyer et al. (2008) found that some students learned more from purely cognitive feedback than from cognitive feedback with praise, although students' perceptions of self-efficacy benefited from the praise. These studies complicate the role of motivational scaffolding. Cromley and Azevedo's (2005) experienced tutors may have been more selective in their use of motivational scaffolding than inexperienced tutors and, hence, may have avoided offering unwarranted praise and other encouragement. Boyer et al.'s (2008) results suggest that motivational scaffolding does not have an immediate effect on learning outcomes, but students' increased self-efficacy could positively influence learning in the long run. More research on the role of motivation in learning in general and in learning how to write in particular would help untangle mixed and complicated results.

Motivation, Politeness, and Writing Center Tutoring

Besides our own research, few empirical studies have investigated motivation in writing center tutoring. In fact, we found only two. DeCheck (2012) defines motivation from a different perspective and examines a single case of a tutor working with a student writer. However, Williams and Takaku's (2011) study adopted a definition of motivation similar to ours. Williams and Takaku conducted an eight-year longitudinal study of the effects of writing self-efficacy and help-seeking behavior (writing center visits) on writing performance. They found that high levels of help-seeking behavior—frequent writing center use—best predicted high grades in composition classes. This finding is particularly striking in that about half of the 671 undergraduate participants were L2 American English speakers. Calculating the relationship between help seeking and self-efficacy, they found an inverse correlation: the students with the lowest self-efficacy scores upon entering the university used the writing center most frequently. This finding runs counter to Bandura's (1997) view that people with high self-efficacy are more likely to seek assistance than those with low self-efficacy. However, as Williams and Takaku point out, it may be "related to the students' perceived need as well as to the attributional style associated with Asian students" (13). Williams and Takaku's study serves as a basis for further research on the relationship between writing center tutoring and student writers' self-efficacy.

In their synthesis of writing center qualitative research, Babcock, Manning, and Rogers (2012) discuss the importance of the relationship developed during a conference between the tutor and the student writer. They say that, "this relationship is characterized by solidarity, trust, and comfort (or the lack thereof) and is displayed in the tutoring session through collaboration and conflict, authority, and empowerment" (91). Clearly influenced by Brown and Levinson (1987), they add that solidarity relates to connectedness, rapport, and chemistry. Similar to tutor–student intersubjectivity (Puntambekar and Hübscher 2005), solidarity, as Babcock, Manning, and Rogers say, stems from "a unified sense of purpose and mutual respect rather than, say, affection" (92).

Tutors use politeness to generate solidarity and to help student writers save face, the latter need sometimes generated by tutors' telling and suggesting. However, the concern to offset directiveness with politeness can sometimes result in misunderstandings. Analyzing 11 tutors' evaluations of student writers' texts, Thonus (1999b) found that juggling three important goals—comprehensibility, politeness, and effective tutoring strategies such as those prescribed in tutor training—led tutors to face a "triple bind": to be comprehensible, tutors may have to sacrifice politeness and what they have been taught is effective tutoring practice (275). Further, in outlining characteristics of successful writing center conferences, Thonus (2002) identified 10 "necessary, but not sufficient conditions" for success. Three conditions relate to politeness: movement toward solidarity between tutors and student writers, tutors' mitigation of directiveness, and development of tutor–student intersubjectivity (126). Bell, Arnold, and Haddock (2009) observed two experienced tutors' politeness strategies in repeated conferences with the two student writers that extended across at least six weeks. They found that, in early conferences, tutors used positive politeness to relate to the student writers as peers, laughter to ease FTAs, and negative politeness when assuming authoritative roles. In later conferences, they used fewer negative-politeness strategies but continued to use positive-politeness strategies. Clearly, politeness, particularly positive politeness, plays a substantial role in building a sense of goodwill.

In an analysis based on positive- and negative-politeness theory and Goffman's (1955) views of self-presentation to shed light on directiveness in tutoring, Murphy (2006) discusses four cases, each demonstrating a different form of self-presentation a tutor might enact: the linguistic expert, the educated-but-confused reader, the uninformed reader, and the mentor/co-learner in literary analysis. She found that, "being nondirective moves irregularly and sometimes recursively along a continuum as a session progresses" and that, "consultants and students both adopted various forms of self-presentation to appear nondirective but at the same time set an agenda, establish authority, and/or gain trust" (63). Focusing on positive politeness, Mackiewicz (2006) analyzed the 107 compliments tutors used in writing center conferences with engineering students. She found, as expected, that most of the compliments were formulaic and used to fill pauses and avoid silences, particularly in conference closings. They "allowed tutors to provide instantaneous positive feedback by retrieving prefabricated language from memory" (25). Non-formulaic compliments demonstrated that the tutors were paying attention to the students as individuals and pointed to specific effective textual elements. Finally, examining conference attributes that might influence tutors' and student writers' satisfaction, Thompson et al. (2009) found that student writers' feelings of comfort and the amount of positive feedback that they received strongly influenced their satisfaction; on the other side of the coin, tutors' perceptions that they provided comfort and positive feedback to student writers strongly influenced their satisfaction with conferences. These studies indicate as well the important role that positive politeness plays in the relationship that tutors and student writers co-construct during conferences.

Motivational Scaffolding Strategies in Our Coding Scheme

We identified five motivational scaffolding strategies:

- *Showing concern*: Tutors built rapport with students by demonstrating that they cared. Such demonstrations of concern could be formulaic, as when a tutor asked about a student writer's understanding with a collocation: "Does that make sense?" Demonstrations of concern could also be nonformulaic, as when a tutor attended to a student writer's emotional well-being: "You're feeling less overwhelmed now that you've found it's not hard at all?"
- *Praising*: Tutors pointed to student writers' successes with positive feedback and verbal rewards. Praise, too, could be formulaic: "That's good." It could also be nonformulaic: "I think it has a subtlety to it, which is . . . very nice. And I think that's a difficult thing for lots of students to achieve in their writing."
- *Reinforcing student writers' ownership and control*: Tutors increased student writers' developing self-regulation and self-efficacy by asserting that the student writer ultimately made the decisions: "Well, I mean . . . that's something that is ultimately up to you."
- *Being optimistic or using humor*: Tutors reduced student writers' anxiety with light-heartedness and built confidence by asserting a student writer's ability to persevere in the task. "Uh, consequences for your actions. Wrong and right. Whatever. I can't spell consequences": a tutor used this self-deprecating humor when jotting down a note.
- *Giving sympathy or empathy*: Tutors expressed their understanding that the task was difficult: "And it's a difficult thing to analyze senses."

Conclusion

In this chapter, we have reviewed research that informed our macro- and microlevel analyses. We have discussed how Wood, Bruner, and Ross's (1976) work on scaffolding and Vygotsky's (1978, 1987) notion of the ZPD provide the educational framework and how additional research from education, psychology, and linguistics augment our framework and our analyses.

We began the chapter by discussing research to analyze conferences at the macrolevel. Writing center conferences consist of an opening stage, a teaching stage, and a closing stage. The teaching stage consists of a chain of topic episodes, defined according to the content of the talk. Topic episodes can consist of a single turn or begin and end during a turn, and they can also comprise a sequence of tutor and student writer turns.

We continued our review with a discussion of scaffolding and the ZPD. These two concepts describe the co-construction of meaning that occurs in writing center conferences for both tutors and students. Effective tutoring begins and continues with intersubjectivity, where the tutor and student share knowledge of the topic the student wants to discuss and begin to develop trust in each other's good will to move forward from that shared topic to new understanding for the student and often for the tutor as well. The moving forward occurs in the student's ZPD developed during the collaborative agenda setting. While tutors lead students from existing understanding to greater mastery, they rely on active participation to diagnose students' errors and misunderstandings.

In operationalizing scaffolding and instruction, we discussed the three categories of tutoring strategies—instruction, cognitive scaffolding, and motivational scaffolding—that we target in our microlevel analysis. Prohibited in early writing center mandates because of its association with directiveness, instruction requires expertise from tutors and can lead to tutor dominance. However, as we argue, instruction and the resulting directiveness are essential for student writers to move along in developing understanding. Instruction can protect student writers from frustration in trying to answer questions they do not understand and can save time in conferencing.

Research about scaffolding and the ZPD applies particularly to our coding of cognitive and motivational scaffolding. Both are vital to the process of co-construction of meaning between the tutor and the student—on the one hand, to the co-construction of understanding and, on the other, to the co-construction of rapport and solidarity. Cognitive scaffolding, with its co-construction of meaning and performance, usually constrains students' responses and then supports those responses to help students avoid failure and frustration. It often begins with a closed question, where the tutor evaluates the student's response as appropriate or not. The early writing center admonition to use only open-ended questions and to avoid leading student writers to appropriate responses can leave student writers floundering and anxious.

Motivational scaffolding strategies offer encouragement and thus can save student writers from anxiety and enhance their comfort during conferences through feelings of rapport and solidarity with tutors. Unless student writers are already intrinsically motivated to improve their writing, tutors likely can hope only to stimulate situational interest in a writing task, such as interest based on student writers' extrinsic motivation to get good grades.

In other words, based on research conducted primarily about areas other than writing center tutoring, we can establish a theoretically grounded framework for discussing tutors' talk in conferences. In the rest of *TAW*, we demonstrate our coding scheme devised from this framework, as it can be applied quantitatively and qualitatively to better understand writing center conferences.

3

METHODS

In this chapter, we describe and explain our methods of data collection and quantitative and qualitative analysis. We also explain some of the challenges we encountered as we collected and analyzed the data, particularly as we worked to develop discrete, reliable codes. In discussing these challenges and our imperfect responses to them, we try in this chapter to do more than report our methods; we also try to facilitate the research process of others who are conducting or will conduct similar research on natural-language data.

The Conferences

We recorded the 10 writing center conferences from 2005 to 2008 in the writing center (then called the English Center) of Auburn University in Auburn, Alabama. At that time, funded entirely by the Department of English, the writing center served only students enrolled in FYC and in world literature (WL)—required core-curriculum courses (see Table 3.1). Later, from 2010 to 2011, we recorded conferences and collected other data. Specifically, we again studied T9. She had graduated with a bachelor's degree and was at that point a graduate student in the Master of Technical and Professional Communication program. From 2010 to 2011, she worked as writing fellow in the Business Writing Prototype (BWP), a WID program that ran within Auburn University's College of Business (COB) from 2010 to 2012. As a writing fellow, T9 met with all of the students enrolled in a supply-chain management (purchasing) course. We recorded her conferences with S12, a junior-level business student enrolled in the course. In Chapter 8, our case-study chapter, we examine T9's strategies as she worked with three student writers (S9, S11, and S12) during four conferences. The institutional review board at Auburn University approved both phases of the data collection.

When we collected the writing center conferences, the writing center operated under a 30-minute, loosely enforced guideline for conferences. The 10 conferences that we analyze in Chapters 4–7 ranged from 17 to 40 minutes, totaling approximately 5.5 hours of conference talk. Nine of those 10 constituted

TABLE 3.1 Description of the Conferences in Both Phases of the Study

Tutor (T)/ Student Writer (S)	Conference Duration (minutes)	Course	Agenda	Conference Topic
Writing Center (WC)				
T1–S1	37	FYC I	Revising/ Proofreading	Spatial description of floors in the library.
T2–S2	32	FYC I	Revising	Description and discussion of a change in S2's life.
T3–S3	23	FYC I	Brainstorming	Rhetorical analysis of a magazine.
T4–S4	47	WL II	Brainstorming	Comparison of two short stories.
T5–S5	16	FYC I	Brainstorming	Argument to limit smoking areas and portrayal of smoking in media.
T6–S6	39	FYC I	Proofreading	Description and analysis of the importance of a personal experience.
T7–S7	39	FYC I	Revising/ Proofreading	Argument about the value of running and other physical activity.
T8–S8	38	FYC II	Revising/ Proofreading	Persuasive essay about a class reading.
T9–S9	24	WL I	Brainstorming	Analysis of a creation myth other than Genesis.
T10–S10	41	FYC II	Proofreading	Persuasive essay advocating safe-sex education.
T9–S11	27	FYC II	Revising	Persuasive essay about presidential candidates' views on cultural diversity.
Business Writing Prototype (BWP)				
T9–S12	24	Purchasing	Planning	White paper analyzing the merits of Coca Cola's supply chain.
T9–S12	26	Purchasing	Editing	White paper analyzing the merits of Coca Cola's supply chain.

Note: FYC = first-year composition; WL = world literature

first-time meetings for the tutor and student writer; one of the conferences (T3–S3) we believed to be a first-time conference, but we cannot be certain. Before we could verify that it was, the database of the writing center was lost in the transition from a center run by the English Department to one administered at the university level. We used this tenth conference because it allowed us to include another male tutor and because it allowed us to include another brainstorming conference. In addition, as Chapter 4 shows, the frequency counts of tutoring strategies in this conference exhibit no outlier data.

As we noted in Chapter 1, we selected the writing center conferences from a larger corpus of 51 video-recorded conferences because the participants in each evaluated them as very satisfactory in postconference surveys. We determined tutor and student writer satisfaction through two 6-point Likert-scale items on the matching postconference surveys:

- How would you rate the success of the conference? (tutors and student writers; 6, "very successful" to 1, "not successful")
- Will you incorporate the ideas discussed into your writing? (student writers; 6, "very much" to 1, "none")
- Do you think the student will incorporate the ideas discussed into his or her writing? (tutors; 6, "very much" to 1, "none")

The majority of tutors and student writers rated their conferences as a 6, "very successful." The rest rated their conferences as a 5. Similarly, the majority of tutors and student writers indicated 6, "very much," on the question of the extent to which the student writers would likely implement the conference discussion. The rest assigned a rating of 5. We concluded that both students and tutors were quite satisfied with the conferences. The two conferences that we analyze in Chapter 8, our case-study chapter, were satisfactory too, as judged by the tutor, T9, and the student writer, S12, with whom she worked.

Along with the video recordings of the writing center conferences, Thompson collected postconference interviews with most of the tutors. Thompson conducted these interviews within three days after the conference—as soon as tutors' schedules (filled with classes and other jobs) would allow. She played back the recorded conferences and asked tutors to comment freely on their reasons for using certain strategies. At times, she also stopped the video recording to ask tutors questions about why they said certain things (that is, made certain discourse moves). She also asked them to stop the recording whenever they wished to make comments about their tutoring strategies. As with all of the conferences, we transcribed the interviews.

Gass and Mackey (2000), writing about what they call "consecutive recall interviews," postconference interviews occurring with little or no delay, note that "the length of time period that lapses between the event and the recall, what sort of memory structures are being accessed, and the efficacy of the support in overcoming any delay are all key issues" (49–50). Interviews that occur with little or no delay, they say, allow better access to information in memory structures. However, interviews occurring after some delay still provide access to participants' memories, particularly when the interview involves video or audio playback of the original event (in this case, a conference).

As we mentioned above, the data we analyze in Chapter 8 consisted of four conferences with T9. We collected the two writing center conferences that we analyze in Chapter 8 during the first phase of data collection. In Chapter 8, we refer to these conferences with abbreviations that stand for writing center-unfamiliar student writer (WC-U) and writing center-familiar student writer (WC-F). WC-U was part of the analysis of Chapters 4–7 (T9–S9), whereas WC-F was not included in that analysis. In the second phase of data collection, we collected the other two conferences. We refer to these as Business Writing Prototype-unfamiliar student writer (BWP-U) and Business Writing Prototype-familiar student writer (BWP-F).

During the second phase of our data collection, the former writing center tutor, T9, was a writing fellow in the BWP. She worked with Dr. Gary Page, the instructor of a participating purchasing course. In the two BWP conferences, she met with the same student writer, S12, three times. We video recorded their first conference, which took place close to the beginning of the semester, and we video recorded their third conference, which took place closer to the end of the semester. In addition to video recording the conferences, we conducted postconference interviews using the same procedure as described above.

Dr. Page's purchasing class was one of four undergraduate and two graduate classes participating in the BWP, a program begun in part to address the accreditation requirements of the Association to Advance Collegiate Schools of Business. In the spring of 2010, the COB's Office of Professional and Career Development initiated a partnership with writing studies faculty to develop a program that built on prior work of other colleges of business that had already incorporated writing into their curricula (Bowers and Metcalf 2008; Cyphert 2002; Tuleja and Greenhalgh 2008) but also experimented with other strategies for improving students' disciplinary writing. In spring 2010, Mackiewicz worked with administrators and faculty in the COB to plan the BWP and ensure its viability for fall 2010.

BWP writing fellows worked 15 hours per week during the academic year. Thus, like the other participating writing fellows, T9 worked 225 hours, both in fall 2010 and in spring 2011. After some trial and error in scheduling conferences in fall 2010, Mackiewicz, COB faculty, and the writing fellows revised the conference schedule for spring 2011. In spring 2011, T9 spent her 225 hours working with a class of 58 purchasing students as follows:

- Commenting on drafts (30 minutes × 58 papers × 2 times per semester) = 58 hours.

- Attending class = 20 hours (roughly half of the class meetings).
- Administering pretests, grading pre- and posttests, entering data, writing emails, creating materials = 25 hours.
- Holding office hours during planning, revising, and editing conference blocks (12.5 hours per week × 9 weeks) = 113 hours.
- Holding (limited) office hours during other weeks = 9 hours.

T9 and the other writing fellows found this schedule fairly workable, particularly because the business students had to schedule their planning, revising, and editing conferences within a certain block of time during the semester, a requirement that kept them from trying to squeeze mandatory meetings in at the end of the semester.

In the BWP, each writing fellow worked with an individual class on a multi-component, semester-long writing project. As mentioned above, T9 worked with Dr. Page's purchasing class (SCMN 3730 Purchasing: Supply Management and Servicing), a junior-level, required course in the supply-chain management program. Even before Dr. Page's participation in the BWP, he incorporated writing into his courses, and, in each of the two semesters that T9 worked with Dr. Page, she helped students with a variety of assignments that involved writing besides the semester-long writing project, including case studies and presentations. The major writing assignment for the class—the one developed and shaped during discussions of ways to make the purchasing course part of the BWP—was a researched and designed white paper. The assignment, as explained in the spring 2011 syllabus for the purchasing class, was as follows:

> Research, organize, and write a formal report (white paper) characterizing a selected company regarding its supply-chain management operating philosophy and strategy. Choose a company from the attached list of companies that have been recognized for their excellence in designing and managing their respective supply chains. Structure your paper like a magazine article from a supply-chain trade magazine. You will supply some company background, but the main focus of your article should be how the company's supply chain works and what supply-chain best practices put your company in AMR's [Advanced Market Research's] top 25. Your paper's overall purpose will be to subjectively assess your company and predict their future success or failure (based on evidence you supply through research). The white paper submission . . . must be 1200–1500 words, not including tables, figures, reference list and appendices.

This multicomponent assignment required an executive summary, a corporate profile, an analysis of the company's supply-chain design, a summary of the company's recognized best practices, and an assessment of the potential of the company for continued success. A semester-long project, it required a total of five deliverables: research summaries; a complete rough draft; two more draft versions, each with a bulleted list of changes from the last version; and the final version. As we discuss in Chapter 8, students' lack of familiarity with the white paper genre, along with the complexity of the assignment, strongly influenced the frequency of T9's instruction strategies, particularly her use of explaining.

The Participants

At the time of the first phase of the data collection (2005–2008), Thompson was the director of the writing center (the English Center). She evaluated as highly competent all 10 of the tutors whose talk we studied. In the first phase of our data collection, the tutors were all in their second year or more of working in the writing center.

All 10 tutors had completed a semester-long training practicum. The training consisted of weekly hour-long meetings. In these meetings, the tutors role-played agenda setting and conference closings, scaffolding, and working with difficult, confused, or special-needs students. Thompson and the tutors also discussed the assignments for FYC and WL courses, and they discussed what the tutors could expect to see students bring in the following week, based on the course syllabi for FYC and WL. Several of the 10 tutors participated in the training practicum a second time as assistant writing center directors or as mentors for inexperienced tutors. Optimally, as Cromley and Azevedo (2005) argue is possible with expert tutors, Thompson intended the training to enable the tutors to "create opportunities for students to be generative when students have the knowledge and skills to do so but provide instruction when students lack sufficient knowledge" (104). In other words, the tutors should have been able to diagnose student writers' needs and employ tutoring strategies to meet those needs.

During this training, Thompson talked with the tutors about potential roles, such as teacher and peer. She asked tutors to avoid enacting either of these roles. Rather, she trained the tutors to be "apprentice" writing teachers, as Trimbur (1987) discusses the term to differentiate it from a paraprofessional or preprofessional role:

> For me, tutor training is a matter of timing and community allegiance. The apprentice model of tutor training invokes a kind of knowledge—the theory and practice of teaching writing—that pulls tutors toward the professional community that generates and authorizes such knowledge. . . . We need to treat peer tutors as students, not as paraprofessionals or preprofessionals, and to recognize that their community is not necessarily ours. (27)

Thus, Thompson's tutor training recognized that tutors, like student writers, were learning from their writing center experiences.

In addition, as we noted above, this writing center served only students enrolled in the required English core courses—FYC and WL; all of the tutors had taken those courses, and some of them had taught those courses. Therefore, as we analyzed the data, we considered the tutors to be very proficient, not only in essay and literary analysis genres, but also frequently in the content of student writers' papers. Even if tutors were not familiar with all of the assignments that student writers brought in, the tutors knew a great deal about the required readings, their uses in those courses, and instructors' expectations. Also, the tutors were not peers in age with the student writers whom they served. All 10 tutors were at least junior undergraduates, and many were graduate students. Most of the student writers were first-year and second-year undergraduates—around 19 and 20 years old (see Table 3.2).

The 10 tutors followed a common set of procedures and policies, delineated in the tutoring handbook that Thompson had developed in conjunction with tutors (Auburn University English Department 2008). Appendix A contains the handbook section "Conducting a Conference with a Student." This section provides detailed advice about suggested discourse moves for each stage of the conference, although it allows tutors some latitude and autonomy. Also from the guidebook, Appendix B includes the "Notes for Students" form, as well as instructions for filling out the form. Just as Clark (1988) describes, some of the FYC and WL instructors worried about plagiarism—student writers using language that tutors had supplied. Therefore, to mitigate the potential for such charges, Thompson told the tutors not to write on student writers' drafts. Instead, she encouraged tutors to use the "Notes for Students" form to describe the agenda for the conference, to summarize the topics (with the student writer's help, if possible), to develop a schedule for finishing certain composing tasks, to establish goals for completion before the next conference, and to jot down the date and time for the next conference, if the student writer had scheduled one. Unless student writers showed them the forms, instructors did not have access to them. However, at the end of each conference, tutors wrote reports for student writers' instructors. In the training practicum, Thompson emphasized the differences in what tutors should include in the notes that they wrote for student writers and the summary report that they wrote for instructors.

At the end of their first semester working in the writing center, for assessment, each tutor audio recorded a conference and reflected back on that recorded conference, addressing questions related to best practices in writing center tutoring. Thompson listened to the conferences, responded to the reflections, and met with each tutor individually to discuss the conference. Tutors who performed poorly during the recorded conference or did not complete the reflection repeated the recording requirement during their second semester of employment. Thompson terminated the employment of the few who did not improve.

TABLE 3.2 Description of the Conference Participants

Tutor (T)/ Student Writer (S)	Gender	Race/Ethnicity	Education Level
T1	Female	White non-Hispanic	PhD candidate in English
S1	Male	White non-Hispanic	First-year undergraduate
T2	Female	White non-Hispanic	MA candidate in English and English Center assistant director
S2	Female	White non-Hispanic	First-year undergraduate
T3	Male	White non-Hispanic	PhD candidate in English and English Center assistant director
S3	Female	White non-Hispanic	First-year undergraduate
T4	Female	White non-Hispanic	MA candidate in English
S4	Female	White non-Hispanic	Second-year undergraduate
T5	Female	White non-Hispanic	MA candidate in English
S5	Male	White non-Hispanic	First-year undergraduate
T6	Male	White non-Hispanic	PhD candidate in English
S6	Female	White non-Hispanic	First-year undergraduate
T7	Male	White non-Hispanic	Undergraduate psychology major/English minor
S7	Female	White non-Hispanic	First-year undergraduate
T8	Female	White non-Hispanic	PhD candidate in English
S8	Female	White non-Hispanic	First-year undergraduate
T9	Female	White non-Hispanic	Undergraduate English major with S9 and S11; Master of Technical and Professional Communication candidate with S12
S9	Female	African-American	Second-year undergraduate
T10	Female	White non-Hispanic	Undergraduate English education major
S10	Male	African American	First-year undergraduate
S11	Female	White non-Hispanic	First-year undergraduate
S12	Male	White non-Hispanic	Undergraduate business (supply-chain management) major

Table 3.2 describes the writing center tutor and student writer pairs in the conference data. As shown in Table 3.2, seven of the tutors were graduate students or, more specifically, graduate teaching assistants (GTAs), teaching the courses (but not the student writers) that generated the assignments in the conferences; three were advanced undergraduates, pursuing either English majors or English minors, with overall GPAs of at least 3.5 (on a 4-point scale). The graduate students worked in the writing center without being screened, as their employment in the writing center was a component of their work as GTAs in the English Department. The undergraduates, however, were rigorously screened—nominated by an instructor, interviewed, and required to provide a satisfactory writing

sample and pass a proofreading test. Therefore, we considered all of the tutors accomplished writers (and students) and trained and experienced tutors. All 10 tutors were non-Hispanic white. Seven tutors were female; three were male. We mentioned before that T9 had worked in the writing center before becoming a writing fellow in the BWP. Her writing center experience consisted of two years as an undergraduate tutor and one as a graduate student tutor. After her first year in the writing center, Thompson appointed her to be a mentor for inexperienced tutors. Later, Thompson nominated her as a writing fellow based on her superior tutoring skills.

To familiarize T9 and the other already experienced tutors participating in the BWP with specific genres that COB faculty wanted students to learn, Mackiewicz held 60–90-minute training sessions during the first two weeks of fall 2010. These sessions focused on business genres, design of graphs and charts, and paragraph structure. They familiarized the writing fellows with genres often discussed in business and technical communication and helped them to relate those common genres (for example, the feasibility report) to the assignments that the faculty had developed. In addition to receiving training in business genres and the design of common visuals in business documents, T9 and the other writing fellows delved into business communication research. They read reports on writing-to-learn versus learning-to-write programs, assessments of business communication programs, and studies of business communication such as linguistic and rhetorical analyses of business reports and emails.

All the tutors and the students were native speakers of American English. Although this lack of diversity certainly influences the applicability of our findings, we wanted to limit the variables in this study as much as possible to clarify the utility of the coding scheme. As Lepper, Drake, and O'Donnell-Johnson (1997) mentioned in discussing their selection of students to be tutored in their studies, we wanted "to ensure that all tutees fell in an appropriate 'window for learning'" (113). In their research, they pretested students to be certain that they had mastered the prerequisite skills necessary for the tutoring to be useful but had not mastered the material for the tutoring. We strongly believe that future studies should include more linguistic diversity, examining the talk of tutors and student writers interacting in languages other than English, as well as tutors and student writers (interacting in English) who speak languages other than English as their first language.

Identifying and Analyzing Topic Episodes for Macrolevel Analysis

As we noted in Chapter 2, to identify and analyze topic episodes within the teaching stage, we looked to definitions and descriptions used in research about instructional discourse and multiparty conversations (Chafe 2001; Johnson et al. 2003; Korolija and Linell 1996; Novick, Andrade, and Bean 2009). Based on such research, we defined a topic episode as a single turn, a segment within a turn, or a string of turns that focuses on a single topic. Thus, we identified topic episodes by content, but we also looked to commonly occurring discourse markers such as "O.K.," "now," and "let's," markers that frequently signaled the beginnings of topic episodes and often signaled the endings as well.

To characterize multiturn topic episodes, we also closely examined the sequence of turns within each episode. Along with the cognitive scaffolding strategies that often initiate the three-part IRF sequences described in Chapter 2, topic episodes can begin with instruction or motivational scaffolding. Yet, like topic episodes comprised of three-part IRF sequences, such topic episodes are indeed collaborative, but collaboration within them can manifest itself in different ways. This difference is due in part to the fact that topic episodes beginning with instruction or motivational scaffolding (or consisting entirely of either) do not necessarily demand that students respond orally. Student writers' responses can be nonverbal—head nods, smiles, or looks of confusion—expressing student writers' understanding or lack of understanding.

To differentiate between topic episodes that correspond to earlier research about the three-part IRF sequences and those that do not, we decided to use the term "initiate" to discuss topic episodes beginning with tutors' pump questions and other cognitive scaffolding strategies. We decided to use the term "launch" instead of "initiate" to indicate topic episodes that tutors started with instruction or motivational scaffolding strategies. Further, we found that student writers began some topic episodes. We use the neutral term "introduce" to discuss these cases. In short, we found that discussing topic episodes, including the ways tutors launched and initiated them and student writers introduced them, helped us describe our data more accurately than if we had attempted to analyze our data solely in terms of three-part IRF sequences.

To get some measure of the extent to which we agreed on the boundaries of topic episodes, we separately coded the teaching stage of two conferences, marking the boundaries of the topic episodes and assigning an informative title to each episode (for example, "A problem with Microsoft Word" and "Using a comma after an introductory prepositional phrase"). We also marked the ending of the opening stage and the beginning of the closing stage. Our codes mostly matched, but we coded another conference separately to determine a percentage of agreement. In coding that third conference, we achieved 88% agreement. As was the case with the first two conferences we coded, discrepancies in our coding stemmed from times when the talk shifted in level of generality, for example, talk about places where smoking is banned (for example, restaurants) that shifted into talk about the scope of smoking bans (for example, local versus national). After we had identified topic episodes across the teaching stages of all 13 conferences, we were able to analyze the chains of topics these episodes created across the teaching stages they composed.

Developing the Coding Scheme for Microlevel Analysis

As we mentioned before, to code and eventually to analyze tutoring strategies, we modified Cromley and Azevedo's (2005) classification and descriptions of strategies. Called "elaborative coding," this top–down process of refining a previous scheme for another use further develops existing theory, as opposed to the bottom–up process of developing grounded theory (Auerbach and Silverstein 2003, 104; Saldaña 2013, 229). As we refined our scheme for use in analyzing writing center tutoring, we modified Cromley and Azevedo's (2005) scheme in three important ways.

First, in relation to instruction strategies, we differentiated between telling and suggesting based on a framework of more direct and less direct language (and less polite or more polite language) available to editors working with writers to improve their drafts. Writing about technical editors working with technical writers and subject matter experts, Mackiewicz and Riley (2003) explain that, in situations in which an editor has not established rapport with a writer, that editor has to balance directness (and its potential accompanying threat to self-image, what Goffman (1959) and Brown and Levinson (1987) call "face") with indirectness (and its potential lack of clarity). In our categories, the most directive utterances, those we refer to as telling, convey an obligation for their recipients to perform the action. They are the least mitigated and the most clear in conveying the speaker's intended meaning. Telling instruction strategies include "bald-on-record" strategies ("Put a comma here"). These unmitigated imperatives clearly and strongly convey the recipient's (the student writer's) obligation to comply, but the speakers' intentions are as clear as possible. Telling instruction strategies also include "locution-derivable" strategies, formed with modal and modal-like verbs that convey obligation such as "should," "must," "need to," "have to," and "ought to" ("You must put a comma here") and "opinion-statement" strategies ("I would put a comma here").

Suggesting instruction strategies carry less obligation, but they are less clear. They include "conventionally indirect" politeness strategies, strategies that convey possibility rather than obligation. These strategies employ modals such as "could" and "might" ("You could put a comma here") and question syntax ("Should you put a comma here?"). Presented as a general rule or an observation usually requiring the recipient's extensive inferencing, hints, or "nonconventionally indirect strategies," are the least clear and most vague of all ("Commas are used to separate independent clauses joined by coordinating conjunctions"). In the open-world domain of writing, the distinction between conveying obligation and conveying a possibility is critical. In the former case, according to the tutor, a student writer who wants to succeed must comply with the advice; in the latter case, a student writer who wants to succeed need only consider the suggestion.

Second, unlike Cromley and Azevedo (2005), we classified suggestions as instruction strategies rather than as hints (cognitive scaffolding). Suggesting is far more directive than hinting. Hints are vague; they allow for several potential meanings. For example, a tutor might say, "Paragraphs containing a lot of numerical data can be difficult to understand." This assertion could hint at any of the following meanings (among others): "You should use a table to organize the numerical data here," "You should cut the amount of numerical data that you provide here," or "You should write a few more explanatory sentences about the numerical data here." We found only few hints in the conference data, and these included statements of writing rules and conventions ("A semicolon separates two main clauses unless a coordinating conjunction is present"). In contrast to hints, suggestions such as "You might put a semicolon here" convey the speaker's meaning more clearly.

Third, we augmented scaffolding research with Bandura's (1997) research on self-efficacy, the findings of which have recently informed discussions about motivation and writing (Hidi and Boscolo 2006), as well as with Brown and Levinson's (1987) politeness theory. Although we defined and exemplified the three categories and the 16 codes of our coding scheme in Chapter 2, for convenience's sake, we provide the definitions and examples in Table 3.3 as well.

Thompson and a trained graduate assistant coded the 10 writing center conferences selected from the 2005–2008 corpus; with a second trained graduate student, she also coded the BWP conferences. Training the graduate student assistants in the scheme—its purpose and in its prototypical and boundary cases— was critical; as Scholfield (1995) writes, "Another answer to most [coding] problems is prior training of measures to a uniform standard" (212). The coders analyzed each conference individually, identifying tutoring strategies and classifying them according to the scheme. They achieved 88% agreement in their coding of the corpus and resolved any discrepancies through discussion to consensus. Although Saldaña (2013) points out that, "no standard or base percentage of agreement exists," he goes on to say that "the 80–90% range seems a minimal benchmark" (35). We were satisfied, then, with our percentage of agreement. In addition, we determined inter-rater reliability by applying the coding scheme to a subset of 60 tutor turns and calculating Cohen's kappa. The kappa statistic was 0.717, a good level of agreement (Landis and Koch 1977) that reassured us that our coding scheme was reliable.

Challenges in Developing a Reliable Coding Scheme

In this section, we describe some of the challenges we encountered as we developed the coding scheme and our coding procedure. Although in the end we were (and are) satisfied with the scheme's usefulness and reliability, we frequently ran into data that were difficult to identify and that lay on the boundaries of our codes' definitions.

TABLE 3.3 The Coding Scheme for Tutoring Strategies

Instruction		
Telling	Tutors use little or no mitigation to direct student writers to lower the face threat of their advice.	"Make sure when you when you've expanded these—Make sure they all relate back to that thesis as well."
Suggesting	Tutors use more mitigation (often negative politeness) to lower the face threat of their advice.	"But since the focus of the paper is law enforcement, you probably want to bring it back to law enforcement here."
Explaining and exemplifying	Tutors offer reasons for and illustrations of their advice.	"Because you kind of end with, 'Ah well, whatever it is, it works' after only telling one."

Cognitive Scaffolding		
Pumping	Tutors ask questions (or use inquiry statements) that get student writers to think out loud. Pumping can be highly constraining (particularly leading questions) or minimally constraining.	"Where does the comma go in this sentence?" "How can you incorporate those ideas into your draft?"
Reading aloud	Tutors read sections of student writers' drafts aloud or read instructors' assignment sheets aloud. They also ask student writers to read their drafts aloud.	[Reading from the assignment sheet] "'You must state your position on an issue and convince your reader that your position is correct.'"
Responding as a reader or a listener	Tutors tell student writers what they take away as readers (or listeners), paraphrasing what they think student writers have written (or are saying).	"You say that, you know, this is the way I like it because it's suitable to my needs in getting things done."
Referring to a previous topic	Tutors refer student writers back to the earlier occurrence of an issue.	"And then, T-O-O, 'too good.' Again, like we talked about in the beginning."
Forcing a choice	Tutors present student writers with several alternatives and expect them to choose one.	"Now, 'the boys tell their friends,' or 'the boys tells their friends'?"
Prompting	Tutors set up responses from student writers by providing partial responses or by leaving a blank for them to fill in, narrowing the possible answers.	"So if you were to, you know, if you were to say '*Cosmo Girl* targets' . . . what?"

| Hinting | Tutors use nonconventional indirectness (rely on context) to raise or refer to an issue. | [Used to get the student writer to see that there is more to "punishment." Student writer elaborated with "Oh, like, right and wrong."] "So it also demonstrates punishment. Just punishment in general." |
| Demonstrating | Tutors show student writers how to do something. | [Showing a website exemplifying APA citations.] "Like this. They give you like 'You should have a cover page that does this.' That we don't want you to pay attention to." |

Motivational Scaffolding

Showing concern	Tutors build rapport with student writers by demonstrating that they care. Such demonstrations of concern can be formulaic, as when a tutor asks about a student writer's understanding with a collocation, or they can be nonformulaic, as when a tutor attends to a student writer's emotional well-being with an individualized comment or question.	Formulaic: "Does that make sense?" Nonformulaic: "You're feeling less overwhelmed now that you've found it's not hard at all?"
Praising	Tutors point to student writers' successes with positive feedback and verbal rewards. Praise can be formulaic or nonformulaic.	Formulaic: "That's good." Nonformulaic: "I think it has a subtlety to it, which is . . . very nice. And I think that's a difficult thing for lots of students to achieve in their writing."
Reinforcing student writers' ownership and control	Tutors assert that the student writer ultimately makes the decisions.	"Well, I mean . . . that's something that is ultimately up to you."
Being optimistic or using humor	Tutors convey positivity with light-hearted joking and by asserting a student writer's ability to persevere in the task.	"But they're politicians. What do you expect?"
Giving sympathy or empathy	Tutors express their understanding that the task is difficult.	"And it's a difficult thing to analyze senses."

Creating Useful Codes and Categories

As any researcher who codes natural-language data in an attempt to understand some construct (such as scaffolding) knows, developing a coding scheme—or modifying an existing scheme for a new purpose—requires iterative testing and revising before all codes in the scheme capture like data and reject dissimilar data. As Stadler (2011) writes, "Naturally occurring data rarely fit into these pre-formed categories neatly" (37). Over the course of several months, we iteratively revised and tested our codes until we were satisfied with each code's internal homogeneity—the extent to which the data ascribed a given code and that code match, as well as our scheme's external heterogeneity—the extent to which the codes differ (Patton 2001, 466). During this iterative testing, we revised codes. In one case, we subsumed one code—what we were calling leading questions—into another code—pumping questions. We made this change when we realized that the leading questions did the same work as pumping questions, but were simply at a very far end of the continuum of minimally constrained to highly constrained responses that characterizes some cognitive scaffolding strategies. For example, we originally coded the question "You're not actually using that name are you?" as a leading question. Because T2 stated the question in the negative (a marker of bias in expectations for a response [Schulz and Schmidt 1993]) and used the discourse marker "actually" (a marker of repair to common conversational ground similar to "in fact" or "really" [see Smith and Jucker 2000, 215]), the question leads S2 to the answer "No." (Indeed, S2 responded thusly: "No. Because there's so many people from there that go here.") A question such as T2's certainly does imply that the tutor has a particular answer in mind, but the question nevertheless pumps the student writer for a response.

As another example, early in our iterative testing, we separated suggesting from telling strategies. We knew that the tasks of the open-world domain of writing differed from closed-world domains in the frequency with which those tasks allowed for a number of paths to an effective outcome. In the open-world domain of writing, student writers often could decide for themselves on a suitable "answer," a course of action; they were not working through problems to find definite, objective answers as in, for example, algebra tutoring for middle school students. Seeing this difference, we separated advice that conveyed possibility (suggesting) from advice that conveyed obligation (telling). We created two codes, breaking from Cromley and Azevedo's (2005) scheme so that our analysis would be more targeted to our purpose and therefore more insightful and useful. However, sometimes, determining whether a tutor's utterance was telling or suggesting was difficult—even though explicitly manifested characteristics (for example, modal verbs) made the distinction relatively easy most of the time. For example, we counted opinion statements such as "I would expand on the—how quiet it is as well" as telling. Our thinking was this: We assumed that, when doing their own writing, tutors would look out for their own self-interests; therefore, in telling student writers what their course of action would be with "I would," they conveyed obligation to comply (while still acknowledging student writers' ultimate decision-making capacity).

In other cases, tutors' syntax seemed to mitigate the obligation of the high-value modal that the tutor used. In the examples below, the tutors use the high-value modal "need to," but they embedded the modal and its subject ("you") in a relative clause, as T2 did: "Well then, what you need to do is the same kind of thing." Cases such as this lie on the boundary of the telling code, because their more complex syntax—the embeddedness of their modal verb of obligation—seems to soften their directiveness.

In contrast, we joined optimism and humor—both strategies that convey a tutor's positivity—into one code. We combined these two moves because we realized that these occurrences of explicit positivity—particularly explicit statements of optimism—appeared less frequently than other strategies. So, we decided to join statements of optimism such as T2's "I think you'll feel proud when you're done" to cases of humor such as T1's "Just keep in mind that your thesis statement is like your Bible."

Determining and Refining Latent Codes

Developing codes and categories for tutoring strategies is challenging, because the strategies consist of latent, or functional, content. We identify them by characteristics that do not reside "on the surface of communication" and are not "easily observable," as manifest, or syntactic, content is observable (Rourke et al. 2000, 6). For example, the modal verbs that signal differences between telling and suggesting and the intonation that signals reading aloud are examples of manifest content. Also, characteristics that commonly signal a particular code—for example, the formulaicity of praise and shows of concern and the question syntax of pumps—are examples of manifest content as well. Manifest content facilitates automated identification of codes and thus simplifies and speeds analysis. Latent content, on the other hand, is interpretive and subjective: "the locus of the variable shifts to the coders' interpretations of the meaning of the content" (8). For example, humor strategies contained no particular semantic content. T7's humor consisted of a question to S7 about whether she too had noted that the sentence they just read together rhymed: "It has a nice little rhyme scheme to it. Did you hear that?" T10 responded to S10's agenda for the conference ("Basically, everything to get an A paper") with an understated (declarative) assertion: "Yeah, I guess that would be good." T9's self-teasing aside and playful note to S9 about how to interpret her writing certainly contained unique semantic content: "And I think I just wrote on myself. Anyway, that's a B, not a heart." In such latent-content cases, all we could do was check for inter-rater reliability and refine codes until we achieved satisfactory agreement.

Determining Unit Size and Type for Analysis

Another challenge in developing the coding scheme was identifying the type and size of the unit to demarcate one code from another in our transcripts. Several options for unit of analysis are available to those trying to understand natural-language data, for example, the sentence, the t-unit (Hunt 1965), and the intonation unit (Chafe 1994). In our case, some tutoring strategies (for example, demonstrations of concern) regularly fell into the easily demarcated unit of the sentence, but other strategies (for example, explaining) regularly crossed sentence boundaries. T6's explanation, syntactically, consumes at least three and possibly four sentences, depending on transcription choices:

> "I just decided on Auburn" is a sentence. "I was almost done with senior year" is a sentence. So we've got, you know, the nice conjunctive word there, "which," which ties that—that second part in, which is fine, but I think here you've got the comma doing the work of a period.

In contrast, T8's explanation for her suggestion that S8 combine two sentences that "kind of say the same thing" consists of just one sentence: "Because you have a quote that's basically saying the same thing."

In the end, we needed maximum flexibility in this regard, as some coded items consisted of a short sentence ("You know?") and some such as explanations consisted of multiple sentences. We coded strategies based on Budd, Thorp, and Donohew's (1967) "thematic unit." We asked the question, "What is the purpose of a particular utterance?" (Rourke et al. 2000, 10) to determine a thematic unit and thus the boundaries of individual codes.

Through iterative testing and refining the definitions and boundaries of our codes, we tried to avoid what Mercer (2010) calls "simplistic coding"—coding that limits analysts' sensitivity to what actually happened because the coding scheme forces poor data-to-code associations or blunts researchers' ability to identify data types (6). We realize that our responses to the coding challenges that we encountered were imperfect, but they were the best responses, we believe, for our data and our purposes.

Conclusion

We employed quantitative and qualitative analysis in this study of experienced tutors' tutoring strategies. Quantitative analysis allowed us to pan out to show the big picture of the ways experienced tutors used strategies; qualitative analysis allowed us to provide fine-grained analysis of tutors' talk. Both approaches have drawbacks: quantitative analysis does not display and explain the moment-to-moment creation of knowledge and the moment-to-moment creation of a relationship (even a potentially one-time, institutional relationship). It does not examine the *how* in relation to tutors' use of strategies. Qualitative analysis, on the other hand, does not display and explain the *how often*. The answer to this question of frequency correlates in part to the relative importance of tutoring strategies—both within a single conference and across conferences. In our analysis, we have combined these approaches to show holistically tutors' talk.

We believe that our coding scheme and the analysis that we performed with it can move writing center research forward. Others do not have to start from scratch from a scheme developed for tutoring in closed-world domains or some other rhetorical situation. Rather, writing center researchers can refine our coding scheme for their purposes. For example, a researcher particularly interested in the role that humor plays in student writers' motivation would want to create two codes from our single optimism/humor code. Indeed, that researcher would likely want to test and use several codes for different types of humor (see Wanzer et al. 2006; Wanzer, Frymier, and Irwin 2010). By openly discussing our methods and the lessons we learned as we carried out our study, we hope to advance not just what we know about tutors' talk but also how we perform writing center research.

4

THE THREE CONFERENCE STAGES AND TUTORING STRATEGIES

The Overall Results

- The Opening Stage of Writing Center Conferences
- The Teaching Stage of Writing Center Conferences
- The Closing Stage of Writing Center Conferences
- Tutoring Strategies: Frequencies of Occurrence
- Conclusion and Implications for Tutor Training

As we noted in Chapter 1, we believe that one of the main contributions of *TAW* is its empirical, micro- and macrolevel quantitative analysis of strategies of experienced writing center tutors. In this chapter, we describe the opening, teaching, and closing stages, including volubility counts (word counts). In addition, we describe topic-episode chains and discuss the tutoring strategies that tutors used to launch (in the case of instruction and motivational scaffolding) and to initiate (in the case of cognitive scaffolding) the topic episodes. Finally, we discuss the frequencies of tutoring strategies across the 10 conferences and, to the extent that we can, juxtapose our data with results from studies of tutoring in closed-world domains.

The Opening Stage of Writing Center Conferences

In the opening stage, tutors and student writers got acquainted and set a conference agenda. To give a sense of the extent to which tutors and student writers contributed to this stage, we quantified the volubility of both tutors and student writers in each of the 10 conferences. Table 4.1 shows the results.

In the opening, volubility ranged from a high of 449 words (T6–S6) to a low of 141 words (T9–S9). More revealing than the total word counts, however, are the word counts for tutors and student writers. In 5 of the 10 conferences

TABLE 4.1 Volubility (Number of Words) in the Opening Stage

	Number of Words		
Conference	Tutors	Student Writers	Total
T1–S1	50	108	158
T2–S2	227	131	358
T3–S3	57	89	146
T4–S4	79	355	434
T5–S5	127	125	252
T6–S6	220	229	449
T7–S7	81	106	187
T8–S8	101	96	197
T9–S9	27	114	141
T10–S10	127	89	216
Total (%)	1,096 (43.2)	1,442 (56.8)	2,538 (100)

(T1–S1, T3–S3, T4–S4, T7–S7, T9–S9), student volubility exceeded tutor volubility by at least 20 words. In three conferences (T5–S5, T6–S6, T8–S8), volubility for tutors and student writers was nearly equal. In just two conferences (T2–S2, T10–S10) did tutor volubility exceed student writer volubility by more than 20 words. On the whole, student writers contributed more words to the openings of their conferences than tutors did, and these volubility results suggest that the student writers actively participated in setting the agenda—collaboration likely vital to conference success.

In examining opening stages more closely, we found that, immediately after the greeting, tutors asked the student writers what they wanted to work on; for example, T4 asked, "What can I help you with today?" Further, in each conference, either the tutor (with another question) or the student writer (with an explanation) followed up the student writer's request for assistance. Then, either the student writer offered or the tutor requested the assignment sheet ("Do you have your assignment sheet with you also, or can you tell me anything about it?"). In their training, the 10 tutors in this study learned to familiarize themselves with the assignment regardless of the conference agenda, so that they might flexibly follow the likely twists and turns of the teaching stage. Finally, at the end of the opening stage, all 10 tutors explicitly stated their understanding of the conference agenda or indicated their willingness to carry out the agenda that the student writer had suggested.

The opening stage provided tutors their main opportunity to determine what student writers wanted to accomplish (or, at least, thought they wanted to accomplish). Tutors determined what the final product should be and where student writers were in the composing process. With the information that they gleaned, tutors could help fill in gaps in student writers' knowledge and figure out what student writers meant when they said they wanted help with "flow" ("I want to make sure, like, everything flows from, like, paragraph to paragraph") and "grammar" ("I just want you to look for, um, grammatical things, as well as just, if sentences are awkward or anything"). Thus, tutors were poised not only to address student writers' concerns but also to provide them with more help than they asked for.

The Teaching Stage of Writing Center Conferences

During the teaching stage, the main pedagogical work of the conference takes place. This stage comprises topic episodes, segments of talk that focus on a single topic. Table 4.2 shows the tutors' and student writers' volubility during the teaching stage.

In the teaching stage of all 10 conferences, tutors contributed more talk than student writers, a result in keeping with tutors' and student writers' need to work toward accomplishing the agenda set in the opening within the time limit of about 30 minutes. If tutors had not worked under a time constraint, they might have been able to use Socratic questioning, a method that almost certainly would increase student writers' volubility. Using this method, the tutor "asks questions that lead students to discover their own misconceptions during the course of answering the questions" (Graesser, Person, and Magliano 1995, 501). The tutor "never tells the students they are wrong, never directly supplies correct information, and never articulates the students' misconceptions" (Graesser, Person, and Magliano 1995, 502). Given the intensity of effort Socratic questioning requires, even if tutors had time to use this questioning method, they likely would find the method difficult to sustain and exhausting (Rosé et al. 2003; Tienken,

TABLE 4.2 Volubility (Number of Words) in the Teaching Stage

| Conference | Number of Words | | |
	Tutors	Student Writers	Total
T1–S1	2,497	1,310	3,807
T2–S2	3,068	1,054	4,122
T3–S3	1,638	881	2,519
T4–S4	1,748	1,273	3,021
T5–S5	938	229	1,167
T6–S6	3,343	1,455	4,798
T7–S7	2,020	922	2,942
T8–S8	2,483	1,372	3,855
T9–S9	2,320	751	3,071
T10–S10	1,771	150	1,921
Total (%)	21,826 (69.9)	9,397 (30.1)	31,223 (100)

Goldberg, and DiRocco 2010). That tutors talked more than student writers did, then, seems understandable, given the parameters of the conference situation.

Overview of Topic Episodes

Analyzing conferences at the macrolevel for us meant intra-analysis and inter-analysis of topic episodes. We analyzed the internal structures of topic episodes, as well as the chain of topic episodes that together composed the structure and flow of a conference's teaching stage. Analysis of a teaching stage's chain of topic episodes also reveals the changes—sometimes slight and sometimes radical—in the conference agenda.

In this section, we present summary data. First, we present the inter-analysis, starting with the frequency with which tutors and student writers launched, initiated, or introduced topic episodes and the number of words the topic episodes contained on the average. Then, we look more closely at individual differences among topic episodes, focusing primarily on those that tutors began. Finally, we examine the topic-episode chains of the teaching stages in two conferences. After presenting this inter-analysis, we carry out intra-analysis, examining the structures of individual topic episodes to identify patterns of tutoring strategies.

Table 4.3 shows the total number of topic episodes in each teaching stage, the number of those episodes that tutors and student writers began, and the mean number of words per topic episode.

TABLE 4.3 Launch/Initiation/Introduction of and Volubility in Topic Episodes

| Conference | Topic Episodes | | | |
	Tutor Launched/ Initiated	Student-Writer Introduced	Total	Mean Number of Words[a]
T1–S1	27	12	39	98
T2–S2	20	4	24	172
T3–S3	24	4	28	90
T4–S4	18	4	22	137
T5–S5	12	1	13	90
T6–S6	10	12	22	218
T7–S7	26	2	28	105
T8–S8	36	2	38	101
T9–S9	23	5	28	110
T10–S10	25	0	25	77
Total	221	46	267	1,198
Mean	22.1	4.6	26.7	120

a Rounded to the nearest word

As Table 4.3 shows, on average, almost 27 topic episodes composed each teaching stage, with an average of 120 words per episode. The total number of topic episodes ranged from a high of 39 in the T1–S1 conference, primarily concerned with revising and proofreading, to a low of 13 for the T5–S5 conference, primarily concerned with brainstorming. The T5–S5 conference contained just 1,619 words (in all three stages) and lasted just 16.16 minutes; it was the shortest conference.

As we noted in Chapter 3, we use the term "introduce" for the first discourse move with which student writers began topic episodes; we use "launch" or "initiate" for the first move with which tutors began topic episodes. We use these terms to differentiate between the student writers' intent as learners and tutors' intent as supporters and teachers. Table 4.3 shows that tutors launched or initiated topic episodes over five times as often as student writers introduced them, a finding that suggests the control that tutors exerted over conference structure. Even though this control indicates tutors were, in a sense, the dominant participants, it also indicates tutors' roles as experts in writing, as conference managers, and as tutoring conversation facilitators—all roles that tutors must enact to generate successful conferences (Kiedaisch and Dinitz 1993; Mackiewicz 2004). In addition, student writers were able to introduce topic episodes if they chose to do so. In fact, S6 introduced more topic episodes than T6. Launching, initiating, and introducing topic episodes appeared strongly related to tutors' responsibilities and student writers' rights.

The lengths of the topic episodes varied greatly within conferences. The shortest topic episodes consisted of a segment of a turn, as shown in the long excerpt below with T9 (TE16 "Mm-hmm. Yeah, exactly that."), or a single turn. Here are two examples of short, single-turn topic episodes in which tutors gave student writers advice about process and product. First, in TE16 in T1's conference with S1, T1 expressed concern that S1 use the time in the conference to ask questions before breaking off to make way for S1's turn: "O.K. Do you want to go through the rest of that, or do you feel, like—." Besides short episodes related to process, as shown in this second example, the shortest single-turn episodes could also provide quickly stated advice, as in TE19 from T8's conference with S8: "Now, when you have—When you're talking about people, it's going to be 'who.'" Such short topic episodes contained only a few words—4 in the segment of a turn from T9–S9 and 16 and 14 in the two single-turn examples. In contrast, the longest topic episodes stretched to 750 words.

Because content—as opposed to turn-at-talk boundaries—defines topic episodes, new topic episodes could begin within a tutor's or a student writer's turn at speaking, as well as between turns, constituting intra-turn topic switches. For example, in the T9–S9 (brainstorming) conference, T9's turn includes the end of TE16 and the entirety of TE17, TE18, TE19, and TE20:

TE16 T9: Mm-hmm. Yeah, exactly that.

TE17 T9: See, that's what we have to question, unfortunately, for this essay. It's like, why do I believe this? And that's an important point to the question. Um. That's why we're using philosophical exile, or whatever. Um. Not to question it.

TE18 T9: So, why is imagery important to prove that we came from something? More specifically, that something being something human-like instead of say, a rock. Um. You know, and it takes faith to do that. So. Back to how does it use the element to explain?

TE19 T9: Let's kind of go back to the actual story here. Um. [18 seconds] Um. [Laughs.] Um. I still do kind of think that you should relate the actual story to, you know, what—what it explains to the fact that we were cut up, or they were cut up. And I think, actually, we kind of did that here. Not [unclear]—Because you say we have a need for a superior being. O.K. So. And we established that we have a need to explain why we're here. Otherwise it would just be, poof. Here. Um. And this story shows us that we came from something like a human. Um. I think we've got something good going here. Um.

TE20 T9: The hard part—It's an interesting, interesting assignment. Um. The hard part is going to be organizing it into a kind of something that's understandable and something that's not like, here's an idea, here's an idea, here's an idea. It has to be this idea leads to this idea, leads to this idea, leads to this idea. Do you see what I'm saying?

In TE16, T9's long turn begins with the short response to S9 discussed above. Then, T9 begins an intra-turn series of topic episodes about the main point of the essay (TE17), the myth's use of human-like imagery (TE18), finding evidence in the text to support the analysis (TE19), and the difficulty of the assignment (TE20). Although tutors' and student writers' topic episodes could fall along turn-taking boundaries, such co-occurrence certainly was not a given.

Before leaving this description of topic episodes, we should note one other finding. Like T8's use of the word "now" in TE19 ("Now, when you have— When you're talking about people, it's going to be 'who'"), T9 began TE17 and TE18 with typical markers of topic-episode initiation—"see" and "so"—what Schiffrin (1987) and others since call "discourse markers." Discourse markers are commonplace and brief words and phrases such as "O.K." and "so" and "now" but also "yeah," "you know," "well," and "I mean," and others. As Louwerse and Mitchell (2003), paraphrasing Schiffrin (1987), put it, discourse markers "instruct discourse participants in how to consider an upcoming utterance, providing a path toward the integration of different components of language use into one coherent discourse" (201). In other words, discourse markers indicate points of transition. Thus, tutors' frequent use of discourse markers such as "O.K." at episode boundaries makes sense and provides important cues for students.

Chains of Topic Episodes in Writing Center Conferences

Analysis of the chain of a given conference's topic episodes revealed the linguistic twists and turns that tutors' and student writers' discourse can take—maneuvers that may lead to learning. Here, we analyze the chains of topic episodes in the teaching stage of a brainstorming conference and in the teaching stage of a conference focusing on revising and proofreading. (Appendix C contains the coded T5–S5 conference in its entirety.)

In T5's conference with S5, the tutor and student writer brainstormed ideas for S5's FYC 1 essay about reducing or eliminating smoking. S5 had talked to his instructor about his subject matter, banning smoking, and his instructor had told him that the idea was done to death and needed a new twist. T5 agreed with the instructor and tried to lead S5 to a more complex yet narrower focus for his essay. As the list of topics in Table 4.4 shows, in the teaching stage of this conference, T5 and S5 progress quite directly from the first topic, leaving behind the essay topic of banning smoking, to the last topics—shifting to the subject of banning the portrayal of smoking in movies (particularly ones aimed at children) and general advice for revising a paper.

T5 began the teaching stage of the conference quickly, getting to the point by mentioning curbing smoking rather than banning it (TE1). She followed up in the next two topic episodes (TE2 and TE3) by pumping S5 to determine what he knew about banning smoking. Then T5 needed to know whether S5's instructor required any secondary source research for this assignment (TE4). After being told that the instructor did not require secondary sources, T5 moved toward narrowing the topic by suggesting that S5 might want to examine smoking in

TABLE 4.4 The Chain of Topic Episodes in the T5–S5 Conference's Teaching Stage

Topic Episode	Topic Content
1	T5 initiated the idea of curbing rather than banning smoking.
2	T5 asked where smoking is currently banned.
3	T5 asked if there are places where smoking is not banned but should be.
4	T5 asked where the information for the essay should come from.
5	T5 suggested that topic needs narrowing.
6	T5 suggested Hollywood as a means for narrowing.
7	T5 identified two directions for narrowing.
8	T5 asked what new laws would lead to banning smoking; S5 moved from banning to advertising.
9	T5 moved back to focus on Hollywood.
10	S5 wondered about portraying smoking in movies aimed at kids.
11	T5 gave advice about composing and responding to the prompt.
12	T5 suggested that S5 talk to the instructor.
13	T5 suggested doing a Google search for images related to smoking.

movies (TE5). By TE8, S5 had talked himself out of using the topic of banning smoking and moved on to the problems related to advertising. He then appeared able to shift easily to the negative influence of actors smoking in movies. In the last three topic episodes (TE11–TE13), T5 provided standard advice about beginning an essay—follow the prompt, talk to the instructor, search for images (of smokers). In this conference, it appeared that the instructor had set the final destination, and S5 was willing to allow T5 to lead him there. The topic episodes in the conferences formed a straight chain, beginning with the idea of a new focus of the paper, moving sequentially though potential subject matter, and ending with a new focus for the paper.

In contrast, as shown on Table 4.5, the topic episodes in the T7–S7 conference created a chain with more twists and turns across its length. The T7–S7 conference focused on revising and proofreading. Fairly early in the conference, T7 realized that, even though S7 had asked for help with proofreading, her draft lacked a thesis statement and needed further revising, specifically, further development of ideas. T7 worked in this conference to fulfill S7's request for help with proofreading and, at the same time, to convince her that she should develop her ideas more fully and create a thesis statement.

As Table 4.5 shows, from TE1 to TE9, T7 focused on the sentence- and word-level problems in the draft. However, as he said in his postconference interview, during TE9, he realized that S7 was not defending a belief and thus not adhering to the assignment. Instead, S7's paper discussed exercise as "a necessity." In TE10, T7 asked whether the instructor required a thesis for the paper. S7 said that the instructor had not mentioned the need for one. Rather than trying to persuade S7 that the essay needed a thesis, T7 allowed S7 to determine the course of the conference. He went back to the original agenda of revising and proofreading, bringing up the need to elaborate the ideas contained in the essay during TE14, TE16, and TE17. By TE20, S7 got the message, and she was able to predict the advice T7 was about to give. However, she did not know how to expand the ideas (TE21), and so T7 and S7 brainstormed. During the last topic episode of this teaching stage (TE28), T7 suggested that maybe one of the new ideas S7 had added to the draft could be the essay's theme, thereby raising the chances of meeting the instructor's expectations.

Although T5 moved S5 steadily forward through the topic episodes of their brainstorming conference, the teaching stage of the T7–S7 conference consisted of a more circular, less direct chain of topic episodes. T7 worked at the sentence level for a while, then moved to the global level, then moved back to the sentence level, and so on, until S7 understood that she needed to expand the ideas in the draft. These two examples suggest the diversity of the teaching stage of a writing center conference, specifically, the directness or indirectness of progression from initial observations immediately following agenda setting in the opening stage to potential solutions.

TABLE 4.5 The Chain of Topic Episodes in the T7–S7 Conference's Teaching Stage

Topic Episode	Topic Content
1	Reading aloud, T7 brought up a sentence that needed revision.
2	S7 believed a Word default caused the problem; both laughed at the trouble Word can cause.
3	T7 told S7 that the writing center rules prohibited his writing on her paper.
4	T7 read again, then asked about a part of speech.
5	T7 told S7 to avoid contractions.
6	S7 asked about use of colloquial language in quoted dialogue.
7	T7 read again and returned to the need to avoid contractions.
8	T7 asked S7 if she had ever identified by name the friends she discussed in her paper in order to make the writing more specific.
9	T7 led revision of "It is my belief that exercise should be a necessity."
10	T7 asked S7 whether the instructor required a thesis statement in this essay; S7 said the instructor did not.
11	T7 led the revision of another sentence: "It could possibly be due to the fact that people are so worried about making it through their workout or getting by that every other previous worry gets set aside."
12	T7 suggested that they discuss diction.
13	T7 asked what the page length of the essay should be.
14	T7 suggested that S7 should elaborate by adding another reason why exercise makes people forget their worries.
15	T7 pointed out the phrase "that's so" is colloquial.
16	T7 suggested that S7 add more details about the reasons exercise "lengthens your lifespan."
17	T7 explained (claimed) that instructors give higher grades to longer papers.
18	T7 read, "It also makes life more fun." S7 thought that "fun" is too colloquial, and they tried to find another word.
19	T7 stopped reading, and S7 identified a missing comma.
20	T7 asked S7 to guess what he will say next; S7 realized after that T7 wanted her to expand the ideas.
21	S7 did not know how to expand, so T7 suggested that they brainstorm.
22	T7 told S7 to relate her ideas back to each other as part of the expansion.
23	T7 suggested ordering the ideas in the thesis the way they appeared in the paper.
24	T7 suggested revision of the sentence beginning "Not only are they missing out on a lifetime of accomplishment."
25	T7 led revision of the sentence.
26	T7 showed S7 how to "flesh out" the meaning of "accomplishment."
27	T7 suggested that the fleshing out could lead to expansion of the ideas in the paper.
28	T7 suggested that maybe one of those ideas could be the "theme."

Sequences within Topic Episodes

As shown in the previous section, analysis of topic episodes can reveal patterns or chains in the messiness of the macrolevel constituting the teaching stage. Here, we look more closely at the microlevel of the teaching stage by examining the elaborated three-part IRF sequence of tutoring strategies in TE2 from T5's and S5's brainstorming conference. (We will show other sequences within topic episodes in Chapters 5–7.) TE2 begins with T5's initiation:

I T5: So, O.K. Um, like, let's talk about where it's being banned. You know. Um, like, what are some places that you—?

R S5: There's um, most restaurants. [Sometimes, the band and, [um, I guess
   T5:   [Uh-huh.   [Yeah.
   S5: at bars but just really in public. They can't ban private, so.

F T5: O.K. Is it, um, all over the United States or do you know, is it just [in—

R S5: [It's—I think it depends on the local—the local, um, government. I don't think there's like a national law that has banned smoking.

F T5: O.K. O.K. Um, so, you know this is mostly local, right?
   S5: Yeah.

T5 initiated this variation on the elaborated IRF sequence with a combination of a telling strategy—a directive that announced the topic—and a pumping question (a cognitive scaffolding strategy). S5 responded to the pump question ("There's um, most restaurants . . ."), and T5 backchanneled S5's response with "uh-huh" and "yeah," signs of attentiveness. As part of her follow up to S5's response, T5 asked another (pumping) question ("Is it, um, all over the United States or do you know, is it just in—"). After S5 responded to this question, she again followed up, this time in the form of a leading question that summarized what S5 had previously said.

A variety of other topic-episode structures appeared across the 10 conference teaching stages. Some topic episodes, for example, consisted almost entirely of instruction. In these, tutors gave advice and explained concepts. In many cases, pumping questions or some other cognitive scaffolding strategy followed the instruction, soliciting student writers' participation and moving them forward in their thinking, as opposed to testing their understanding of the instruction.

Tutors' Launching and Initiating of Topic Episodes

As we stated previously, on average, tutors launched or initiated far more topic episodes per conference than student writers introduced: 22.1 to 4.6. However, the tutor roles of expert, manager, and facilitator—roles tutors enact to generate and maintain the productivity and efficiency of conferences—make this difference in control of topics rather expected. Even so, this ratio did not manifest itself consistently across the 10 conferences: T6 launched or initiated 10 topic episodes, whereas S6 introduced 12. We examine the anomalous T6–S6 conference later; first, however, we discuss the tutoring strategies that the tutors used to launch and initiate topic episodes.

We found that, for the most part, tutors launched and initiated topic episodes in fairly consistent and thus predictable ways. By far, tutors used instruction—telling and suggesting—most often to launch topic episodes; sometimes they followed up on these launching strategies with either an explanation or with a cognitive scaffolding strategy. In terms of initiating topic episodes with cognitive scaffolding, pumping questions and reading aloud were common strategies, and tutors often followed these up with further cognitive scaffolding or with instruction.

Launching Topic Episodes with Instruction Strategies

Tutors launched topic episodes with advice—both telling and suggesting strategies. For example, in TE21, T7 told S7 that they would talk about expanding a paragraph on the merits of exercise and then followed up with two cognitive scaffolding strategies: reading aloud and responding as a reader: "Well, let's talk about it then. 'Not only is exercise a vital part of life, but it makes life more enjoyable.' O.K. So it makes life more enjoyable according to what you imply through your rhetorical questions here through sports and competition." Tutors also mitigated their advice when launching topics. For example, before TE6, T2 had read S2's draft and had seen problems with the paper's coherence. In TE6, T2 suggested an approach—a rather general one—for revising: "O.K. So I think what you need to think about is do you want to focus on, you know—These are the two transitions you went through. From public to private and then from private to college." In TE12, T1 used telling to convey a more local revision than the one T2 offered S2: "So, you cram a lot of images into this paragraph. And so my main suggestion would be to slow down this paragraph a little bit." In TE11, T8 suggested that S8 combine two sentences, and then she explained why: "And since these two sentences kind of say the same thing, you might want to combine them. Because you have a quote that's basically saying the same thing." These examples of telling and suggesting to launch new topic episodes reveal tutors' roles as managers ("[L]et's talk about where it's being banned"); facilitators ("I think what you need to think about is what do you want to focus on"); and experts ("[Y]ou cram a lot of images into this paragraph. And so my main suggestion would be to slow down this paragraph a little bit") and concomitantly reveal the ways tutors worked to achieve the goal of productive and efficient conferences.

Initiating Topic Episodes with Cognitive Scaffolding Strategies

Tutors' cognitive scaffolding strategies constrained student writers' responses to varying degrees and thus guided their thinking to various degrees as well. When tutors used cognitive scaffolding strategies to initiate topic episodes, they set in place some guideposts for a topic episode's scope. For example, in T1 and S1's TE4, T1 scaffolded S1's thinking with a question aimed at getting S1 to think about the paper's purpose: "O.K. So what is kind of the purpose? What is it you're wanting to explain to us about the library?" T5's pump question to begin brainstorming in TE1 constrained S5's response more than the pump question from T1: "O.K. Well, um, just to get some of your ideas on it. Um, have you really thought about maybe another way, um, we could kind of curb cancer—curb smoking. Um, other than, you know, banning the smoking?"

Another frequent way tutors initiated topic episodes was through reading aloud from student writers' drafts or from the assignment sheets their instructors had given them. As a cognitive scaffolding strategy, reading aloud, like pumping, sets boundaries and helps guide thinking. For example, in TE4, T8 read aloud from S8's draft and then followed up with a pump question: "Now. 'By Randall Kennedy it says.' Is it the article that's saying it or do you want to just give Kennedy credit, and say 'Kennedy says' or 'Kennedy writes'?" Tutors also used other cognitive scaffolding strategies as initiators of topic episodes, such as referring back to a previous topic and responding as a reader or listener by paraphrasing something a student had written or said.

Launching Topic Episodes with Motivational Scaffolding Strategies

Rarely, tutors launched topic episodes with motivational scaffolding strategies. For example, T1 began TE5 with the motivational scaffolding strategy of praise, but then she followed up that praise with criticism. Researchers in business communication have discussed this technique of placing compliment before critique—a technique called buffering—in analyses of business letters (for example, Limaye 1988; Locker 1999) and book reviews (Mackiewicz 2007), but writing instructors commonly use the technique in conferences and in writing evaluatory comments on papers as well. T1 buffered a criticism about a mismatch between the thesis and the introduction with formulaic praise (discussed in greater depth in Chapter 7) about the quality of S1's thesis statement: "Right. The thesis statement is good. I would say that it's maybe not matching up with the introduction here." Tutors' use of motivational scaffolding strategies to launch topic episodes allowed them to lead with encouragement before moving further into the discussion of the new topic.

Student Writers' Introducing of Topic Episodes

Although tutors typically initiated and launched topic episodes, student writers sometimes introduced topic episodes as well. Their first topic introductions mainly occurred after their tutors had begun to pursue the agenda set in the opening stage—generally after TE5. By far student writers' most frequent method of introducing topic episodes was to ask questions, to express misunderstanding, and to request information or advice. For example, S7 asked T7 to explain why her instructor had deducted points from his last paper for use of slang—even though the slang was in dialogue:

S7: Sorry, this is a whole different topic. On the last paper, she counted off because I had dialogue, but I did like my brother was talking, and he used slang. . . . And she counted off points for that. Is that right? Cause I thought that I was right.

Tutors responded to student writers' topic introductions with a variety of tutoring strategies: pumping questions, telling, suggesting, praise, as well as other strategies. (T7 responded with advice after noting that he could not second-guess the instructor: "And you can always go and talk with her.") Understanding when and how student writers took charge of topics during the teaching stage might help tutors encourage them to do so more often and respond to them more effectively.

Table 4.6 shows topic-episode introductions from S6—an exception to the general finding that student writers seemed content to let their tutors raise most of the topics. The list contains S6's 12 topic-episode introductions. As expected, most of the 12 introductions consist of knowledge-deficit questions, which we discuss in greater detail in Chapter 8.

Except to assure T6 that he could write on her draft, S6, like the other student writers, listened quietly in the first five topic episodes of her conference; however, unlike the other student writers, once S6 began introducing topic episodes related to her draft—fairly early in the conference—she continued to do so, guiding the chain of topics, even though T6 talked more (3,343 words to S6's 1,455) than she did. S6's control began in TE9. At that point, she overlapped T6's long explanation of comma rules, directing his attention back to her draft ("O.K. And what about this one?"). Then, in TE10, TE11, and TE12, S6 continued to introduce topics—sentences that concerned her—by reading from her own paper (the only student writer in our study to do so).

The point at which T6 and S6 finished proofreading the paper would have been a natural point for the conference to end. However, not having finished getting her questions answered, S6 changed the agenda, switching to global-level concerns about content. What she wanted, it seems, was for T6 to confirm that her analysis was sufficient as it stood. When T6 made suggestions rather than

TABLE 4.6 Student-Writer-Introduced Topic Episodes in the T6–S6 Conference

T6–S6 Topic Episode	Context and S6's Introduction of Topic Episodes	
2	*Context*:	T6 had begun to point out comma errors.
	S6:	So feel free to write on this [the draft paper].
6	*Context*:	T6 had explained commas as "grammatical elements" in detail.
	S6:	So, O.K. So where would I—[use a comma]?
9	*Context*:	T6 had explained the use of a comma before "and."
	S6:	O.K. And what about this one? Because, like, that just kind of jumped out at me, like every time. But I never really changed it.
10	*Context*:	T6 had explained problems with the sentence S6 asked about, and then T6 tried to sum up the types of comma errors in S6's draft.
	S6:	O.K. This one. I'm just reading it right now, and is that confusing, as far as like, who's playing and who's walking?
11	*Context*:	T6 and S6 had discussed the problems with a sentence, particularly the lack of clarity in what or who is doing the action.
	S6:	And then here, um. [3 seconds] [Reads aloud.] "At that moment, I experienced a flashback of that freezing cold December night sitting in my car sobbing my eyes out." Should there be a, like, a—I feel like I'm missing a subject.
12	*Context*:	T6 had told S6 that the sentence did indeed have a subject and that the sentence "works pretty well."
	S6:	O.K. What about—What about this? [Reads aloud.] "Slowly and a little timid [unclear]." And then over here?
14	*Context*:	T6 and S6 had finally finished proofreading the essay.
	S6:	So tell me. As far as—As far as content goes, and my actual sentences—Now that we've kind of weeded out the co—Wow. That's a lot of commas. [Laughs.]
16	*Context*:	T6 had asked S6 to specify what about the draft worries her. S6 had said that her instructor mentioned connecting the personal narrative to analysis. S6 had thought the draft was already adequate, but she asked T6 to confirm her assessment.
	S6:	What do I do?
17	*Context*:	Rather than confirming, T6 had suggested ways to increase the amount of analysis in the draft.
	S6:	Uh-huh. Um, definitely I just—I really don't want to put something so specific like "I got back into horseback riding" or something like that, that's just kind of—Because it takes away from—I just like how it's so—I don't know. It's general in a way that people can relate to it. And as soon as I attach something really, really specific to it, I don't think it does that anymore.
19	*Context*:	T6 had suggested that S6 make the ideas more concrete and had discussed ways to achieve that. S6 asked which ideas lacked concreteness.
	S6:	Here in the first?

20	Context:	T6 and S6 had discussed how to make the ideas more concrete.
	S6:	Um. O.K. Well, I mean, anything else?
21	Context:	T6 had praised the ideas in the draft and had asked S6 if she learned anything about comma usage.
	S6:	[Laughs.] O.K. I just want to make sure that there's a sense of finality here, I guess.
22	Context:	T6 had said that he liked the two short sentences they wrote to end the essay.
	S6:	And then one of the guys in my, um, little group that we had, like editing group or whatever, said I should change this, um, maybe to "me" instead of "myself," just because I used that in other parts of the paper. But I don't know how I feel about that.

providing such confirmation, S6 at first rejected his suggestions ("I just like how it's so—I don't know. It's general in a way that people can relate to it") before, in TE19, accepting his advice about making her ideas more concrete. In TE20, with a question that tutors as opposed to student writers usually ask—"Well, I mean anything else?"—S6 asked T6 whether he saw any other problems in her draft, extending the teaching stage further. Afterwards, once again as the conference appeared to be ending, S6 began a new topic (TE21): "I just want to be sure there's a sense of finality here." And again, in TE 22, S6 brought up yet another entirely new topic: her use of the objective pronoun "me," as opposed to the reflexive pronoun "myself." Even though we found that, as student writers' familiarity with their tutors grew, they were more likely to introduce topic episodes, S6's persistence in getting her questions answered—her willingness to begin new topics—is an anomaly.

In first-time conferences, student writers, often polite and deferential young people who are well schooled in classroom behavior, typically assumed the secondary role to which they were accustomed: they allowed tutors to manage a conference's topics. But, as Thompson et al. (2009) found, student writers want their questions answered. When tutors provide the answers that they seek, student writers have little reason to introduce new topics. However, as in the T6–S6 conference, when tutors prolong explanations of concepts rather than focus on correcting errors in drafts, student writers—particularly those with some extra audacity—may introduce topic episodes to move the tutor back to the draft. In this move, S6 countered T6's priority—helping her improve her writing ability—in order to work toward her own priority—improving the paper as quickly as possible.

The Closing Stage of Writing Center Conferences

The beginnings of closing stages were easy to determine; most often, tutors asked student writers about whether they had received answers to their questions. For example, T9 asked, "Is there anything else I can help you with?" and T7 (somewhat dramatically) inquired, "Now, before you answer, just think about it. Do you have any other questions?" As with the opening stages, the closing stages of the conferences varied in the total volubility (see Table 4.7).

In the two longest closing stages (T1–S1, T8–S8), tutors helped student writers summarize what they had discussed and set goals for what student writers should try to accomplish postconference. Tutor training materials have emphasized the importance of summarizing and setting goals; however, only two tutors—the most experienced of the 10—performed these tasks or helped students perform them. In contrast, the shortest closing stage (T10–S10) occurred at the end of a conference focused on proofreading a paper due later that day; unsurprisingly, summarizing the proofreading that they had carried out was not a priority. And, because the student writer had little time to work on the paper further, goal setting was not a priority either. Summarizing and goal setting are valuable closing activities, but the need (or want) for them depends on the student writers' intentions for further work on the paper.

TABLE 4.7 Volubility in the Closing Stage

	Number of Words		
Conference	Tutors	Student Writers	Total
T1–S1	229	194	423
T2–S2	50	14	64
T3–S3	28	118	146
T4–S4	257	26	283
T5–S5	162	38	200
T6–S6	38	44	82
T7–S7	43	173	216
T8–S8	241	46	287
T9–S9	118	14	132
T10–S10	16	11	27
Total (%)	1,182 (63.5)	678 (36.5)	1,860 (100)

Tutoring Strategies: Frequencies of Occurrence

As a basis for further analysis of the 10 satisfactory conferences, we calculated the frequency with which tutors used instruction, cognitive scaffolding, and motivational scaffolding strategies. Although these strategies occurred predominantly in the teaching stage of the conferences, tutors used them in the closing stage as well. To account for the different lengths of the conferences, we relativized the strategy counts, reporting the number of strategies per 10 minutes. Overall, tutors used 31.16 strategies per 10 minutes of conference interaction—or just over

3 strategies per minute. This general finding shows that the experienced tutors in these satisfactory conferences saturated their sessions with discourse moves that had the potential to facilitate student writers' learning by conveying information, moving student writers' thinking forward, and encouraging student writers' continued efforts at their writing task.

A second main finding was that the tutors used instruction strategies far more often than they used either cognitive or motivational scaffolding strategies. This finding suggests that the tutors saw the utility in directing student writers in what to do by telling, suggesting, and explaining. The tutors used instruction strategies on average 13.86 times per 10 minutes. Put another way, close to half (44%) of the tutoring strategies that tutors used were instruction. In contrast, tutors averaged 10.54 cognitive scaffolding strategies (34%) per 10 minutes and 6.76 motivational scaffolding strategies (22%) per 10 minutes. Table 4.8 shows the frequencies of strategies in the three categories, as well as each category's percentage of the total strategies that the tutors used.

A third main finding was that tutors used four strategies from across the three categories far more frequently than the other types: telling (instruction), pumping (cognitive scaffolding), suggesting (instruction), and showing concern (motivational scaffolding). Table 4.9 shows the frequencies and percentages; it reveals that tutors used about the same percentage of pumps and suggestions: 18% of tutors' total strategies each.

As Table 4.9 shows, although tutors were quite directive, using telling and suggesting strategies often (together 37% of their total strategies), they also

TABLE 4.8 Frequency and Percentage of Tutoring Strategies per 10 Minutes

Category of Tutoring Strategy	Frequency	Frequency per 10 Minutes (% Total)	
Instruction	438	13.86	(44)
Cognitive scaffolding	326	10.54	(34)
Motivational scaffolding	214	6.76	(22)
Total	978	31.16	(100)

TABLE 4.9 Frequency and Percentage of Tutors' Most Frequent Strategies

Tutoring Strategy	Category	Frequency per 10 Minutes (% Total)	
Telling	Instruction	5.97	(19)
Pumping	Cognitive scaffolding	5.91	(18)
Suggesting	Instruction	5.68	(18)
Showing concern	Motivational scaffolding	3.32	(11)
Other strategies	All categories	10.28	(34)
Total		31.16	(100)

balanced their instruction with pumping questions, to get students to generate content and to reconsider the content and form of their writing, and with signals that they cared about student writers' comprehension and well-being. With these four most frequent strategies, the tutors varied their pedagogical approaches to create satisfactory conferences.

As we discussed in Chapter 3, although we based our coding scheme on the coding scheme Cromley and Azevedo (2005) developed for analyzing tutoring in closed-world domains, we modified their scheme substantially, particularly in relation to the strategies that we call suggestions and that they call hints, to create a valid and useful scheme for the open-world domain of writing. The differences between our coding scheme and theirs make impossible direct and obvious comparisons between our results and results from prior research on closed-world-domain tutoring. We can, however, juxtapose our results against the prior research, keeping the complexities of doing so in mind. For example, Cromley and Azevedo (2005) found that instruction constituted 23% of experienced tutors' total moves. Indeed, even Cromley and Azevedo's less experienced tutors used a lower percentage of instruction strategies than the experienced writing center tutors in our study: 34%.

Some cognitive scaffolding strategies that seem fairly common in the tutoring of closed-world domains occurred rarely or did not occur at all in our 10 writing center conferences. For example, the tutors in our study hardly used the forced-choice strategy at all. This excerpt from VanLehn et al.'s (2007) study exemplifies a forced-choice strategy in physics tutoring: "Can it be applied to experiments with just one group, or do you need two or more groups?" (11). Areas of study such as physics—and likely other STEM fields too—may more readily lend themselves to offering a student two potentially objectively correct choices from which to choose a single answer.

The writing center tutors in our study did not employ prompting very often either. With prompting strategy, a tutor leaves a word or phrase off an answer so that the student can supply it or fill in the blank: "That's a . . ." Like forced choice, this strategy lends itself to soliciting objectively correct answers (ones that a tutor already has in mind). It does not lend itself particularly well to the open-world domain of writing. When it occurred in our 10 conferences, prompting was moderately to highly constraining on student writers' possible responses, not always requiring a single answer but establishing clear and limited boundaries.

Some motivational scaffolding strategies appear to occur infrequently during tutoring—no matter the subject matter. For example, expressions of sympathy ("I know that you don't want to hear that") occurred infrequently across tutoring studies. Cromley and Azevedo (2005) give the name "acknowledging difficulty" (see also, Lepper et al. 1993) to the moves that we coded as sympathy and empathy, and this strategy accounted for small percentages of their literacy tutors' strategies: 2.7% of the experienced tutors' strategies and 5.3% of the less experienced tutors' strategies (101).

Also, like the tutors in Cromley and Azevedo's study, the writing center tutors in our study used humor infrequently. Perhaps tutors sense what prior research has borne out: using humor can be risky. As Wanzer et al. (2006) found in their study of teachers' use of humor in the classroom, inappropriate humor can be verbally aggressive or offensive. Research has also shown that humor in pedagogical settings has myriad benefits. It can obtain and retain students' attention (Davies and Apter 1980; Ziv 1979), and it can help them recall information (Wanzer et al. 2006). Writing center directors and others who train tutors might encourage tutors to use humor related to the subject matter of their writing—humor that students find appropriate.

Direct comparisons between our study and prior studies are not possible, but it is possible to juxtapose our findings with those from prior research and to consider the differences and similarities we see, keeping in mind the variations in coding schemes. As writing center directors and other administrators more often collaborate with other tutoring support services to provide tutor training, they may want to consider differences between the needs of writing center tutors in training and the needs of other tutors who are likely to represent a wide range of disciplines. Juxtaposing our results with those results from prior research on tutoring in closed-world domains revealed some differences in the strategies that tutors employed, differences likely arising from focus on well-structured problem solving during tutoring in closed-world domains. Directors and administrators training writing center tutors might familiarize tutors with strategies from both repertoires to help writing center tutors understand and appreciate their colleagues and to broaden their own skill sets.

Conclusion

In this chapter, we first described the three stages in our writing center conferences and reported volubility counts for each stage and, for the teaching stage, we also described topic episodes. Second, we reported results about the frequency with which the tutors in our study employed tutoring strategies within the three categories of instruction, cognitive scaffolding, and motivational scaffolding.

In the opening stage, student writers often talked more than tutors did, because they needed to explain why they were seeking help. For their part, tutors tried to gain as much knowledge as possible about the assignment and student writers' progress thus far, as well as to collaborate with student writers to set an agenda.

In the teaching stages, as appropriate for their roles as experts, facilitators, and managers, tutors always talked more than the students. They also launched and initiated the most topic episodes, almost five times as many as students introduced. Analyzing topic episodes closely, we found that some followed the prototypical IRF sequence and its elaborations, but mainly we found variable sequencing in topic episodes. Further, we also found that tutors launched topic episodes more often with instruction strategies than they initiated topics with cognitive scaffolding strategies.

In the second group of findings reported here, we analyzed the frequency of instructional, cognitive scaffolding, and motivational scaffolding tutoring strategies. We found that writing center tutors employed tutoring strategies frequently, saturating the conferences with them: they used just over three strategies per minute. They also used a range of tutoring strategies from across the three categories, showing that they "can adapt the balance of moves to the needs of individual students" (Cromley and Azevedo 2005, 104). Another main finding was that the tutors used instruction strategies far more often than they used either cognitive or motivational scaffolding strategies. Close to half (44%) of the strategies that tutors used were instruction strategies. Also, they used four strategies from across the three categories far more frequently than the other types: telling, pumping, suggesting, and showing concern.

Tutors' talk manifested indictors of dominance: they talked the most, initiated and launched the most topic episodes, and usually signaled the end of conferences. However, tutors dominated the conferences only as long as the student writers allowed them to do so. Not only did students typically lead the initial agenda setting, but, once the teaching stage was underway, student writers participated actively, responding to tutors' questions and sometimes using questions to introduce topic episodes. Further, tutors could not signal the end of conferences until students allowed them to. As shown in the T6–S6 conference, unless tutors enforce a time limit or refuse to continue, student writers can extend conferences until they are certain that all of their questions are answered. Our analysis revealed greater control over the conference from student writers than we had anticipated.

5

INSTRUCTION STRATEGIES

In this chapter, we begin our three-chapter analysis of specific categories of writing center tutoring strategies. We start with the instruction strategies that tutors used in satisfactory conferences. We first discuss the idea of directiveness in tutors' advice, a term we use to refer to the instruction strategies of telling and suggesting together. Then, we move to our data, examining at the macrolevel and microlevel tutors' instruction strategies. In terms of macrolevel analysis, we examine instruction strategies within the chain of topic episodes that constitutes the teaching stage and within the closing stage. In terms of microlevel analysis, we discuss the frequencies with which experienced tutors employed the three instruction strategies and closely analyze excerpts that exemplify the ways in which they used them. We end the chapter by discussing the implications of our findings and analysis for tutor training.

Directiveness: Worrisome but Necessary

As discussed in Chapter 2, much writing center lore mandates that tutors avoid directiveness in conferences. Two instruction tutoring strategies in our coding scheme—telling and suggesting—are directive, with the third instruction strategy—explaining and exemplifying—used to follow up. Mackiewicz and Riley (2003) discuss the balance between what they call "directness" and politeness that editors have to maintain in working with writers. They describe the use of negative politeness—mitigation—as a means for lessening the face threat of a directive. However, as editors mitigate with politeness, their advice becomes less clear. We used the levels of directness that Mackiewicz and Riley (2003) discuss to code telling and suggesting strategies. As we discussed in Chapters 2 and 3, telling is more direct and less mitigated; suggesting is less direct and more mitigated. Whether telling or suggesting, though, with these strategies, tutors instruct student writers in how to begin or improve their writing.

Over the past 15 years, researchers have investigated the influence of directiveness on student writers' and tutors' conference satisfaction. The results agree: tutors' directiveness in itself does not negatively influence student writers' satisfaction (Clark 2001; Thompson et al. 2009; Thonus 2002). Further, although tutors worried about being too directive, they were not so concerned that they were dissatisfied with their conferences (Clark 2001). Clark (2001) suggests that directiveness exists upon a continuum; directiveness, she says, is "a matter of degree, and, to some extent, perception" (35). The most directive tutor "will tell the student exactly what to do" and dominate the conference; the most nondirective tutor "will say nothing at all except for making a few encouraging noises" (35). Clark measured tutors' directiveness through (1) perceptions about the extent of tutors' contributions to the conference; (2) perceptions about the extent of tutors' error corrections; and (3) perceptions about the extent of tutors' and student writers' individual control of the conversation. Clark (2001) did not specifically study negative politeness or distinguish between telling and suggesting. However, the continuum that she posits neatly corresponds to the idea of levels of directness that Mackiewicz and Riley (2003) discuss and that undergirds our analysis.

Regardless of the mandate to avoid directiveness (and some squeamishness about it today), few writing center directors would advise tutors never to use telling and suggesting. However, few would encourage tutors to dominate conferences. Instead, when tutors decide to instruct, they must balance telling's clarity with suggesting's politeness.

Instruction Strategies in the Opening Stage

During the opening stage, the tutors all engaged in agenda setting and attempted to develop rapport with students, but, as they did so, they used no instruction strategies. Rather, they used knowledge-deficit questions to negotiate agendas with students, as well as motivational scaffolding strategies such as praise to start building rapport.

Instruction Strategies in the Teaching Stage

In this section, we analyze at the macro- and microlevel tutors' use of instruction strategies during the teaching stage. In regard to the macrolevel, we focus on tutors' use of instruction strategies in topic episodes. (In Chapter 4, we described in general tutors' and student writers' topic episodes and chains of topic episodes.) After this macrolevel analysis, we look to the microlevel, examining the frequencies with which tutors used instruction strategies and closely analyzing excerpts that exemplify the ways they used those strategies to give and explain advice.

Instruction Strategies in Topic Episodes

As we noted in our analysis of topic episodes in Chapter 4, topic episodes varied greatly in length. TE5 from the conference between T7 and S7 contained just 37 words; T7 launched the episode with an instruction strategy: a suggestion to avoid contractions:

T7: Now, "wasn't," and all contractions—This is a more laid-back type [that
S7:   [Right.
T7: you probably want to begin avoiding—Right. To begin avoiding contrac-
    tions. Because in formal papers [usually that is a definite no-no.
S7:   [Was not.
T7: Right.

TE5 exemplifies the ways that topic episodes launched with instruction could mimic the IRF sequence—a sequence that we discuss in relation to cognitive scaffolding strategies, strategies that tutors use to obtain a substantive response. In TE5, T7 launched the episode with instruction. S7 responded to T7's suggestion (though she did not have to do so), overlapping T7's turn and showing that she understood how to solve the contraction problem: "Was not." T7 followed up with an evaluation, assessing S7's prior turn as "Right."

These two topic episodes—TE8 and TE9 from the T2–S2 conference—show instruction working with cognitive and motivational scaffolding. They also show a student writer who responded minimally until she, in a more substantive response, discounted the instruction the tutor had painstakingly provided. T2 launched TE8 with the suggestion to put check marks next to sentences and paragraphs that fail to support the newly determined focus for the paper. She continued on after S2's backchannel ("O.K.") with her explanation of that suggestion:

T2: Why don't you put a check next to that because now since you're going to
    focus on, like—I think part of—with C papers, it's usually that the paper it
    meets the assignment. It does what the teacher has asked, but something is
    missing. Whether it be focus or whether it be a real clear thesis or something
    like that. And it seems to me after reading your paper what's missing is focus.
    So if we put a check mark next to the things that are not related [as much.
S2:   [O.K.
T2: Then maybe that will help you when you go back and try to take those things
    out.

TE8 exemplifies an advice-dominated topic episode with minimal input from the student writer. It also demonstrates one of Wittwer and Renkl's (2008) guidelines for effective explanations—to move quickly from explanation to application. In the previous topic episode, T2 and S2 decided on the essay's focus, so here T2 quickly moved to a revising strategy.

After the rather short TE8, T2 moved on to a new (albeit related) topic in TE9—the need to focus the paper solely on the change S2 made from her private school to college:

T2: "The first year of private school has been a drastic change for me." So we think when we read that is what you're talking about is this change. [2 seconds] Does that make sense?

S2: Uh-huh.

T2: This whole paper now needs to be focused about the way that the private school is and the change that you went through to college. So this kind of language, "drastic change for me," is confusing and maybe is somewhere we need to put a check mark as far as it's not making the paper not seem quite as focused. [Reading for 30 seconds.] And maybe instead of focusing on the private school as being a changing time, just focus on the negative things about it. Just focus on the things without saying it was a change. Just focus on things that were difficult for you. [5 seconds] Does that make sense, or is that kind of confusing?

S2: It's kind of confusing to me.

This topic episode demonstrates another of Wittwer and Renkl's guidelines about effective explanations: along with her telling and suggesting, T2 used cognitive and motivational scaffolding. In fact, T2 initiated TE9 with cognitive scaffolding strategies—by reading aloud from S2's paper and responding as a reader ("So we think when we read that . . .")—and afterwards moved right into a motivational scaffolding strategy—a demonstration of concern ("Does that make sense?"). T2's demonstration-of-concern question generated a minimal reply from S2 ("Uh-huh"). After this response from S2, T2 began to give advice, stringing together suggesting and telling strategies aimed at getting S2 to differentiate between content relevant to the change she went through in college and content irrelevant to that change (content about the change she went through at the private school and thus content potentially confusing to the reader). T2 concluded her advice with another demonstration of concern—another question aimed at assessing S2's understanding of the advice she had just given: "Does that make sense, or is that kind of confusing?" S2's substantive response to T2 ("It's kind of confusing to me") finished this topic episode and negated T2's instruction.

To sum up this section, topic episodes such as the ones above illustrate how instruction strategies can begin topic episodes and how tutors use instruction within topic episodes to give advice.

Quantitative Results: Frequencies of the Instruction Strategies

The category of instruction contains three strategy types, including the two most frequently used strategies in our corpus. As we noted in Chapter 4, 45% of tutors' strategies fell into the instruction category. Table 5.1 shows a breakdown of the frequency with which tutors used the three types of instruction strategies.

Table 5.1 shows that the tutors employed telling and suggesting strategies with almost equal frequency: 43% of instruction strategies were telling, and 41% were suggesting. They used the explaining strategy far less frequently—about 2.2 times per 10 minutes of conference talk (16% of instruction strategies). When they explained and exemplified, they tended to do so in conjunction with telling and suggesting, thereby clarifying their advice.

Explanations and examples might occur less frequently than telling and suggesting because tutors sense during their ongoing diagnosis, or possibly from their previous experience, that student writers are not interested in or, at least, see no immediate use for explanations. Student writers might be less interested in the "why" behind tutors' advice than they are in the "what," as in what to do. Student writers' motivation is often extrinsic—targeted on the grade—rather than intrinsic—targeted on learning that might transfer to other assignments (Boscolo and Hidi 2007; Hidi and Boscolo 2006). We can compare student writers with students seeking tutors' help with tasks from closed-world domains. Unlike students in writing center conferences, if such students want to get good grades on tests, they need to understand the "why," the explanations behind the answers. However, because they can follow tutors' advice to improve their essays and therefore their grades, student writers do not need explanations. Their attitudes that explanations waste time, whether implicit or expressed, might limit the number of explanations that writing center tutors give.

Another potential reason for fewer explaining and exemplifying strategies than telling and suggesting might be the relative difficulty of generating an explanation (or conveying an example) in the moment. Although tutors usually have punctuation and grammar rules at the ready, explanations for global-level issues such as cohesiveness, coherence, and organization do not abide by rules delineated in guidebooks. However, as writing center tutors gain experience, they likely

TABLE 5.1 Instruction Strategies per 10 Minutes

Instruction Strategy	Frequency per 10 Minutes (% Total)	
Telling	5.97	(43)
Suggesting	5.68	(41)
Explaining and exemplifying	2.21	(16)
Total	13.86	(100)

become more skilled in analyzing the "why" of global-level concerns and then articulating those concerns to student writers.

Qualitative Results: Close Analysis of the Instruction Strategies

Quantitative analysis of tutoring strategies gets us only so far. Here, we move into close, qualitative analysis of conference excerpts to determine how the experienced tutors employed strategies and, in the process, helped create conferences that they and student writers considered to be satisfactory. Here, we focus on how the tutors used telling (for example, "Let's start with the cover" and "So focus on this and focus on that") and suggesting (for example, "I think that you could do either one" and "We could kind of look at um, what messages Hollywood is telling us?) to convey advice, with and without accompanying explanations such as these:

- "Because see, something like this. This is kind of an example. Right here where you say 'I was not used to sitting with girls at lunch anyway.' That's a reference to your private to your public school."
- "Because you're saying, you know, they cause their life to be or feel meaningless. And it seems like from what we talked about here you're going to say, like, however, in *Notes from the Underground*, the author does show that there's hope for a better life."

As we discussed in Chapter 2, according to writing center research on tutors' politeness and on writing center lore, when tutors use directive language to tell students what to do and how to proceed, they risk imposing their views on students. In some conference situations, they might decrease opportunities for student writers to think through and make decisions for themselves about potential content, organization, and rhetorical choices, and they risk usurping control over the focus of the conference, potentially disengaging student writers from the conversation. They also risk instructors' accusations of plagiarism, disastrous for students, not to mention troubling for tutors and writing center directors (see Clark 2001). Tutors might also limit opportunities to build rapport and a sense of goodwill in that students might perceive them to be pushy or overbearing. Tutors are right to worry about problematic outcomes such as those discussed above, but they will, without a doubt, need to use instruction in some instances. For one thing, telling and suggesting take less time than cognitive scaffolding. Also, as theorists from Vygotsky (1978, 1987) to Henning (2005) point out, helping students through a discovery process in order to get at objective knowledge (in writing centers, knowledge such as comma rules) might not be worthwhile. Close analysis of how tutors used these strategies can reveal whether such potential problems arising from instruction arose during the conferences that we studied.

Suggesting for Politeness and Optionality

We found that, even during topic episodes that focused on grammar, punctuation, and other issues for which guidelines and rules exist, tutors often mitigated their instruction, using suggestions. Given that student writers were, for the most part, obligated to follow tutors' advice about such matters (if they wanted to do well on the assignment), tutors' mitigation seemed to arise from a drive to be polite.

The excerpt below shows an example case. In this excerpt, T7 offers advice about punctuation, specifically, commas after introductory phrases. In focusing on commas, T7 was responding to S7's request for help with "grammatical type things." Such a request from a student can tempt a tutor to enact a teacher-like role (reminiscent of Bruffee's [1978] warning against tutors acting as "little teachers" [446]). A topic such as commas with introductory phrases gives a tutor an opportunity to demonstrate expertise—an attractive scenario for many tutors and others who love the combination of a captive audience and an opportunity to talk about matters such as correct punctuation.

When asked in his postconference interview about how he deals with the quite common request for grammar help, T7 said that his response depends on the amount of time a student writer has to work on the paper before the deadline:

> Typically, if a student is adamant about focusing on grammar, I will try to accommodate them unless I see something that I am concerned with. For example . . . if it is due in an hour, I will focus on grammar. But they are ultimately in charge of the session, and I am there to serve them.

About requests for grammar help, T8 said much the same thing, but she also recounted a strategy she used for dealing with grammar:

> I want to facilitate them figuring out what they need to do. If there are rules about mechanical issues or grammar issues, I can obviously try to teach them those and try to point out the first couple ones. My goal would be to have them start to identify them after that point. As far as the more global issues, I want them to see where the errors are and figure them out for themselves how to fix them. So I try to keep myself out of it if I can.

T7 followed S7's request in this conference and focused on reading through S7's draft paper. After reading for a few minutes, he stopped at a four-word prepositional phrase that led in to a sentence. He stopped to give a short lesson on comma use with introductory phrases and clauses, and he used a suggesting strategy—advice with mitigation—to convey what S7 should do:

T7: So a good thing to do would be to put a comma [there because you put a
S7:   [O.K.
T7: comma after a four-or-more-word prepositional phrase.
S7: O.K.

T7 delivers his instruction, "So a good thing to do would be to put a comma there," by eliding the agent of the action ("you") completely. He then moves right into an explanation of a punctuation guideline in his suggestion, "Because you put a comma after a four-or-more-word prepositional phrase," thus justifying the action he has advocated. Both the mitigation and the justification of it signal deference toward S7's right and ability to decide for herself about this punctuation matter, even as T7 conveys his opinion that using a comma is the better choice because doing so follows common practice.

Besides mitigating the force of their advice to convey politeness, tutors also used a variety of syntactic and lexical choices to convey optionality—linguistic choices useful for conveying that a student writer is not obligated to carry out a suggestion. Indeed, at many points in the conferences that we studied, as in most writing scenarios, multiple choices for effectively communicating an argument or idea existed. For example, in the excerpt below, T2 discussed an option for concluding a paper that described a sad time in S2's life—a switch from one school to another. The tutor presented S2 with the option of concluding the paper on a more positive, upbeat note. The tutor suggested that S2 mention that her life had since improved:

T2: And so it's kind of sad to write a paper about such a sad change, but you
     might even could say in your conclusion, "since then." You know?

T2 used low-value modal verbs "might" and "could" to soften the force of her advice, thus conveying possibility rather than obligation. After all, for all T2 knew, S2 had no problem with writing an essay that focused exclusively on the sadness she felt during a difficult time in her life. The suggestion here, then, stems at least in part from authentic optionality.

T2's modal-verb-mitigated suggestion in the excerpt above contrasts in an interesting way with the advice T1 delivers in the excerpt below. T1 mitigated her advice, but, in this case, T1 first buffered her advice with a liberal helping of praise. Then, she made explicit the optionality of her suggestion:

T1: I like, um—You say that, you know, this is the way—I like it. "I come here
     because it's suited—it's suitable to my needs in getting things done." So,
     when I'm first reading your introduction, I feel like that's the way you're—
S1: Uh-huh.
T1: going to go. [You're going to explain the library as suitable [for study. And
S1:   [Right.   [Suitable. O.K.

T1: then you throw this sentence in, which is a great sentence and a great thesis. But do you see how [maybe it doesn't necessarily—
S1:   [Yeah. I understand. Uh-huh.
T1: So what I would suggest is going back and reworking the first, um, especially the second two sent—Like the first sentence or two.

The clarity of T1's suggestion at the end of this excerpt comes from her use of the illocutionary-force indicating device (IFID), "I would suggest." IFIDs explicitly mark what a speaker is doing with his or her words; they identify a speaker's speech act. For example, a judge would say, "I pronounce you husband and wife," in order to make a pronouncement about the new marital status of two people. T1's IFID identifies her advice as a suggestion and thus conveys its optionality. T1's observation, specifically, her criticism about an unmet expectation about the paper's argument—given its introduction—provides evidence and thus impetus for heeding the suggestion.

Telling to Show Engagement

Even so, tutors did indeed use telling, even stating their advice bald-on-record, with no mitigation at all. We found that one of the main ways that tutors used such directives was to indicate heightened engagement via the efficiency of bald-on-record directives (Lafuente-Millán 2014; Myers 1989), particularly to respond to something a student writer had just said. For example, T8 used a bald-on-record directive in responding to S8, whose contribution had just proven that she understood the point T8 had been making about pronoun antecedents:

T8: But be careful about the "it," because that "it" is still the confusing part.
S8: Race should not be a factor in decisions that are made because, um—
T8: What does the "it" refer to?
S8: The suspecting criminals—Or—
T8: In this paragraph does "it" refer to "suspect"?
S8: Well, no.
T8: Exactly. So—
S8: [Reading quietly.] Um. [15 seconds] Because—
T8: Specifically, like, generally your pronoun refers right back to a noun that comes before it. "So race should not be a factor in decisions that are made." Are you saying [race should be—
S8:   [Decisions.
T8: Right. Decisions. Good. So when you combine it, try to take that "it" out because it [gets a little
S8:   [O.K. Race should not be an effect on decisions that are made because decisions should be solely on the person's actions.
T8: Good.

Responding to S8's identification of the noun "decisions," T8 coupled an unmitigated telling strategy ("try to take that 'it' out") to a series of one-word responses. When paired with the quick, syncopated rhythm of the one-word responses that preceded it ("Right. Decisions. Good."), the efficient bald-on-record telling strategy conveyed that T8 was engaged in the interaction. T8 likely sensed that S8 could handle the efficient and clear instruction, as she had just shown that she understood what T8 had told her about pronoun antecedents.

Like T8's bald-on-record telling in the example above, the short excerpt below illustrates how the conversational context makes all the difference in the stance telling conveys and constructs. Rather than imposing the tutor's will, the telling strategies combine with motivational scaffolding (praise) and cognitive scaffolding (referring to a previous topic) to acknowledge and reinforce the student writer's prior good work:

T10: So, like you've done a really good job so far of like, introducing um, your quotes and stuff, so I would do that here. Say um, so-and-so says, comma. This report should serve. Or whatever. Just introduce that somehow.

T10 led into telling the student writer what to do by praising him on his consistent use of lead-in phrases to his quotations. After this praise, T10 used an opinion statement to remind S10 of his own earlier practice ("I would do that here"). Such strategies typically begin with "I would," explicitly referring to the speaker's point of view. In writing center settings, because that point of view is usually an expert, institutionally sanctioned one, the strategy often conveys some sense of an obligation (or, at least, the student writer's best interest) to comply. T10 used the opinion statement to convey advice for using a comma after an introductory phrase, and then followed up with an even more direct telling strategy to reiterate ("Just introduce that somehow"). Her use of the understater "just" implied that following the advice would be an easy thing to do.

These last two excerpts in particular make clear how tutors' use of telling strategies did far more than convey an obligation to comply with advice; they also played a role in ratifying what student writers had previously done and said.

Instruction's Potential Role in Tutor Dominance

In this chapter so far, we have examined how tutors used suggestions to convey politeness and lack of obligation to comply. We have also examined how tutors' telling strategies could signal their engagement with student writers' texts and how those strategies did not appear to constitute attempts to take ownership of student writers' work. But of course, because conversation is complex, no analysis is so straightforward; some exchanges between tutors and student writers did indeed appear to be tutor dominated. In this section, we examine two longer excerpts from two conferences. Both of the excerpts contain long tutor turns at talk, but only one appears to be tutor dominated. In the first series of excerpts, the tutor took and maintained control most of the time, without requiring the student writer to contribute as much as she probably could have. We juxtapose the excerpts to examine the role instruction strategies played in generating tutor dominance.

The first excerpt we examine is from the T4–S4 conference. T4 contributed multiple long turns to the exchange; in these turns she laid out an introduction, including a thesis, for S4. We examine this excerpt because in it T4 appears to go too far in telling and suggesting ideas for the paper. When reading this excerpt, it is possible to visualize S4 with pen in hand, poised and ready to write down whatever T4 might say, thus saving herself the effort of having to think about the thesis and the introduction. That T4's long turns did not include any questions for S4—such as pumping questions that could prompt S4's participation and scaffold her learning—strongly suggests that T4 took too much control of the paper's content.

The excerpt begins as T4 suggested that the thesis statement for S4's paper should consist of two parts and offered a long explanation for that suggestion. In her explanation, T4 thought out loud about *Notes from the Underground* and its author's (Fyodor Dostoevsky's) stances toward life's meaning—knowledge she had just gained in conversation with S4. T4's long turn broke only when S4 cut in to ask a question. Specifically, S4 wanted to know how T4 would compose what she had just said out loud as she was describing the proposed two-part thesis. S4 wanted T4 to give her the exact words to use:

T4: And I would say too, there's probably going to be—It's probably going to be sort of like a two-part thesis statement because you're saying, you know, they cause their life to be or feel meaningless. And it seems like from what we talked about here, you're going to say, like, however, in *Notes from the Underground*, the author does show that there's hope for a better life, [or, however, while one of them seems, you know, that there's no chance

S4: [Mm-hmm

T4: for the human condition to improve, *Notes from the Underground* shows that there is. Because when you get to this section on meaninglessness, even though these are the same up here—these ideas of absurdities and pretenses—when you get down to the idea of meaninglessness, from what you mentioned, it sounds like you're going to kind of have it split, you know, that—

S4: O.K. So how will I say that, like, in the introduction?

Rather than turn the tables and ask S4 how she might construct the thesis, thereby getting S4 to do some thinking for herself, T4 continued with more instruction:

T4: Um, I don't know. I mean you could just introduce it as, uh, you know, like—While both of these works use the ideas of absurdities and pretenses to, uh, show that life is meaningless, in *Notes from the Underground*, you know, the character, the underground man, or the author, you know, shows that there is hope to improve their life, or that [there is a way to change, or that

S4:   [Mm-hmm

T4: you know, you can find a way to overcome. [And you want to have, I think,

S4:   [O.K.

T4: some specific example. Like a specific example of that. Like, where do you feel, like, at the end of the work that the author and the character sort of shows that there's a chance that you can change and there's a chance that he can make something out of his life and that things will get better. [And then,

S4:   [O.K.

T4: at the same time I think you'll want to show that the cockroach thought that things were going to get better. But in the end, he just, I think the word you used was he accepted that his life wasn't going to change, so. [I think it'll be

S4:   [Mm-hmm

T4: important to show like, to give two specific examples of those things. And don't forget too, that you don't always have to use, you know—Sometimes, there's really long sections that talk about one idea. And you can't put, like, block quote. The whole [page of text but you know, you can summarize

S4:   [Mm-hmm

T4: and get the main idea across or like paraphrase those ideas. Um, if you can't find like one—

S4: O.K.

T4: specific quote that really [like sticks out that you want to talk about—

S4:   [O.K. I think I just need to, like, read some more about it. Like all day today. [Both laugh.]

Throughout T4's lengthy turn, S4 simply backchanneled ("Mm-hmm" and "O.K.") as T4 went on to point out that S4 needed examples to support the new thesis. Once, in discussing a potential example, T4 nearly asked S4 a question ("Like, where do you feel, like, at the end of the work . . ."), but, as the potential pump question rambled on, it turned into yet another suggestion ("And then at the same time . . .").

S4 continued to backchannel, even as T4 went on to hone her suggestion about using an example ("I think it will be important to show, like, to give two specific examples of those things") and then to provide yet another suggestion ("You don't always have to use . . ."), a suggestion to summarize sources rather than to use block quotations. Indeed, T4 began yet another suggestion on top of the last, this time about what to do if no particular quotation stood out for summarizing ("If you can't find, like, one . . ."). At this point, though, S4 once again cut in, this time with some humor: "I think I just need to, like, read some more about it. Like all day today."

In the excerpt above, we see in T4's talk some of writing center researchers' concerns about tutor dominance made particularly salient, and the tutor's use of instruction certainly influenced the control she demonstrated. Before we look at the role instruction played in her talk, though, we think it is important to point out characteristics of tutor dominance in this excerpt: what is it exactly that makes us think the tutor took and maintained control, as opposed to making way for the student writer's potential contributions?

First, clearly, T4 did nearly all of the talking, and so the ratio of tutor-to-student writer volubility shifted far in favor of the tutor's contributions. Second, S4 contributed mainly backchannels, those minimal responses that people use to show that they are attending as their interlocutors talk (for example, "Mm-hmm"). Third, S4's longest contribution to this exchange is a question, and it is one in which she asks T4 for the words to use in her introduction. Multiple variables point to the assessment that T4 was the dominant participant in this sequence.

As to the ways instruction strategies played a role in how T4 dominated this excerpt, we start with T4's suggestion and explanation of a two-part thesis statement. At its start, the suggestion itself is no more controlling than other tutor suggestions. But T4's suggestion went on, and in it T4 provided specific words and phrases that S4 could use in her introduction. Then, T4 moved into a lengthy explanation of absurdities and pretenses and the idea of meaninglessness. Indeed, S4 broke in to ask about how to write out in the introduction all that T4 had just said—likely because neither would be able to recall the words T4 had used if she continued to talk. So, while T4's suggestions and explanation did indeed go on too long, the main problem with T4's talk was the way she specified too much content for the paper's introduction.

After S4's question, T4 strung suggestions together, one after the other, about specific examples, the cockroach's thoughts, and paraphrasing rather than using long quotations. What we see here is a tutor who forgot to encourage and push the student writer to think for herself about the thesis statement that she wanted to argue and the introduction that she wanted to craft around it.

Contrast T4's long turns with T9's in the next excerpt, in which T9 helped S9 figure out a thesis about a creation myth. Like T4, T9 dominated the conversation in terms of volubility, and yet her talk does not come across nearly as dominant as T4's. A main reason for this difference, as we discuss below, was the way T9 consistently incorporated cognitive scaffolding pump questions that pushed S9 to think about the assignment and to contribute to the conversation, even as T9 used instruction to tell S9 what to do.

To address the question of how a myth's fantastical elements responded to the problem of philosophical exile, T9 thought out loud for a while before putting pumping questions to S9:

T9: And then just the—You mentioned, um, the body with the four heads and thousand eyes—Like the use of um, obviously, the cutting up. And then— And then the, um, using kind of strange body-type imagery. So that we visualize this man with four heads. It's crazy. Um, you don't have to call it "body imagery" in your paper. That's the word that came to my mind. Um, so, how—how does this story use these images of this savior cutting up everyone's body? How—how does that explain the problem of our existence? Well, first of all, actually, why don't—Before we do that, what problem of our existence does it explain? Then we'll talk about the how.

S9: What is a problem of existence?

After telling S9 that she did not have to use the term "body imagery" and posing two pumping questions, T9 backed up to address a more basic question to S9: "Before we do that, what problem of our existence does it explain?" That T9 backtracked to ask a different question shows that she had some measure of control over the progress of the conference. She seemed to realize that her first question assumed S9 understood the "problem of our existence" that she needed to address. To shift gears, she told S9 how they would proceed: after they had determined the problem of existence, they would figure out how the creation myth that S9 had chosen responded to this problem: "Then we'll talk about how."

However, T9's cognitive scaffolding questions revealed that S9 did not at all understand what the instructor meant by a "problem of existence." To answer S9's question, T9 continued telling her about the reasons for creation myths; unlike T4, T9 once again ended her long turn with a pump question: "So which problem of existence did this solve?"

T9: I think what they're referring to here is, you know, one of the fundamental concerns of mankind is why are we here? How did we get here? You know, that's—that's—that's how we, you know, discover religion in the first place. Um, and, um, that's why different people come up with different creation myths. And you know, some of them are part of our faith and some of them are not. But these people at one time felt the need to explain our existence and this is how they did it, with this myth. Um. So which—which—problem of existence did this solve?

S9: I guess the need for, like, a superior being. And, um, once you have that, it starts to, like, grow into a conflict sort of thing. Because, like, this person. And then this person. So it starts to create like tension, I guess you could say. And then that, from the tension part, is the resolution. And once you get to the resolution, it's, like, in order to—Creation, you know, put humans on earth. It's kind of—that's what I got from it.

This time, T9's pump question set off a long turn from S9. S9 began to think out loud about the problems that creation myths solve, such as the (rather big) mystery of human existence. S9's in-depth response is one many of us would consider a sort of ideal response to a tutor's pump question.

These two extended excerpts show that not all long tutor turns and not all instruction strategies are created equal. T4 used instruction strategies to give advice, including advice about exact words that S4 could use in her paper, and to explain that advice. She did not integrate that instruction with pumping questions or other strategies that might have prodded the student writer to contribute more than backchannels to the interaction. T9 took long turns at talk as well, but she refrained from providing exact wording for S9's paper, and she integrated her instruction with pumping questions. The difference in the student writers' responses is particularly salient in S9's lengthy turn in response to T9's pumping question ("So which—which—problem of existence did this solve?"). Our analysis here showed that, although instruction strategies (and tutor volubility as well) could certainly play a role in a tutor's dominant behavior, their use did not automatically generate tutor dominance.

In addition, these excerpts reveal tutors' use of their expertise in literary analysis and writing to advise the two student writers about their WL essays—even though neither tutor had read the texts that S4 and S9 were analyzing. Like the tutor in Mackiewicz's (2004) study who had worked as a technical writer, T4 and T9 knew the right questions to ask because they were English majors who had analyzed numerous literary texts in their own coursework. Their general disciplinary knowledge and writing knowledge trumped their lack of knowledge of the particular texts.

The two conferences we have excerpted above show the dangers of tutors' expertise as well as the benefits. Like one of the tutors in Kiedaisch and Dinitz's (1993) study, T4 used her expertise to tell S4 exactly what to do, a situation S4 was happy to embrace. T9, however, used her expertise to ask questions and help S9 explore her thinking.

Instruction Strategies in the Closing Stage

In their training, all 10 tutors learned that they should end conferences by preparing student writers to continue working on their papers after their conferences. To help organize student writers for their future efforts, tutors were supposed to summarize what they had covered and to create a plan of action—a set of goals—for continued work on the paper. As mentioned in Chapter 4, only two of the 10 tutors followed both of these mandates.

T8, one of the two tutors who summarized and set goals, closed the conference by using bald-on-record telling and pumping questions to remind S8 of important points for composing paragraphs:

T8: O.K. So the big things that we've kind of talked about today. Transitions
between paragraphs [to kind of show a logical link. And with those transitions I
S8:   [O.K.

T8: think come a topic sentence and your concluding sentence. [So make sure

S8:   [O.K.

T8: your topic—What do you want to do with your topic sentences?

S8: Um, make sure that they are, like, setting up the whole paragraph.

T8: Right. So they're kind of forecasting. And what about your concluding sentences?

S8: They need to end the sentence, or end the paragraph, and um kind of link to—

T8: Good. And tie it back to your thesis statement to remind us what the theme point is. And then also supporting—integrating your support. So, avoiding—I completely understand what she's telling you, you know, you've got to support [everything they say. But—So try to support it without saying it twice,

S8:   [Right.

T8: and try to put the support in possibly instead of what you've said that's exactly the same. And then look at the pronouns. Um, pull out every time you use "it," and make sure "it" clearly is referring to something.

T8's series of bald-on-record directives ("Tie it back . . .," "try to support it . . .," "try to put the support . . .") make clear T8's certainty about what S8 should do when she began work on the paper after the conference. T8's directness seemed to signal that she and S8 were on the same page and that, at this late stage in the conference, T8 felt she could provide efficient and clear advice without worrying too much about S8 taking offence.

The second tutor who made sure that the student writer left the writing center with a conference summary and a plan for what to do next, T1, used more cognitive scaffolding strategies to close the conference. We examine an excerpt from T1's conference with S1 in Chapter 6, the chapter that focuses on cognitive scaffolding strategies.

Conclusions and Implications for Tutor Training

We examined tutors' use of instruction—telling, suggesting, and explaining and exemplifying—and the directiveness of their advice. Our analysis indicated that tutors' instruction serves several pedagogical and practical purposes and, as also indicated by prior empirical research in writing center pedagogy, definitely has a place in writing tutoring. Indeed, even the most directive telling strategies had benefits: when tutors used bald-on-record or other directive telling to respond to student writers' contributions, they showed engagement with what student writers had said.

In this chapter, we have examined how tutors showed deference by using suggesting strategies to convey their advice. Tutors appeared to use polite suggestions when the context made clear that failing to follow the tutors' advice would be detrimental to the quality of the writing or to the grade, for example, during topic episodes focusing on punctuation, grammar, and citation style. Tutors also used suggestions to indicate the optionality of their advice, such as when a student writer could address an issue in multiple ways—any of which could potentially be effective—such as rewording a sentence, organizing a paragraph, and deciding upon a thesis statement. Further, we found that some topic episodes consisted solely of instruction and contained minimal input from student writers.

Our results have implications for tutor training. Most obviously, we think that writing center directors and others who conduct tutor training should make clear, not just the acceptability of instruction, but also its appropriate use. For example, they might discuss with tutors Wittwer and Renkl's (2008) research review and guidelines for using explanations and possibly expand those guidelines to telling and suggesting as well.

Because directors conducting training as well as teaching courses in tutoring practices will likely ask new tutors to read critical writing center scholarship and because those older articles tend to advise against instruction in favor of a hands-off approach, those overseeing tutor training and writing center pedagogy should ensure time in training or class to discuss the appropriate and effective use of instruction strategies. Tutors certainly should know and understand the thinking behind important work such as Brooks's (1991) "Minimalist Tutoring: Making the Student Do All the Work," but they should understand it in light of current research and practice.

We found that tutors sometimes told students how to correct errors in grammar, punctuation, and citation style, among other writing-related topics, but we also found that, at other times, they used suggestions to convey such advice. Directors might convey to tutors that mini-lessons on such topics are perfectly reasonable, but they might also point out the efficacy of ensuring that student writers can apply the lesson themselves. Therefore, tutors might ask student writers to read a paragraph out loud and respond to that paragraph, or they might use the referring back strategy (discussed in Chapter 6) when they encounter the same error or issue later in the draft.

Our analysis of tutors' suggestions shows that ensuring clarity when using them can be tricky: their mitigation can convey either politeness or a lack of obligation to comply with the advice (Thonus 1999b). In tutor training, writing center directors can help tutors ameliorate some of the ambiguity of their suggestions by using the IFID "I suggest" or some variant of it. Tutors can explicitly mark their suggestions with phrases such as "This is my suggestion" or "Here's one option."

Directors might also want to spend some time talking to tutors—both new and experienced ones—about explanation strategies. The tutors in this study explained just 16% of their advice. We think that more explanation could be worthwhile, as explanations can facilitate student writers' understanding of the "why" behind their advice, as opposed to just the "how." However, as our analysis of instruction in tutors' long turns shows, explaining, like telling and suggesting, can work the other way, factoring into tutor dominance over a student writer's text and over the interaction—particularly when a tutor supplies too much in the way of content and neglects to bring in the student writer as an active participant. We also recognize that explaining consumes time, and so tutors trying to explain a bit more often will need to be judicious in choosing advice deserving of explanation. In addition, directors might want to work with tutors so that they are better able to help students generate explanations themselves, as Chi et al. (2001) advocate.

The tutors in our study all engaged in agenda setting in the opening stage of their conferences, negotiating conference goals with student writers. However, their negotiation did not involve instruction. Rather, tutors primarily used knowledge-deficit questions and motivational scaffolding strategies, reserving instruction for the teaching stage. Directors might point out and reiterate to tutors in training that cooperative and collaborative agenda setting requires engaging student writers and not telling them what to do.

Although all of the tutors knew that they should end conferences with summary and goal setting, just two enacted their training. Even though the student writers appeared to know what they needed to do postconference, tutors' use of explicit summaries and statements of goals would decrease potential confusion later. Tutors and student writers could also write down the summary and goals, safeguarding against forgetfulness.

In sum, instruction played a critical role in the 10 conferences that we analyzed. In the chapters to follow, we examine other ways that tutors used it in conjunction with cognitive and motivational scaffolding.

6

COGNITIVE SCAFFOLDING STRATEGIES

- Cognitive Scaffolding Strategies' Constraint on Responses
- Cognitive Scaffolding Strategies in the Opening Stage
- Cognitive Scaffolding Strategies in the Teaching Stage
- Cognitive Scaffolding Strategies in the Closing Stage
- Conclusions and Implications for Tutor Training

One of the hallmarks of one-to-one tutoring across all disciplines is the opportunity to move away from the directiveness of instruction strategies to more collaborative strategies that typically are difficult to practice in one-to-many classroom teaching. Cognitive scaffolding strategies can push and probe students' thinking by getting them to reflect on their own reasoning and by guiding them to answer questions or perform tasks they could not otherwise perform. These strategies lend student writers the support they need to advance in their composing abilities. The experienced tutors in our study took advantage of the one-to-one pedagogical situation—the individualized attention and feedback it affords—to use cognitive scaffolds that got student writers to think and make decisions about their writing, to analyze their aims for their papers, and to generate content for their own purposes.

In this chapter, we discuss the constraints that cognitive scaffolding strategies put on student writers' responses. We then describe tutors' use of cognitive scaffolding strategies in the opening stage, the teaching stage, and the closing stage. We end the chapter by discussing our conclusions and the implications of our analysis for tutor training.

Cognitive Scaffolding Strategies' Constraint on Responses

In Chapter 2, we discussed the degree of constraint that cognitive scaffolding questions can impose on student writers' responses. In this chapter, we expand the discussion and provide examples of tutors using cognitive scaffolding strategies to set boundaries on student writers' responses. In constraining student writers' responses with such strategies, tutors helped protect student writers from failure and frustration and simultaneously required them to interact (Chi et al. 2001). Cognitive scaffolding strategies exist along a continuum defined by the degree of constraint they put on a response. At their most constraining, they solicit answers that are easy to identify as either correct or not correct, and they have single correct answers (for example, "What is the subject of that sentence?"). Cognitive scaffolding strategies that highly constrain responses include referring to a previous topic, forcing a choice, using single-answer pumps, and in some instances, particularly those related to correct punctuation, reading aloud.

At the other end of the constraint continuum, the least constraining cognitive scaffolding strategies can lead to a wide range of possible responses from student writers. In some instances, pumping questions, responding as a reader or listener, and reading aloud can support student writers while allowing them a range of appropriate and thoughtful responses. However, unlike truly open-ended questions, even cognitive scaffolding strategies that allow (and probably encourage) a range of responses set some limits, and tutors can and do evaluate the appropriateness of student writers' responses.

Some examples help clarify how cognitive scaffolding strategies range from most to least constraining. T7's pumping question was highly constraining because it had a single correct response: [Pointing at a sentence.] "How do you punctuate that?" In contrast, T2's prompting question—"So he transitioned fine because of . . . what?"—was moderately constraining. Even though more than one correct answer was possible, an appropriate response would have addressed reasons the person referred to transitioned easily. Having read the rest of the essay, T2 could determine the appropriateness of S2's response. Other cognitive scaffolding strategies imposed minimal constraints on student writers' responses. However, minimally constraining cognitive scaffolds require more time for students to consider and then to formulate appropriate responses. In fact, minimally constrained pumping questions such as T8's "What's the big argument about?" and T9's "Where do you think you should go with that?" can potentially demand so much cognitive effort that student writers may struggle to formulate responses at all.

Cognitive Scaffolding Strategies in the Opening Stage

Analyzing opening stages shows that tutors read aloud from assignment sheets, paraphrased what they read and what student writers told them, and asked questions. However, they most often seemed to be trying to understand the assignment and to collaborate in setting the agenda. They were not pumping student writers in order to help them understand problems with their drafts or to brainstorm new ideas. Cognitive scaffolding requires that tutors can identify appropriate or correct responses, but, in the opening stages of conferences, tutors did not know the background of the student writers' assignments or student writers' individual understandings of their assignments. For example, in the talk excerpted below, T7 paraphrased the assignment for S7 to ensure his understanding matched S7's:

T7: [Reads through the assignment.] O.K. So this is just expository in the sense that you are going to tell what you believe?
S7: Right.

Questions such as the one above that T7 used in the opening stage make clear that not all tutor questions are cognitive scaffolding. As we explained in Chapter 2, some questions serve the purpose of filling in a tutor's knowledge deficits. Later in the conference, while T7 read S7's draft, T7 (like other tutors) used similar interrogative syntax when responding as a reader and when asking pumping questions, both cognitive scaffolding strategies. The difference between cognitive scaffolding questions and knowledge-deficit questions lies in their context and in the tutor's intentions.

Cognitive Scaffolding Strategies in the Teaching Stage

In this section, we analyze at the macrolevel and the microlevel tutors' use of cognitive scaffolding strategies. We first consider cognitive scaffolds at the macrolevel, examining tutors' use of these strategies in a topic episode. Then, we focus on cognitive scaffolds at the microlevel, examining the frequencies with which tutors used them and closely analyzing examples to show the ways tutors used them to move student writers' thinking forward.

Cognitive Scaffolding Strategies in Topic Episodes

As we have discussed in Chapter 2 and elsewhere, Mehan (1979), Nassaji and Wells (2000), and others have described and analyzed the prototypical three-part IRF sequence. Although they use different terminology, they show that instructors use forced-choice, prompting, and pumping questions—strategies that require a response from students—to initiate a sequence to push student writers' thinking forward. In the excerpt below, TE3 from the conference between T8 and S8, T8 used a pumping question to initiate the IRIRF sequence:

I   T8: O.K. So, this is your main point of this paragraph? [2 seconds] Like your topic sentence, you think?

R S8: Um, like my thesis?

I T8: Or do you think it's the topic—that's the topic sentence of that particular paragraph? [Reading.] ["That it's the person inside that the time."

   S8:   [Um.

   T8: I'm just wondering because—

R S8: Well, I don't know. A lot of this is like, it's four pages, so you have to just kind of like—

   T8: Get out what you can?

   S8: Yeah.

F T8: O.K. The only reason I'm asking is because you have the exact same wording here that you do up there, so it's a little bit redundant. Um, so let's continue reading and maybe see what the main point is.

   S8: Yeah. O.K. And then change it.

   T8: Yeah.

T8 initiated the sequence with a single-answer pumping question, but S8 did not seem to understand and could not respond correctly. Using another pumping question, T8 rephrased the original question. Both questions require "yes" or "no" responses ("So, this is your main point of this paragraph? Like your topic sentence, you think?" and "Or do you think it's the topic—that's the topic sentence of that particular paragraph?"). After the second question, T8 read aloud the sentence to which she referred. However, S8 still could not answer. T8's follow up, as opposed to functioning mainly as an evaluation of S8's response to the reformulated pump question, was really an explanation of the reason that she asked the initiating question in the first place. As Nassaji and Wells (2000) point out, explaining and justifying are appropriate forms of follow up in IRF sequences. In any case, even though the main function of T8's follow up was explanation, it did contain some evaluation as well, pointing out a problem with the draft rather than with the student writer's response: "You have the exact same wording here that you do up there, so it's a little bit redundant." After giving this explanatory follow up, T8 backed off from the topic she initiated (the paragraph's focus, as opposed to the paper's thesis), seemingly with the idea of returning to her question and the topic later. The excerpt above exemplifies how writing center tutors used cognitive scaffolding strategies to initiate elaborated IRF sequences. It further illustrates how a tutor might need to recast an initiation of the IRF sequence before a student writer understands it and responds.

Quantitative Results: Frequencies of the Cognitive Scaffolding Strategies

Table 6.1 shows that the frequencies with which tutors used cognitive scaffolding strategies varied widely. Tutors used pumping more often than any other cognitive scaffolding strategy. In fact, they used it more often than all of the other cognitive scaffolding strategies combined. Pumping was also the strategy that tutors used third most often overall. In contrast, tutors rarely used prompting (six occurrences), hinting (four occurrences), and demonstrating (one occurrence). Because the tutors hardly ever used these three strategies, we grouped them together in Table 6.1 and discuss them just briefly. In this section, we discuss the frequencies and percentages of the eight cognitive scaffolding strategies. In the next section, we will provide qualitative analyses of excerpts from the 10 conferences.

Pumping

As we noted before, depending upon the constraints they wanted to impose on possible responses, when tutors used pumping questions, they withheld their advice or part of the answer. The tutors averaged 5.91 pumping questions every 10 minutes of conference talk. The frequency with which tutors used this strategy ranged quite widely—from 12.82 to 1.71 occurrences per 10 minutes of talk. One tutor, T8, used this strategy 33% more than the tutor who used it second most often. T8's conference with S8 focused on revising and proofreading a response to a class reading about racial profiling. We analyze this conference in more detail in the next section on qualitative results.

Reading Aloud

The procedure of reading silently (as opposed to reading aloud) through a student writer's draft and stopping periodically to fix errors has received its share of criticism (for example, Capossela 1998, 11; Ryan and Zimmerelli 2010, 49). Writing center researchers point out that, when tutors read silently, stopping to comment and correct, they for the most part fail to engage student writers in the process of improving their own work. For example, Ryan and Zimmerelli (2010) proscribe against tutors reading silently while student writers sit (passively) and watch them. Research on tutors' and student writers' preferences for reading aloud versus silently

TABLE 6.1 Frequency and Percentage of Cognitive Scaffolding per 10 Minutes

Cognitive Scaffolding Strategy	Frequency per 10 Minutes (% Total)	
Pumping	5.91	(55)
Reading aloud	2.18	(23)
Responding as reader or listener	1.27	(11)
Referring to a previous topic	0.54	(5)
Forcing a choice	0.40	(3)
Prompting, hinting, demonstrating	0.24	(3)
Total	10.54	(100)

showed that silent reading—whether with tutor comments throughout or at the end—was not favored by tutors or student writers (Adams 2009, 6). Ryan and Zimmerelli's (2010) admonition is strong because they, like most others, feel that silently reading a student writer's paper makes the writer into a passive and likely quite bored spectator. Chapter 1 of Block's (2010) dissertation nicely summarizes the scholarly discussion about reading aloud, describing researchers' "concerns about how reading methods affect client control and engagement, audience awareness, and attention to local versus global issues" (4). Many writing center researchers, she says, prefer that student writers read their own papers out loud "to reify their sense of agency and control" and to ensure their attention (4). For these researchers, the act of reading aloud constitutes a student writer's active participation in his or her conference—an opportunity that a tutor should not miss.

On the other hand, other writing center researchers, such as Gillespie (2002), feel that student writers can benefit more from tutors reading their papers aloud, because they do not have to expend the extra cognitive resources on pronouncing words and because they hear their words and punctuation the way their audience would understand them. That is, with the reading-aloud strategy, tutors give students another mode—the aural mode—of input. In addition, current reading research suggests that the phenomenon of mind-wandering may in fact be more prevalent in reading aloud than in silent reading. Franklin et al. (2013) write, "Reading aloud actually promotes mind-wandering, relative to silent reading" (4). Such results suggest that writing center tutors rather than student writers should read aloud, and that the strategy can be a good pedagogical choice.

The experienced tutors averaged 2.18 reading-aloud strategies per 10 minutes of conference talk, ranging from 0 to 5.61 strategies per 10 minutes. Not surprisingly, the conferences focused on revising and proofreading contained far more of these strategies than the brainstorming conferences did. T1, T2, T6, T7, T8, and T10 averaged 3.06 reading-aloud strategies per 10 minutes of conference talk. Three tutors, T10 (5.61 times per 10 minutes), T7 (5.00 times per 10 minutes), and T8 (4.10 times per 10 minutes), used this strategy most often during their revising and proofreading conferences.

Responding as a Reader or a Listener

When experienced tutors used the responding-as-a-reader-or-listener strategy, they read from a student writer's draft (or outline or notes) or assignment sheet or listened to something the student writer said and then told the student writer what they had taken away. Tutors paraphrased what they had read or heard and, in doing so, made it possible for student writers to compare their intended meaning to their conveyed meaning. The tutors averaged 2.18 of these strategies per 10 minutes of talk, ranging from 0 strategies to 3.33 strategies. Two of the three tutors who used this strategy most often were T3 (2.61 times per 10 minutes) and T9 (3.33 times per 10 minutes). Both of these tutors participated in brainstorming as opposed to revising- or proofreading-focused conferences and, as the student writers had no drafts, these tutors were usually responding as listeners rather than readers. The other tutor who used this strategy most often, T2 (2.81 times per 10 minutes), participated in a conference about revising (as opposed to proofreading or a combination of revising and proofreading).

Referring to a Previous Topic

Tutors used the strategy of referring to a previous topic in two ways. First, they referred to a previous topic when they saw that students were having the same problem (such as difficulty formulating a topic sentence) more than once. In these situations, tutors referred back to the earlier occurrence and reinforced the advice that they had provided before. Second, tutors referred back to student writers' previous contributions—particularly contributions in which student writers had articulated their own approaches to problems that they were having. Tutors did not use this strategy often, averaging just 0.54 occurrences per 10 minutes of conference talk and ranging from 0 to 1.28 occurrences per 10 minutes.

Forcing a Choice

As we discuss in a prior study of tutoring strategies (Thompson and Mackiewicz 2014), the forced-choice strategy seems to arise more naturally in closed-world domains where discrete, objective answers to student writers' questions exist. In the open-world domain of writing, tutors did not use the strategy of forcing a choice very often. When tutors used this strategy, they presented student writers with (usually) two alternatives and asked students to choose one. In presenting student writers with a limited set of possibilities, tutors severely constrained student writers' possible responses. Four of the tutors did not use the forced-choice strategy at all, and the other six tutors used the strategy between 1 and 3 times. The tutors averaged 0.40 occurrences of this strategy per 10 minutes of conference talk and ranged between 0 and 1.25 occurrences per 10 minutes.

Prompting, Hinting, Demonstrating

We coded prompting, hinting, and demonstrating strategies because these strategies occurred in prior studies—research that focused mainly on closed-world domains (for example, Chi 1996; Lepper, Drake, and O'Donnell-Johnson 1997). As we noted above, though, the writer center tutors in our study used very few of these strategies—just 11 occurrences of the three strategies in the 10 conferences (prompting = 6, hinting = 4, demonstrating = 1). Because tutors did not rely on these three strategies, we grouped them together and spent little time examining them, except in cases where they occurred in conjunction with other strategies. However, demonstrating did occur more frequently in T9's conferences when she worked as a writing fellow. In Chapter 8, we discuss this strategy in more detail.

Qualitative Results: Close Analysis of the Cognitive Scaffolding Strategies

In this section, we analyze conference excerpts to show how writing center tutors used cognitive scaffolding strategies in our corpus.

Pumping

In a brainstorming-focused conference, T3 used minimally constraining, pumping questions to help S3 analyze the audience of the magazine *Cosmo Girl*:

T3: What else? I mean what kind of traits or whatever does the average *Cosmo Girl* reader have? I mean, what would they all have in common?
S3: Um, I guess popularity. Probably money.

T3 began with what appears to be a minimally constrained pump question ("What else?"), though he likely did not mean for it to be so wide open. He quickly followed up with a more constraining pump question and then another pump that explained the previous one. Similar to the notion of writing as a discovery process, T3 appeared to be pumping his own question, gathering steam in his inquiries to diagnose and thereby help himself clarify how best to lead the student forward to analyzing the audience of *Cosmo Girl*. T3's pumping questions pushed S3 to list common characteristics of the magazine's readers in order to help S3 eventually to map these characteristics as evidence. To help student writers home in on a particular topic, tutors asked minimally constraining pumping questions that prodded student writers to think about potential areas of focus for their papers.

Tutors also used slightly more constraining pumps—moderately constraining pumps—to help focus student writers' responses while simultaneously pushing them to think about their writing. In the excerpt below, T4 leads off with a suggestion ("And so maybe you want to talk about both relationships") and then moves to moderately constraining pumping questions that set boundaries on a potential response:

T4: And so maybe you want to talk about both relationships. Like the comments between both the king and queen cockroaches [and then also the comments
S4:   [Mm-hmm

T4: that happen between the husband and wife. [What's another possibility here?
S4:   [O.K.
T4: Besides the dinner party. Is there another?

Throughout this conference and in the talk excerpted above too, T4 brainstormed with S4 to develop ideas for her essay, turning to moderately constraining pumps to help S4 generate ideas: "What's another possibility here? Besides the dinner party. Is there another?" Although these pumps opened the conversational floor to S4, they also established some clear boundaries for S4's response. T4 pumped S4 for a short response—another specific example. In doing so, T4 continued her data gathering about relationships in one of two short stories that S4 analyzed for her essay. T4's moderately constrained pumps facilitated an easy and fast response from S4.

One challenge for tutors who used pumping questions that allowed for a range of responses was that they had to be ready to grapple with whatever response student writers generated to determine its appropriateness. Another excerpt from the T3–S3 conference shows how such a pumping question can temporarily stump a student writer. When T3 asked a moderately constraining pump to get S3 to generate support for her claim about *Cosmo Girl*, S3's response did not address the magazine but instead commented on the ability of the magazine's readership to achieve the lifestyle the magazine endorses. This excerpt shows an IRIRFRFR sequence, with the student writer adding an atypical final response.

I T3: O.K. Um, so then the question, you know, the next question would be, how does it go about that?
R S3: Wait. How does it go about what?
I T3: How does it go about reflecting this lifestyle, but then also encouraging that lifestyle?
R S3: I'm not really sure. I think it—I think you honestly need to have like a lot of time on your hands.
F T3: [Laughs.] O.K.
R S3: I think . . . Let's say you're in that popular crowd where, like, all of your friends are like cheerleading and sports and then you're just like "Hmm, I guess I'll watch E News tonight."
F T3: O.K.
R S3: I guess.

T3 moved from the moderately constraining question—one made unclear by an unclear pronoun referent ("And how does it go about that?") to a much more constraining and thus more specific question. In this instance, he seemed to be responding to S3's confusion ("Wait. How does it go about what?"). In reacting to S3's confusion and modifying his approach, T3 was, it seems, particularly tuned in to the contingency of tutoring. In response to T3's revised question, S3 formulated at first only "I'm not really sure," before extending that response with an analogy.

In her brainstorming conference with S9, T9 used minimally constraining pumping questions such as "So why, why do you think it's, it's effective?" T4 also used minimally constraining pumps in her brainstorming conference with S4, including "So what is sort of like the main idea that you feel like you are going to be working with when we talk about these two ideas?" and "O.K. So what are some specific ideas that you want to talk about when you talk about this idea that they are living like these fake, meaningless lives?" However, a conference focused on brainstorming did not always generate frequent, minimally pumping questions from tutors. In her conference with the chain of topic episodes shown in Chapter 4, T5 focused on helping S5 think through the viability of his proposed thesis: smoking in public places should be illegal. S5's instructor had pointed out that smoking in public places is already illegal in many areas, making S5's argument a moot point. During the conference, T5 used pumping questions that moderately constrained the range of possible responses for S5, moving him along in considering options for modifying his proposed thesis so that it would acknowledge current smoking laws: "Um, are there maybe some places where it's not banned that, you know, it should be?"

As we noted above, T8, on the other hand, worked in a conference geared toward revising an existing draft, as opposed to brainstorming ideas for a draft that did not yet exist. As she and S8 moved through the paper together, T8 used pumps frequently. In particular, she used minimally constraining pumps, questions that allowed a wide range of response, such as "How else could you say it?" and "O.K. What do you think the main point is here that you're making?" Also, T8 used pumps to respond to questions from S8, a student who participated quite actively by both asking and answering questions. T8 tossed S8's questions back to her to get her to make an attempt at formulating her own answers:

S8: [Speaks under breath as she writes on paper.] Um. Especially crime based. Does that make sense?
T8: Hmmm, what do you think?

Certainly, in some discourse situations, answering a question with a question conveys evasiveness and even a potential mask of deceit (for example, Knapp, Hart, and Dennis 1974). But, as Walton (1988) points out, "In some cases it is highly appropriate to reply to a question by posing another question," although he acknowledges that continuing to do so "could frustrate the aims of a reasonable dialogue" (210). In this case, T8 answered S8's question with another question to give S8 the opportunity to think through and then supply an answer for herself.

Even T8's more constraining pumping questions—ones aimed at getting S8 to generate content for her paper—usually allowed S8 leeway in responding. In the excerpt below, T8's pump required a response consisting of potential content, a sentence or two about racial profiling. T8's intervening suggestion for formulating a potential response ("Maybe as a clause in one of these sentences") somewhat restricted T8's pumping questions ("How might you bring in racial profiling for a crime back into this?" and "But how could you add it in there?"), but an appropriate response from S8 could have been just about any relevant phrase or clause about racial profiling. The exact phrase or clause was up to S8:

T8: Yeah, and how might you bring in racial profiling for a crime back into this?
S8: Um. [5 seconds] Um. "Racial profiling—" [9 seconds]
T8: Maybe as a clause in one of these sentences. So it doesn't actually have to be a new sentence. But how could you add it in there?
S8: [5 seconds] Should I say, "Race should not be an effect on the decisions that are made but should be on a person's personality scales or actions"? Like make those two one sentence?

After S8's halting start to a new sentence that included a mention of racial profiling and T8's suggestion for embedding the idea into an existing sentence, T8 produced a potential sentence in response to T8's pumping questions.

Although it appeared that minimally constraining pumps had the greatest potential to stump students, the following excerpt shows that student writers at times had difficulty formulating responses to highly constraining pumping questions as well. It also shows how an experienced tutor can salvage such a situation by moving to another strategy, in this case, a forced-choice strategy. The topic episode here follows an IRIRIRF sequence, with the student writer unable to answer.

I   T7: [Whispering, reading draft, and then speaking aloud to S7.] O.K. Now here you have a—Do you know what part of speech this is?
R   S7: What part of speech?
I   T7: Uh huh. Subject, verb, preposition. Multiple choice.
R   S7: O.K.
I   T7: Which one do you think?
R   S7: Uh. That would be a verb?
F   T7: Well, actually, I meant choice A, subject. Choice B, preposition. So a preposition "from." You begin with that preposition [and you end with
    S7:   [Right.
    T7: the object of your preposition is "basketball." So a good thing to do [would be to put a comma [there because you put a comma after an
    S7: [Right.   [O.K.
    T7: introductory four-or-more-word prepositional phrase.

T7 began with a highly constraining pump question: "Do you know what part of speech this is?" Although the literal answer is either "yes" or "no," S7, like most L1 American English speakers, moved to the intended question: "What part of speech is this?" This pump has only one answer. However, S7 did not understand, so T7 adapted by switching to the forced-choice strategy—a strategy of providing alternatives. When S7 guessed incorrectly ("Would that be a verb?"), T7 provided the answer and moved on quickly to his real point: the need to put a comma after an introductory phrase of four or more words. This excerpt points to the importance of contingency, as we saw previously in T3's tutoring, a tutor's ability to adapt to and wrestle with a student writer's response, as opposed to simply trying to get past that response.

Reading Aloud

As we noted above, tutors working with student writers on revising and proof-reading used the reading-aloud strategy far more often than those working in conferences focusing on brainstorming. The tutor who used this strategy most often, T10, worked on proofreading with S10. Throughout the conference, T10 read S10's paper, stopped, gave sentence-level advice, and then moved on. Because the paper was due later that day, the tutor had little choice except to focus on proofreading, and she had little time to employ much pumping. The excerpt below exemplifies T10's approach to interacting with the text and S10 throughout the conference:

T10: O.K. And here you have, "The estimated total number of people living in the US with a viral STD is over 65 million. At least 25 percent of them were teenagers." So I would change this to [are teenagers.
S10:   [Are teenagers.
T10: Yeah.

The example above shows how T10 used the strategy as she and S10 moved through the paper together to focus S10's attention on a particular line or section. In this case, T10 read two sentences, focusing S10's attention and helping S10 hear the difference in tense between the two sentences. The strategy appeared to work, as S10 supplies the correct verb phrase at the same time that T10 states it.

In a somewhat more substantial use of the strategy, T7 moves from reading aloud to pumping questions that seem aimed at getting S7 to think about the implications of her word choice on her thesis statement:

T7: [Reading.] "It is my belief that exercise should be a necessity."
S7: I actually think that she wanted me to—Oh no [unclear].

T7: O.K. Do you think you might—Looking at "necessity"—Do you think that fits there well? Do you feel comfortable with that or maybe—?

S7: Hmmm. Not really. I mean, like, it should be maybe "a part of people's everyday life" instead of "a necessity."

After he finishes reading the sentence ending with the problematic word "necessity," T7 uses pumping questions, seemingly aimed at getting S7 to reconsider her word choice. Once again, the reading-aloud strategy works: S7 hears the problem with the word "necessity," even though neither she nor T7 attempts to explain the problem.

As these excerpts indicate, at times, the experienced tutors in our study—like many writer center tutors—used the approach of reading through student writers' draft papers out loud, commenting as they progressed through the papers. As writing center scholars have pointed out, this practice tends to compel tutors to focus overwhelmingly on student writers' drafts at the sentence level (Block 2010). Writing center scholars think that this approach and the focus that it encourages create conferences that look like tutor-directed editing sessions, rather than collaborative pedagogical activities. However, as these excerpts also indicate, reading aloud to student writers from their own work can serve an important purpose: it can help them hear and identify grammatical and lexical problems in their drafts. It seems, then, that the key to using this strategy well would be to use it purposefully and to avoid doing a student writer's work.

Responding as a Reader or a Listener

Tutors responded as readers to student writers' draft papers, notes, and outlines, and they responded as listeners to things that student writers said—their thoughts about their papers and their attempts at putting those thoughts into writing by saying them out loud first. As previously stated, working in conferences focused on brainstorming, T3 and T9 used the responding-as-a-listener strategy, paraphrasing what the student writers had said. In the excerpt below, S9 told T9 about the creation myth she was to address in her paper. T9 paraphrased what S9 told her, allowing S9 to determine whether T9 had understood her correctly:

S9: Like, it's like, it is about creating man out of the one who unties him and, like, cut off his butt to create mankind from his butt. Something like that. And then it just goes bye-bye.

T9: [Laughs.] O.K. So you could say that, basically, the concept is the gods got to war.

With this responding-as-a-listener strategy, T9 showed she attended to what the student writer had just said by summing it up quite pithily. At the same time, T9 also gave S9 what Brown and Levinson (1987) call the gift of understanding (or, at least, the gift of attempted understanding). With the responding-as-a-reader-or-a-listener strategy, tutors described what they took away from listening or from reading a draft, and they were able to do some motivational work as well.

Of course, tutors who helped student writers to revise and proofread draft papers (as opposed to brainstorming ideas for papers) also used this strategy to show their understanding of student writers' intended meanings. For example, T8 summarized a point in S8's paper to lead in to a pumping question:

T8: I mean, this paragraph is saying any case. But you're specifically saying in the case of law enforcement. So what if you were to make that clear?

In this excerpt, similar to the excerpt from the T9–S9 brainstorming conference, the tutor conveyed her understanding of the student writer's text and, in doing so, gave the gift of understanding, building the student writer's positive face and a sense of rapport and solidarity. Again, as in the previous example of responding-as-a-listener, the responding-as-a-reader strategy does double duty.

Referring to a Previous Topic

Tutors also scaffolded student writers' development as writers and development of their papers by referring back to previous points of discussion in the conference. Tutors used two variations on this strategy. First, they referred back to advice that they had given earlier in the conference, such as T6's advice that S6 make her main point clear (even if it was the case that S6's goal was to be subtle in stating her main point):

T6: And I think that, again—Like, trying to—to find that—that line between, um, you know, between being so abstract that we don't know what you're talking about and still retaining that—that that kind of subtlety and giving us at least a sense of what you're talking about is an important thing to—to try to develop.
S6: Oh yeah. Definitely.

As this excerpt shows, this strategy was useful when tutors wanted to reinforce their advice, trying to ensure that the student writer had registered the point they had tried to make before.

Tutors also used this strategy to refer back to something a student writer had previously articulated, as T4 did when she referred back to something S4 said at the beginning of their conference:

T4: Well [Laughs.] that the absurdity in itself is that, like, I mean what you said in the very beginning. Which is that the cockroaches sort of like represent the relationship.

This second variety of the referring-back strategy is particularly powerful. First, it scaffolds student writers' development by recalling important points from earlier in the conference and making them available once again, so that the tutor and the student writer can apply them in another situation. Second, it also does positive-politeness work, in that it clearly shows that tutors not only attended to what student writers had said but also were able to recall it. Similar to using the responding-as-a-reader-or-a-listener strategy, when tutors recalled and discussed again student writers' contributions, they gave them the gift of understanding and, in the process, likely built a sense of rapport.

Forced Choice

The forced-choice strategy—presenting a student writer with two or possibly more options—did not occur with any frequency in writing center tutoring. Unlike closed-world domains, writing generates fewer objective and definitively right answers that can be paired up with a parallel, constructed alternative choice. Of course, that is not to say that such opportunities never arose. For example, in a conference focused on revising and proofreading, T7 used the forced-choice strategy to point out disagreement between the subject and verb:

T7: Now, "The boys tell their friends" or "the boys tells their friends"?
S7: I had "tell," but the computer wouldn't let me do "tell." It kept underlining it and saying "tells." [Laughs.]

Here, T7 used the forced-choice strategy to point out a sentence-level error, while still making S7 actively engage in the conference by doing some of the work to correct the error. Not only does a forced choice such as T7's—one focused on a discrete error—do the work of identifying the error for the student, but also the forced choice limits the student writer's response and thus greatly increases the likelihood that the student writer will be able to correct the error.

More often, though, writer center tutors used forced choice in more substantive ways than identifying and correcting punctuation and grammar errors. They used the forced-choice strategy to reign in and make manageable student writers' options for the direction in which they could take their papers. For example, T4 used forced choice to start up a line of inquiry into the main focus of the paper:

T4: Like, would it be easier for you to talk about like, this is how the underground man represents, you know, the meaninglessness of life, or do you think it would be easier to talk about the story, like, more generally? As a whole?
S4: I think maybe the story, like, saying like, like, the fakeness of him and his friends [and then, like, fakeness of, I think, why the husband's relationship maybe—
T4: [O.K.

S4: I could do that or—And then, I was thinking about maybe, if after I did that *both* of them feeling because of because of that they both feel meaningless.

T4: O.K.

The excerpt above shows how an experienced tutor used forced choice to constrain higher-order choices, including choices about a possible thesis. In this way, the tutor balanced two goals for writing center conferences that sometimes conflict: helping the student writer focus the writing and making way for the student writer's preferences and decision making.

Prompting, Hinting, Demonstrating

As we noted above, unlike tutors working in closed-world domains (for example, Chi 1996; Lepper, Drake, and O'Donnell-Johnson 1997), the experienced tutors in our study used prompting, hinting, and demonstrating infrequently. We include an example of each strategy here to illustrate how these strategies manifested in the tutors' talk. The first of these three uncommon strategies, prompting, occurred just six times overall. One of these occurrences appears here:

T8: O.K. So what do you think the main point of that paragraph is?

S8: Um. [3 seconds] That police aren't doing their job, I guess.

T8: Police aren't doing their jobs because—What?

Rarely, tutors such as T8 (with her "What?" question) let student writers "fill in the blank," as they attempted to get students to contribute to the conversation. When they used this strategy, they constrained student writers' potential responses to answers that would complete their prompts. Thus, they supported student writers while they helped them to develop their writing for themselves.

Hinting occurred even less frequently than prompting—just four times in the 10 conferences. However, as we noted in Chapter 3, hints are (almost by definition) difficult to identify: they consist of words (in linguistic terminology, locutions) that do not match their underlying speech acts (their illocutions). The following excerpt shows an example. When T9 said "Just punishment in general," she hinted that S9 could extend her answer, possibly to be more specific:

S9: He basically—It was, like, to [unclear] human beings. That's your punishment.

T9: Mm-hmm. For—for starting all of this?

S9: Yes.

T9: O.K. Um, so it also demonstrates punishment. Just punishment in general. So—

S9: Oh, like, right and wrong.

T9: Uh-huh. Right and wrong.

S9 picked up on T9's hint that she could say more about what the creation myth demonstrates and offered a relevant response. But hints are extremely dependent on context, and they can be difficult for student writers to recognize (and for researchers to identify and code). Student writers may miss them altogether (see Mackiewicz, 2005, for a discussion of such miscommunication). We think that tutors, for the most part, eschewed hinting in favor of other strategies that student writers could readily identify and that constrained students' potential responses.

Research on tutoring in closed-world domains shows that tutors used demonstrating with some frequency, but we found just one occurrence of demonstrating in the 10 conferences. In this excerpt, T2 demonstrated for S2 a transition from one paragraph to another, so that S2 could do the same herself next time:

T2: Like, "The halls were not the only place that people made fun of my hair" would be a way to transition to "They also did this at lunch."

Whether a writer center tutor demonstrates a transition, as in the excerpt above, a topic sentence, a figure caption, or whatever the case may be, the potential exists for student writers to simply use tutors' words rather than develop their own way to say (write) what they intend. In writer center tutoring—as opposed to tutoring in closed-world domains—demonstrating might tempt students to avoid developing their own content.

Further, our data-collection process itself (the setup of the video recording) might have limited tutors' use of demonstrating: the tutors and student writers sat at a small table and lacked access to a computer. Therefore, demonstrating tasks such as accessing and using library databases was literally out of reach. We discuss in Chapter 8 how T9, with a computer on her desk, demonstrated design and other report-writing tasks for S12, a business (specifically, purchasing) student.

Cognitive Scaffolding Strategies in the Closing Stage

Cognitive scaffolding strategies played a minor role in conference closings; because these strategies by definition prod students to respond, they invite more interaction. For this reason, it seems, tutors tended not to use them to close. Only T1 and T8, the two tutors who ended their conferences with summarizing and goal setting (as mentioned in Chapters 3 and 5), used pumping questions during conference closings. They wanted to get student writers to participate in making plans to move their writing forward. We excerpted and discussed the initial part of the closing stage of the T8–S8 conference in Chapter 5 to show the use of instruction.

In contrast, T1 used less instruction and more pumping as she began the closing stage of the T1–S1 conference. She began with a pump question to test S1's understanding of the priority for revising that the two of them had determined.

This pump caps a conference spent discussing the connections between the draft's paragraphs and its thesis statement.

T1: What would you say is the main thing you're going to work on when you go home?
S1: Reflecting back to the thesis statement.
T1: I think that's good.

Although cognitive scaffolding did not occur frequently in the closings in our corpus, our analysis suggests that these strategies at conference closings could be useful for making sure student writers can summarize the conference and delineate a plan for revising after the conference.

Conclusions and Implications for Tutor Training

In this chapter, we have seen that cognitive scaffolding strategies played a critical role in supporting student writers' development in the short term—in their work on a single paper. In particular, we have seen that pumping strategies were especially important to tutors' ability to guide student writers' thinking and to prompt responses (and thus more active participation) from them. Tutors used pumping strategies more often than all the other cognitive scaffolding strategies combined.

Pumping questions in particular showed the extent to which cognitive scaffolding strategies could constrain student writers' responses because they required—through adherence to conversational rules—a substantive response. Minimally constraining pumps made room for student writers to think out loud and take some control over the direction of the conversation. A risk inherent in minimally constraining pumps is that the wide range of responses that they allow might hinder student writers' ability to respond correctly or at all. In such situations, to help student writers along, tutors could switch to a more constraining pump or another more constraining cognitive scaffolding strategy. During tutor training, writing center directors might show examples of experienced tutors starting with a minimally constraining pump question and then shifting to another strategy (such as the forced-choice strategy) or a more constraining pump to facilitate a response. In our analysis above of pumping questions used to initiate topic episodes, we saw T8 make a similar move: she recast her initiating pump in an attempt to help S8 understand what she meant by the term "topic sentence."

Writing center directors and others who train tutors often worry that reading aloud will result in sentence-level revising and proofreading. However, most of the experienced tutors used this strategy selectively, with discretion, to focus a student writer's attention on a particular line or section of text and to help the student writer identify the problem by hearing it. This strategy gets its efficacy from the extra boost of attention it delivers to a certain line or section of text via the aural mode. Of course, line-by-line reading of student writers' papers can be problematic. Sentence-by-sentence reading can generate problems in working with student writers who are not sufficiently proficient in English to recognize grammar problems simply by hearing those problematic words and sentences read out loud. Writing center directors already caution tutors about the tendency of sentence-by-sentence reading of student writers' papers to focus attention on local-level issues, but they might during tutor training complicate their position somewhat by noting the potential that the reading-aloud strategy has to focus student writers' attention and make use of the aural mode.

When tutors responded as listeners to what students had said (particularly in brainstorming conferences) and as readers to what student writers had written (notes, outlines, and, of course, draft papers), they did positive-politeness work. They showed student writers that they were engaged with what they heard and read and that they had understood, especially when they responded by paraphrasing their words. Writing center directors might show tutors in training that this strategy has an analogy in guidelines for productive business relations (for example, Pryor et al. 2013), running effective meetings (for example, Malouff et al. 2012), and fruitful teamwork (for example, Decuyper, Dochy, and Van den Bossche 2010). Tutors who hone their facility with this strategy may reap rewards in other discourse situations, including professional discourse situations.

Tutors infrequently referred back to previous points of discussion in the conference. When they did use this strategy, they referred back to advice that they had given to students earlier in the conference and, in doing so, reinforced it. Although they sometimes focused on recurring proofreading errors, tutors also used this strategy to reinforce advice about contentful concerns such as organization and coherence. They also referred back to student writers' comments. When they referred back to what student writers had said earlier, they reinforced the previous topic and connected the current topic to it. In addition, they did substantial positive-politeness work in that they showed their attentiveness and understanding. During training, writing center directors might encourage tutors to employ this strategy, especially the second variety, given its positive-politeness benefits.

The experienced tutors rarely used forced choice, but writing center directors might encourage tutors to employ this strategy more often—particularly to constrain options for student writers at the global level. By constraining possibili-ties, tutors can facilitate difficult tasks such as developing a feasible thesis statement. This strategy could have promise for tutors working with students who seem overwhelmed by their assignments and the challenge of focusing their ideas.

For tutor training on agenda setting in conference openings, directors might show tutors how to paraphrase the assignment in order to force themselves to check that they understand it, to give student writers another means to understand it (via different words), and to ensure a shared understanding. Also, although perhaps not as effective as paraphrasing the assignment, reading the assignment out loud was a popular strategy with the experienced tutors. This strategy appears to be a good choice for tutors familiarizing themselves with the assignment at hand. Writing center directors might encourage both approaches, but make clear that paraphrasing is preferable.

In conference closings, cognitive scaffolding strategies played a quite minor role. That said, T1 used a pump question during a closing in a way that we think writing center directors should consider for tutor training: using a pump at the end of a conference to get the student writer to articulate a plan for writing and revising after he or she leaves the writing center. Leading student writers to set their own goals is tricky. To support them in this complex undertaking, tutors must carefully support and arrange the student writers' goal setting in highly constrained situations to keep them on track. However, leading student writers to develop their own summaries of conferences and set their own goals is worthwhile. In performing these tasks, student writers are more likely to recall the range of topics they covered, to delineate the most important topics, to prioritize those topics, and then to formulate strategies for addressing those topics. These cognitive tasks can help them become better writers.

To conclude, in our study, cognitive scaffolding strategies did the heavy lifting of supporting student writers' thinking about and production of their writing. As the tutors moved between minimally constraining cognitive scaffolding strategies that allowed a wide range of responses to constraining ones that limited and focused student writers' responses, they helped move student writers ahead in their development of single texts, but, more importantly, the tutors may have helped them move forward in their development as more self-sufficient writers.

7

MOTIVATIONAL SCAFFOLDING STRATEGIES

- Motivation's Connection to Learning
- Motivational Scaffolding Strategies in the Opening Stage
- Motivational Scaffolding Strategies in the Teaching Stage
- Motivational Scaffolding Strategies in the Closing Stage
- Conclusions and Implications for Tutor Training

In an article focusing exclusively on motivational scaffolding in writing center conferences, we described how writing center tutors used motivational scaffolding strategies to encourage students to think for themselves about their writing and to continue their efforts after the conference (Mackiewicz and Thompson 2013). Here, as in the study we reported in that article, we acknowledge that motivation has perceptual and cognitive components as well, but we focus on the ways that motivational scaffolding strategies help tutors attend in particular to the affective components of working with student writers. Motivational scaffolding, like Brown and Levinson's (1987) positive politeness, can help generate and support a sense of rapport and solidarity between two people, including two people who have just met. Brown and Levinson write:

> Positive-politeness utterances are used as a kind of metaphorical extension of intimacy, to imply common ground or sharing of wants to a limited extent even between strangers who perceive themselves, for the purposes of the interaction, as somehow similar. (103)

We argue that, like positive politeness, motivational scaffolding can speed up the rate with which two people build up a connection and a sense of goodwill.

In this chapter, we briefly discuss the reciprocal relationship between motivation and learning. We then describe tutors' use of motivational scaffolding strategies in the opening stage, the teaching stage, and the closing stage. As in Chapters 5 and 6, we end this chapter by discussing our conclusions and the implications of our analysis for tutor training.

Motivation's Connection to Learning

As we noted in Chapter 2, motivation is "the desire to achieve a goal, the willingness to engage and persist in specific subjects or activities" (Margolis 2005, 223) and, therefore, it plays an important role in the amount of time and effort that students will put into a task. More specifically, as we discussed in Chapter 2, motivation includes three major components: (1) interest in the writing task, (2) self-efficacy in relation to completing the task successfully, and (3) the ability to self-regulate performance.

Consequently, motivation likely influences student writers' active participation in writing center conferences and other learning situations. As Chi et al. (2001) found, students' active participation—their interaction—plays a critical role in their enjoyment of learning (517). As Puntambekar and Hübscher (2005), Fox (1993), and Chi et al. (2001) point out, when students actively participate in their conferences, tutors can more readily diagnose what they currently know and determine their next steps in learning. In addition, through what Fox calls "collaborative contextualizing" (1993, 1), tutors can begin to develop a shared understanding of the assignment and goals for the conference, as well as trust and rapport. Thus, with student writers' active participation, writing center tutors can more effectively employ instruction and cognitive scaffolding to enhance their learning.

Motivational Scaffolding Strategies in the Opening Stage

The tutors in our study used a range of motivational scaffolding strategies in the opening stage of their writing center conferences. Regardless of the strategies they used, they were all trying to generate goodwill from the outset. For example, in the opening stage, T7 praised S7 for her revising strategy:

T7: O.K. Just to make sure, we are looking more at grammatical type things?
S7: Right. The grammatical and just, if you see—When I read through it, I always read back through it again and again [and I always find sentences that don't
T7:   [Right.
S7: work. That I—that I don't like. [And so I have only read through this—
T7:   [That's the best way to do it.

With "That's the best way to do it," T7 begins the conference by praising the very first thing that he can.

Similarly, when an opportunity occurred during the opening stage, T9 gave sympathy to S9, who assessed her capability to write analytical papers quite harshly:

S9:   And I'm not good at analytical papers. I can write from my view but [unclear]
T9:   Mm-hmm. Everybody says that. I promise.

With her reassurance that all student writers who come to the writing center say something similar about their own perceived lack of ability to write successful research papers, T9, it seems, tried to put S9 at ease about the work they were about to start. By using motivational scaffolding at the outset, T9 contributed to a congenial tone that lasted throughout the conference.

T2—the tutor who used the most motivational scaffolding strategies—also gave sympathy in the opening stage. As shown in other excerpts in this chapter, T2 continued to give S2 sympathy in their conference. In fact, this early excerpt appears to set the stage for their relationship.

T2:   O.K. O.K. Great. So what did she say that your main problem was, or what did she say you needed to work on?
S2:   She gave us the grading criteria. And she gave me a C. And she was like "A C and below you can revise." [So I definitely—
T2:   [You're going to revise.
S2:   Yeah.
T2:   O.K. So. [Reads aloud.] "This essay covers the assignment well." It's pretty sad how this C paper is a pretty good paper. When I first read this rubric, I was like, "Man that's tough."

According to the grading criteria that T2 and S2 examined in this conference, an essay that would likely receive an A grade in a high school class would receive a C grade in FYC. T2, who taught FYC in addition to tutoring in the writing center, knew how shocking such a grading system could be for new under-graduates. In addition, making T2's job in the conference more difficult, the instructor did not justify S2's grade. Instead, she included a copy of the (fairly vague) grading criteria. Therefore, T2 gave S2 sympathy.

In addition to the motivational scaffolding strategies of praise and sympathy, tutors engaged in humor during the opening stage. For example, T10 participated in humor initiated by S10. The following excerpt begins just after T10 asked S10 what he wanted to work on. After mentioning several proofreading-related issues, he jokingly stated this ever-so-important goal:

S10:   Basically, everything to get an A paper.
T10:   [Laughs.] Oh, O.K. Yeah, I guess that would be good. [Laughs.]

With her joking addition, "Yeah, I guess that would be good," T10 helped to set the friendly tone that continued throughout the conference.

Motivational scaffolding was the only category of tutoring strategies that occurred during the opening stage. Along with the knowledge-deficit questions necessary to collaborative agenda setting, motivational scaffolding strategies helped tutors develop intersubjectivity with student writers.

Motivational Scaffolding Strategies in the Teaching Stage

In this section, we analyze at the macrolevel and the microlevel tutors' use of motivational scaffolding strategies. We first turn to motivational scaffolds at the macrolevel, examining tutors' use of these strategies in two rare topic episodes that the tutor launched with a motivational scaffolding strategy. Then, we turn to motivational scaffolds at the microlevel, examining the frequencies with which tutors used them and closely analyzing examples to show the ways tutors used them to encourage student writers.

Motivational Scaffolding Strategies in Topic Episodes

In the two topic episodes we examine below, as we explained previously, S2 and T2 worked on an FYC essay about a change in S2's life, but the draft lacked coherence because S2 had written about two changes in her life instead of one. Through the first half of the conference, T2 and S2 tried to revise the draft so that it would focus solely on S2's move from her private high school, where other students teased and ostracized her, to college, where she found friends. However, S2 could not seem to find a way to accomplish such a revision. As shown below, T2 used encouragement to launch TE14. However, after realizing that S2 did not want to focus on the positive change from private high school to college, T2 moved in TE15 to what she called "Plan B" in her postconference interview—the negative (and earlier) change in S2's life, from a happy existence at a public high school to her unhappy experience at the private high school. T2 used motivational scaffolding to launch TE15 as well.

TE14, as mentioned above, launches with T2's statement of optimism about S2's ability to carry out the revision:

T2: I think you can do it though. I mean I think you can. It will take a lot of work, but I think that—I think that it will be worth it though. I think if you take out these things that focus on the transition from public to private and mainly focus on the negative things at your private school, and then focus on your transition to college, I think you can do it.

S2: Yeah, I hope so. [Looking through draft. Laughs nervously.]

T2: It'll just be—The confusing part will be taking out the first transition part that you have in there. The public to private transition.

S2: Yeah, well I mean, I will have to write a whole new intro, and I'm so weak at that.

T2: Yeah, it will take a whole new intro. And then it's going to take a whole lot of reorganizing with these paragraphs. [3 seconds] Because see, something like this, this is kind of an example. Right here where you say, "I was not used to sitting with girls at lunch anyway." That's a reference to your private— to your public school. Does that make sense? [Pointing to draft.]

S2: Yeah.

T2: Now. "At the public school I was not used to sitting with girls anyway. So it didn't hurt me that much." That's the kind of stuff that makes it focusing back to that original public school. See, that's the kind of stuff you [have to

S2:   [So I'm

T2: look for.

S2: going to edit that whole out and just say I went from the guys. Because that's going to be so hard.

After attempting several times prior to TE14 to help S2 delete unnecessary information and focus on just one change, T2 started TE14 with optimism. However, when S2 did not seem at all confident about her ability to accomplish this revision either, T2 tried again to encourage her by pointing out the limits on the necessary changes ("It'll just be—The confusing part will be taking out the first transition part . . ."). In other words, T2 pointed out that the necessary revisions would not be vast and boundless. Even after T2's statements of optimism, S2 was still not convinced that she could do the revision. At that point, T2 admitted that the second version of the revision would indeed be difficult. However, she lent a hand with the task by pointing out an example passage that S2 would need to edit so that it no longer referred back to her experience at the public school: "Right here where you say, 'I was not used to sitting with girls at lunch anyway,'" and she followed that up with a (formulaic) demonstration of concern: "Does that make sense?" However, this topic episode ended with S2's implicit refusal of T2's advice: "Because that's going to be so hard."

At this point, T2 decided to move to Plan B, and the teaching stage moved into TE15:

T2: Well, how about this then? Would you rather focus it on this? [Pointing to draft.] Even though this change is kind of a negative one—But she didn't say it had to be positive.

S2: Exactly.

T2: She just said it had to change you in some way.

S2: O.K. I'd rather do that then.

T2: O.K. Well then. What you need to do is the same kind of thing, but it might be a little easier. But go through and take out the stuff about the transition [to college.

S2:   [to college.

T2: Yeah. And really focus on what you learned from this transition. [3 seconds] So yeah, let's go find it. Where, where is it at about college? [30 seconds]

S2: And I started the college thing right here.

T2: O.K.

S2: And then this is all college.

T2: O.K.

S2: So, I'll just end the paper here.

T2: Yeah.

T2 launched TE15 with motivational scaffolding—reinforcing S2's ownership in light of S2's reluctance to follow T2's initial advice ("Well, how about this then? Would you rather focus it on this?"). With this motivational scaffolding strategy, T2 attended to S2's confidence in her ability to carry out the revision as opposed to the quality of the revision. She also led S2 to select a direction for the revision, combining cognitive scaffolding and motivational scaffolding, a common occurrence in the findings of Wood, Bruner, and Ross's (1976) research. As she said in her postconference interview, T2 believed that the first revision idea— the one focusing on the positive change—was a better idea, but she wanted to make sure that S2 believed that she could do the revision and, therefore, would actually do the revision work after she left the writing center.

After S2 made her choice ("O.K. I'd rather do that then"), T2 provided more encouragement through optimism, telling S2 that the choice she had made for the focus of her paper (the change from her public school to the private school), "might be a little easier" than the other option. With this optimism (and with the quite cheerleading directive, "So yeah, let's go find it. Where, where is it at about college?"), T2 worked to get S2 revved up about getting to work on looking for any mention of the other, now irrelevant, change. This excerpt exemplifies how tutors could stimulate student writers' situational interest by easing their anxiety and frustration.

These topic episodes—TE14 and TE15 from the conference between T2 and S2—are interesting in the extent to which motivational scaffolding strategies pervade them. T2 had to put forth special effort to encourage S2—a quite dejected and somewhat self-pitying student writer. T2 used motivational scaffolds to launch TE14 and TE15 and continued to use motivational scaffolds (as well as other strategies) to increase the chance that S2 would substantially revise her paper after the conference.

Quantitative Results: Frequencies of the Motivational Scaffolding Strategies

We coded five types of motivational scaffolds. As Table 7.1 indicates, showing (demonstrating) concern was by far the motivational scaffolding strategy that tutors used most frequently. In fact, it was the tutoring strategy that tutors used fourth

TABLE 7.1 Motivational Strategies per 10 Minutes

Motivational Scaffolding Strategy	Frequency per 10 Minutes (%)	
Showing concern	3.32	(49)
Praising	1.53	(23)
Reinforcing ownership and control	0.76	(11)
Being optimistic or using humor	0.60	(8)
Showing empathy or sympathy	0.55	(8)
Total	6.76	(99[a])

a The percentage total equals 99 rather than 100 because of rounding

most often overall (after the instruction strategies of telling and suggesting and the cognitive scaffolding strategy of using pumping questions). Showing concern accounted for nearly one-half of all motivational scaffolding strategies (49%); it occurred 3.32 times per 10 minutes. However, as we discuss below, many of these showing-concern strategies consisted of formulaic expressions such as "Right?" or collocations of words such as "You know?" as opposed to novel, nonformulaic words and phrases. The formulaicity of these strategies certainly contributed to the frequency of their occurrence.

Even though tutors' strategies were often formulaic, tutors nevertheless clearly were cognizant of the motivational facet of writing center work—their responsibility for encouraging student writers. Through their shows of concern, tutors indicated that they cared about the well-being and learning of student writers. In this use, demonstrations of concern closely relate to the positive-politeness strategy of noticing another person's needs, interests, or some other characteristic of the conversational partner's condition.

The motivational scaffolding strategy that occurred second most often was praise, also called complimenting in the relevant scholarship (for example, Mackiewicz 2006). Tutors used praise 1.53 times per 10 minutes. Praise accounted for 23% of tutors' motivational scaffolds. As with the strategy of showing concern, praise too was often formulaic in its lexicon ("Good job") and syntax ("Your thesis is good"), and, similarly, praise's formulaicity played a large role in its frequency. Like the strategy of demonstrating concern, praise relates to the positive-politeness strategy of noticing or attending to a conversational partner's interests or wants: a tutor notices a student writer's accomplishment—anything from using a semicolon correctly to developing a feasible thesis to supporting a claim with substantial evidence. Praise also relates to the positive-politeness strategy of "giving gifts" to a hearer. Although such gifts can be tangible, they can just as often (likely more often) be intangible gifts—fulfilling what Brown and Levinson (1987) call "human-relations wants," including the want for others to appreciate us (129). Tutors' positive evaluations, their praise, fulfill this human-relations want.

Praise, it seems, can have strong positive effects. As Lepper et al. (1993) point out, such positive evaluations can promote students' self-efficacy, their confidence in their ability to perform successfully. Positive evaluations can also raise students' level of situational interest (Hidi and Boscolo 2006) in the writing task, as many student writers tend to be more interested in whatever task they are working on when someone—particularly someone with expertise—appreciates their performance (Margolis 2005). Similar to good grades, praise is more likely to influence extrinsic rather than intrinsic motivation. Praise, then, has important and well-supported pedagogical benefits.

Reinforcing ownership and control occurred about 0.76 times per 10 minutes and was the motivational strategy that tutors used third most frequently. However, distribution of tutors' use of this strategy was quite uneven: three tutors did not use this strategy at all, and four tutors used the strategy just once. In contrast, one tutor (T7) used this strategy 9 times, accounting for nearly 37% of the 24 total occurrences, and another tutor (T2) used the strategy 7 times, accounting for 29% of the total occurrences. Thus, two tutors contributed two-thirds of this strategy's occurrences. In using this strategy, tutors explicitly stated to student writers that they were in charge of their own writing and were free to make their own decisions about it. This strategy, then, was one that probably affected tutors' ability to strengthen student writers' self-regulation, as mentioned in Chapter 2, their sense of control over their ability to achieve their goals. Given the importance that the writing center scholarship places on fostering students' ownership and control of their writing and, concomitantly, on avoiding taking control of student writers' papers, the infrequency with which most of the tutors used this strategy somewhat surprised us.

Demonstrations of optimism and humor, in other words, demonstrations of positivity, occurred just 0.60 times per 10 minutes of conference talk, or just 18 times in our entire corpus. The distribution of occurrences across tutors, however, was far more even than it was in relation to reinforcing ownership and control (or demonstrations of sympathy and empathy, as we discuss below). Although two tutors used no optimism or humor at all, eight tutors used the strategy 1, 2, or 3 times. However, one tutor (T4) contributed one-third of the optimism and humor in the corpus, with 6 occurrences of this strategy. In defining and coding this strategy, again based on positive-politeness strategies (being optimistic and joking) from Brown and Levinson's (1987) work, we combined two means of conveying positivity. With this strategy, tutors signaled that they had confidence in a good outcome for the student writer (with optimism) and signaled shared background knowledge (with humor). With this motivational scaffolding strategy, tutors could foster student writers' confidence and thus their self-efficacy, and they could also increase student writers' interest in the task at hand.

Like praise, the strategy of showing sympathy or empathy relates to the positive-politeness strategy of giving gifts to the hearer—in this case, giving the gift of considering a situation (such as a writing task) and its challenges from the student writer's perspective and acknowledging the situation's difficulties. Demonstrations of sympathy or empathy appeared least often of all motivational scaffolding strategies—0.55 times per 10 minutes, or just 17 times in our entire corpus. As was the case with reinforcing ownership and control, tutors ranged widely in the frequency with which they used this strategy: six tutors did not use it at all, and 13 of the 17 total occurrences come from one tutor (T2). We discuss T2's use of this strategy and the conference with S2 that generated it in more detail below.

Qualitative Results: Close Analysis of the Motivational Scaffolding Strategies

In this section, we closely examine the ways in which tutors used motivational scaffolding strategies to encourage student writers and thereby possibly influence their interest in the writing task and support their self-efficacy and self-regulation. We focus in particular on tutors' use of two strategies: showing concern and praising—the strategies that tutors used most frequently and, as we describe below, the strategies that came in two quite distinct varieties: formulaic and nonformulaic. We also, however, discuss tutors' use of the other three, less frequently occurring, motivational scaffolding strategies.

Formulaic versus Nonformulaic Language

The motivational scaffolds that tutors used to encourage student writers frequently employed formulaic language: "a sequence, continuous or discontinuous, of words or other meaning elements, which is, or appears to be, prefabricated: that is, stored and retrieved whole from memory at the time of use" (Wray and Perkins 2000, 1). Interest in formulaic language has been reinvigorated after a long lapse in which linguists (particularly American linguists) laser focused on finding principles common to all languages in order to understand the universal grammar that allows us to comprehend and produce novel utterances. Now, more linguists recognize that understanding how people comprehend and produce language also means accounting for sequences of language that people have comprehended (often through hearing) and produced (often through speaking) many times before, sequences that have "a unique coherence not present in novel utterances" (Van Lancker-Sidtis and Rallon 2004, 208). In this recognition, linguists acknowledge something that L2 teachers and others have noticed for a long time: people use the same words and syntactic patterns over and over again. Speakers do not construct every contribution to a conversation from scratch on a moment-to-moment basis. In addition, they integrate their formulaic language with novel, nonformulaic language (Altenberg 1990; Butler 1997; Moon 1998; Wray 2002). In fact, some research indicates that, although people integrate nonformulaic and formulaic language, they use different mental and neurological structures to generate the two (Botelho da Silva and Cutler 1993; Hoffman and Kemper 1987; Papagno and Vallar 2001; Van Lancker 2001).

As previously stated, tutors used semantically and syntactically formulaic expressions to show concern and to praise—the two most frequently occurring motivational scaffolding strategies. For example, a tutor who showed concern with the collocation (formulaic string) "Do you see what I mean?" used a group of words that occur frequently together in English (more frequently than chance would dictate), as did a tutor who used the collocation "You know?" Similarly, tutors' praise followed semantic and syntactic formulae too, including these: (1) pronoun + "is a" + adjective + noun phrase ("That is a good idea") and (2) noun phrase + "is" + adjective ("The thesis is good"). Tutors' use of prepatterned language likely contributed to the frequency with which they were able to use these strategies. Indeed, in a previous study of praise (called compliments in that study), Mackiewicz (2006) found that nearly 61% of tutors' praise followed semantic and syntactic formulae. Similarly, in this study, we found that 66% of tutors' praise followed formulae.

The distinction between formulaic and nonformulaic tutoring strategies matters because strategies that are formulaic in syntactic form and their semantic content will likely be limited in their function. People are more likely to interpret formulaic sequences holistically rather than as the sum of their parts. According to Kecskés (2000), when a sequence takes on a holistic meaning and loses its compositional meaning, the meaning its parts contribute to its whole, its social function dominates its meaning; the referential meaning moves into the background (606). The more frequently a sequence of words collocates, the more likely it is to retain only its social function (Coulmas 1981; Fónagy 1961; Kecskés 2000). In the case of writing center conferences, that social function is motivating students.

In the next two sections, we discuss the ways that experienced tutors used the strategies of showing concern and praise, paying particular attention to the role that formulaicity played in the way those strategies functioned.

Showing (Demonstrating) Concern

To show concern, tutors inquired about the student writer's emotional state in relation to the writing task, the student writer's level of satisfaction with the conference so far, and, most commonly, the student writer's understanding of what the tutor has said. When tutors showed concern, they demonstrated care and assured students that the environment of the writing center was a safe and positive one. As Cooper (2003) notes, one way that tutors can show concern is by asking students about their welfare.

One of the most salient characteristics of tutors' demonstrations of concern is the extent to which they demonstrated syntactic and semantic formulaicity. Common words and phrases that tutors used to show concern include "Right?" "You know?" "See what I'm saying?" and "See what I mean?" In fact, nearly 83% of tutors' demonstrations of concern followed a semantic or syntactic formula.

However, as noted above, even formulaic sequences such as formulaic questions serve a purpose. With the discourse marker "you know" (see Schiffrin 1987), a tutor can demonstrate concern by indicating interest in the hearer's comprehension of what he or she has said and a willingness to turn over the conversational floor to listen to a response—even if a change in turn does not occur. In the example below, T2 used "you know" to indicate concern for the student's comprehension and opinion, continuing with her turn without a response from S2:

T2: And so it's kind of sad to write a paper about such a sad change, but you might even could say in your conclusion, "since then," you know? "I don't still feel this way, but this is a time in my life that really changed." You know? Whatever. "This is a time in my life that made me feel these ways."

After both of her uses of "you know" in the excerpt above, T2 continued on, speaking as if she were S2, suggesting content for the conclusion. That she did not wait for a response either time suggests she did not expect S2 to respond. On the other hand, T2's uses of "you know" indicated a willingness to give up the conversational floor if S2 wanted to chime in. T2's formulaic "you know" collocations served a social as opposed to an informative function.

In a dissertation study of the ways people use "you know," Turner (2002) found that, of 103 conversational turns in her data that contained "you know" in the turn-final position, 37 (36%) did indeed elicit responses, albeit backchannel responses such as "uh-huh," "mm-hmm," and "yeah." Similarly, tutors' formulaic demonstration-of-concern questions did indeed generate responses from student writers. T7 used the formulaic question "See what I mean?" to gauge S7's understanding of his advice for revising a sentence so that it would seem less argumentative:

T7: Well, one thing you can do is take out "you." Because "those of you"—
    You don't need that.
S7: O.K.
T7: "For those who chose not"—"For those who opt not to exercise regularly"—
    Or something like that. See what I mean?
S7: Yeah.
T7: And you are totally including all of those who might not exercise without directly addressing them and becoming more confrontational.
S7: Right. O.K.

In this case, unlike the previous one involving the formulaic question, "you know," the tutor got a response from the student writer, albeit a brief one ("Yeah").

Although we have to acknowledge the limitations of questions that demonstrate concern, examples such as this excerpt from the T7–S7 conference show that they can generate at least minimal responses from student writers—responses that can help keep them engaged in the conversation. In addition, such demonstration-of-concern questions offer an opportunity for students to take a turn in the conversation—as well as a subsequent opportunity for students to ask tutors to elaborate.

Formulaic demonstrations of concern carry out several other functions. First, because they are prepatterned, they ease the tutor's interactional burden: the cognitive resources needed to toss them into the conversational mix are fewer than those needed to construct novel, individualized demonstrations of concern (see Conklin and Schmitt 2008). Also, even a formulaic question such as "See what I mean?" indicates concern for a student's state of mind, and, as Ho and Mitchell (1982) and Meyer and Turner (2002) point out, showing concern indicates a positive attitude toward the student and a commitment to helping the student succeed. It also, according to these researchers, helps to create a pleasant and supportive environment. In our study, experienced tutors' demonstrations of concern—formulaic or not—appeared to do similar work.

Tutors' novel, nonformulaic demonstrations of concern certainly seemed to do even more interactional work. Because tutors created these nonformulaic strategies on the fly, the strategies were targeted and individualized; thus they even more clearly did the positive-politeness work of showing tutors' attentiveness to students and their well-being. For example, T4 checked in on S4's state of mind about two-thirds into the conference to determine whether the student could tolerate another conversational topic:

T4: O.K. So what do you feel like at this point? Like, before you leave, I feel like we kind of need to get you a working thesis.
S4: Mm-hmm.

T4's preference clearly was to keep the conference going so that the two of them could develop a viable thesis statement; however, T4 also seemed to recognize the potential for S4 to become overwhelmed if she took on yet another task. With her question "So what do you feel like at this point?" T4 gave S4 an opportunity to opt out of continuing, prioritizing the student writer's well-being and goodwill over her own preferences for the conference agenda. Thus, she used motivational scaffolding to adapt her tutoring to what S4 could tolerate at that time. Nonformulaic demonstrations of concern such as this one allowed tutors to target their assessments of student writers' states of mind—opening up the potential to gather more information than a formulaic "You know?" or "See what I mean?" would likely generate.

Praise

Writing center scholarship has mainly focused on the benefits of praise—particularly its ability to buffer criticism or to mitigate advice. (For interesting complications in relation to L2 students, see Bell and Youmans [2006].)

Writing center researchers have also, of course, noted the positive affective response that praise brings. Thus, the scholarship tends to enjoin tutors to "find things that [they] can honestly praise and then praise liberally" (Wilcox 1994, 13), to "find something nice to say about every paper, no matter how hard [they] have to search" (Brooks 1991, 3), to "begin with samples of the writers' unevaluated work and praise its strengths" (Hurlow 1993, 65). With positive evaluation, especially process praise focusing on students' actions ("It's clear you've worked really hard on this"), as opposed to praise that addresses seemingly inherent qualities ("You're a good writer"), student writers can gain direction (Dweck 2007; Maclellan 2005) as well as confidence.

The writing center scholarship thus far, however, has not as thoroughly examined the role that tutors' talk plays in encouraging student writers by nurturing their interest in the writing task, fostering their self-efficacy as writers, and promoting their self-regulation. As with demonstrations of concern, perhaps the most salient characteristic of the praise strategy was its formulaicity. As noted previously, of 64 occurrences of praise, 42 (66%) followed a semantic or syntactic formula. For example, T2 praised S2 after she explained what she meant in the text of her paper:

S2: Yeah, because I was talking about how this new guy came to school, and I knew of him because I worked with his brother. And his brother and I were really good friends. Then when the guy started being mean to me and stuff, I didn't understand. Because his brother, like, we're exactly alike, but yet his brother and I were best friends. And he's like really mean to me just because the kids at school told him not to be my friend.

T2: O.K. Summarize—That's perfect. That was a perfect summary of that paragraph.

The first instance of T2's praise above ("That's perfect") exactly follows the common noun phrase + "is" + adjective formula. The second instance of that praise—really a reinforcement of the first—closely follows a syntactic pattern as well: pronoun + "is a" + adjective + noun phrase. This second instance of praise deviates from the formula only in that it contains a prepositional phrase, "of that paragraph," that modifies the noun phrase, "a perfect summary." In a post-conference interview about another conference, T7 reflected on praise as a strategy for motivating an unwilling student writer to participate more actively: "Even though she doesn't seem willing to talk, I am going to throw the hook out and see if she bites. And maybe she will say something that I can praise her for. And break down this barrier."

As noted before, tutors generated formulaic praise much like they did formulaic demonstrations of concern. Their formulaic praise followed several common syntactic patterns and frequently drew from a set of common evaluative terms, such as "good" and "great" and upgraders such as "really" and "very." Common words and phrases such as these might at first glance appear vacuous and rather innocuous, but they also appear to have a strong purpose. Although their ability to be uttered automatically might very well detract from the sincerity and information they convey, they give connection, build the relationship, because they can be sprinkled throughout.

In contrast to their formulaic praise, tutors' nonformulaic praise was syntactically more complex and semantically more diverse. T6's praise is an example:

T6: And I think that your paper does a nice job of, of trying to explain you know, that that independence let you go out and do these other things and perhaps to see the world in a different way . . .

The more tutors' praise diverted from formulaicity, the more the praise seemed to have been generated on the spot for the particular situation at hand, instead of being retrieved from memory. Similar to Limaye's (1997) argument that explanations in refusal letters should include specific reasons for the bad news, in addition to general and "depersonalized" reasons (43), our study indicates that nonformulaic praise indicates attention to and approval of student writers' individual cases.

Nonformulaic praise appeared to be more instructive than most formulaic praise, because it not only singled out particular elements of the student writers' composing process or draft that were effective but also gave insight into why specific writing strategies or certain ideas were effective. Even though a tutor who says, "This is good" might be referring to a specific referent, such as a bulleted list, the formula leaves no room for insight into why that specific referent is effective (for example, executed in perfect parallel structure). It seems, then, that nonformulaic praise is likely to constitute feedback that better facilitates learning. Further research, however, is needed to test this idea.

Unlike demonstrations of concern and praise, the other, less-frequent, motivational scaffolding strategies were nonformulaic, novel for the conversational moment. That tutors did not (or could not) draw from discourse formula to employ these strategies may to some extent explain the infrequency of these strategies in comparison with demonstrations of concern and praise.

Reinforcing Ownership and Control

As pointed out in Chapter 2, a repeated refrain across writing center scholarship— really since the beginnings of writing center scholarship (for example, Harris 1992;

Lunsford 1991)—has been the call to help student writers maintain control of their own work. In the context of writing centers, maintaining control means making decisions about focus and content (perhaps while thinking through tutor-supplied advice) and maintaining responsibility for the assignment and the content. The idea has always been that writing center tutors should help student writers think through effective ways to meet the requirements of their assignments and to advise them as they work through the writing process. When tutors used the motivational scaffolding strategy of reinforcing ownership and control, they made clear that the student writer not only had the responsibility to consider options and make decisions but also that the student writer had the competence to do so. In other words, tutors fostered student writers' self-regulation—their ability to monitor their learning. For example, conference T6–S6, in which S6 began more topic episodes than T6, provides an interesting example of a tutor's reinforcement of a student writer's ownership. In TE16 of the teaching stage of that conference, S6 mentioned that her instructor emphasized the importance of analysis in the personal narrative she was writing. S6 appeared to want T6 to confirm that her draft had plenty of analysis. T6 did not supply such confirmation but instead suggested ways to add analysis. The excerpt below starts at the beginning of TE 17:

S6: Um, definitely I just, I really don't want to put something so specific like, "I got into horseback riding" or [something like that, that's just kind of, because

T6:   [Laughs.] Right.

S6: it takes away from—I just like how it's so—I don't know. It's general in a way that people can relate to it, and as soon as I attach something really, really specific to it, I don't think it does that anymore. [So that is my

T6:   [Yeah.

S6: only concern [with doing that.

T6:   [Yeah.

S6: But I mean, you know.

T6: O.K. Well. I mean and that's, you know, that's um, that's something that is ultimately up—up to you, you know.

As in TE16, T6 again did not confirm the accuracy of S6's assessment. Instead, he reinforced S6's ownership—and her responsibility—by reminding her "that's something entirely up to you." S6, who appeared satisfied that her draft met the assignment's requirements, might have had her confidence shaken a bit. But, at the same time, she received an important lesson in developing writing maturity and self-regulation. When tutors used this motivational scaffolding strategy, they may not have given student writers exactly what they wanted (a definite answer), but they may have strengthened student writers' ability to evaluate their options and, in the long run, bolstered their confidence in their own competency.

Being Optimistic or Using Humor

We grouped optimism and humor together in one strategy to capture tutors' statements of positivity. Statements of optimism are one way tutors can help student writers see that they should have hope about their chances of completing the writing task successfully. Tutors' humor conveyed a lighthearted attitude—a sense that writing need not be a dour and solemn process. Tutors' optimism and humor, then, can work to maintain student writers' interest in the task.

As we noted earlier, tutors rarely used explicit statements of optimism. In the following example, one of the few incidences of optimism, T7 bolsters S7's confidence by pointing out that S7's instructor said that she liked S7's paper topic:

S7: No, I think you have answered most of my questions. The main—I mean the only other one was do you think the topic will work? And be fine for a belief paper?

T7: I think—

S7: It's too late. I don't want to go back and have to change now. [But she

T7:   [Plus she

S7: said—

T7: said that she liked your topic.

S7: Yeah. She thought it was fine.

T7: Well, she's the one grading it.

S7: Yeah.

T7's optimism is interesting in that it exemplifies a pragmatic, realistic approach to S7's situation. Rather than provide simplistic and vacuous encouragement, T7 acknowledges that a real person with subjective preferences will grade S7's paper and that part of being successful in completing the task is determining and meeting those preferences. Nevertheless, by reminding S7 that the instructor has already signed off on the topic, T7 gives S7 hope that she can indeed do well on the assignment.

Tutors more often used humor to encourage student writers to continue their efforts. Specifically, with humor, tutors attempted to lighten the mood a bit and, in doing so, they tried to build solidarity and rapport with student writers. In encouraging student writers to laugh, tutors helped to reduce student writers' anxiety, thus allowing them to tap into their extrinsic, if not intrinsic, motivation to complete the writing assignment successfully. Research on humor in classroom settings shows that instructors' humorous messages can facilitate learning. Wanzer, Frymier, and Irwin (2010) found that humor related to the subject area leads to message elaboration—the process by which students add to the message content because they are both motivated and able to do so. They also found that instructors' self-disparaging humor positively associates with retention of information:

Because students do not expect their instructors to use humor, the use of self-disparaging humor may be viewed as even more shocking and unexpected than other types of classroom behaviors. This seemingly positive violation of their expectancies may result in more attention paid to the source's message and ultimately increase students' retention of information. (Wanzer, Frymier, and Irwin 2010, 13)

Humor that is relevant or unexpected, it seems, can have a strong effect on students' interest and thus their learning.

Here, we have chosen two of the tutors' prototypical uses of humor to make conferences more congenial. In the first excerpt, the tutor uses self-deprecating humor (about her ability to spell the word "consequences") to lighten the mood.

T9: O.K. Um, so it also demonstrates punishment, just punishment in general. So—
S9: Oh, like, right and wrong.
T9: Uh-huh, right and wrong. Uh, consequences for your actions. Wrong and right. Whatever.
S9: [Laughs.]
T9: I can't spell consequences.

With this use of humor, though, T9 not only lightens the mood by poking fun at herself, she also conveys to S9 that nobody—not even a writing center tutor—is perfect. T9's ability to joke about her own difficulties shows S9 that it is all right not to be perfect. With such admissions, tutors show students that everyone—all writers—have to struggle to overcome challenges.

Tutors' humor did not always relate directly to the student writer's writing or the writing process; at times, tutors simply cracked jokes related to pop culture. Although Wanzer, Frymier, and Irwin (2010) found that humor unrelated to the subject area did not facilitate learning of the subject matter, in our study, it appeared that unrelated humor did some solidarity- and rapport-building work, as in this excerpt about analyzing a magazine:

S3: Um, let's see. I basically can tell my reader a lot about current, current celebrities and what they're doing, current fashions and what, what designer to wear.
T3: O.K.
S3: Um, latest gossip. Who's pregnant, who's not pregnant. Who got a DUI last weekend. Paris Hilton.
T3: Again. [Laughs.]

In this case, T3 cracks a joke at the expense of Paris Hilton, a celebrity known for frequent encounters with police after nights of drinking and dancing at nightclubs. T3's "Again" response alludes to the ridiculousness of Paris Hilton's lifestyle—an assessment that T3 can count on S3 to share. Humor such as T3's use of it here possibly constructs rapport because it reveals a shared position.

Showing Empathy or Sympathy

As noted above, tutors used the strategy of showing sympathy or empathy least of all the motivational scaffolding strategies. Tutors may have assumed that student writers would know that they empathized, not only with the difficulty of the writing work, but also with the difficulty of having to write papers, hold down a job, attend classes, and do all of the other activities that college students do. Being students themselves, the tutors in this study certainly understood the challenges that faced student writers who came to the writing center to get help.

Even so, tutors did on occasion explicitly convey their sympathy or empathy with student writers, T2 far more than any other tutor. In fact, T2 contributed 13 out of 17 occurrences of this strategy. T2's far more frequent use of this strategy likely stemmed from the topic of S2's paper and from S2's anxiety and frustration. In the paper, as mentioned previously, S2 discussed an emotionally charged situation in which she was harassed and ostracized at her private school. Throughout their conference, T2 provided sympathy both in relation to S2's troubling experiences at the school and in relation to S2's current workload. For example, she responded with sympathy to S2's lament about spending her evening revising the paper—particularly given that she had two papers due to the same instructor on the same day:

S2: I have a feeling of what I'm going to be writing about all over tonight.
T2: Yeah, you probably will be, you know. And with these revisions, it always ends up being, you know—It's always a lot of work in order to try to get a better—to try to write a better paper.
S2: Yeah.

As we discussed earlier, T2's sympathy strategies commenced in the opening stage. They continued at the beginning of the teaching stage of the conference, immediately after T2 had read through part of S2's paper:

T2: [Reading.] An enchilada right on your head! Really? Wow!
S2: Uh-huh. Yeah. It was pretty bad.
T2: [Reading.] Do you mind if I write on your paper?
S2: O.K.
T2: [Reading.] Goodness gracious! What kind of school was this? These people sound terrible.

T2's exclamations conveyed astonishment at the treatment S2 endured. The intensity of T2's sympathy aligns with what Brown and Levinson (1987) call exaggerating sympathy (or interest or approval)—another positive-politeness strategy (104). T2's intonation and exclamations conveyed that she was on S2's side and helped build solidarity between the two.

Just as she used optimism to encourage S2 to struggle through the work she had to do in relation to this emotionally charged paper and through the work she had to do on another paper simultaneously, so too did T2 acknowledge the effort required to do the revising work that the two of them had discussed during the session. T2's comment "It's always a lot work" also pointed out that S2 was not the only one who needed to work hard to improve her writing and get a good grade. As with her optimism, then, T2's sympathy here was grounded, pointing out that S2's struggle to improve her draft was not unique.

Other tutors showed that they empathized with student writers' workload and the challenges they faced in the writing tasks ahead of them. For example, in the following excerpt, T7 conveyed that he knew what S7 wanted (and did not want) to hear about her paper. Such signals of shared understanding show empathy and can build a sense of solidarity. In this case, T7 had throughout the session built rapport with the student writer, so much so that he was confident about asking her to read his thoughts about the paragraph he had just read:

T7: [Reading under his breath. Stops. Looks up at S7. Smiles.] Now, what do you think I am going to say?
S7: Expand some more.
T7: I know that you don't want to hear that but—
S7: I know. It is so hard to expand. But like I do—That's good because I kept thinking that too—that I needed to expand.

At this point in the conference, T7 and S7 had at several points discussed ways that S7 might elaborate paragraphs that make claims about the benefits of exercise but lack adequate support. Because they had been over the topic before, T7 was able to ask a pumping question to get S7 to think about the paragraph that they had just read: "Now, what do you think I am going to say?" This pumping question strongly indicated that T7 and S7 had built up a rapport over the course of their session, so much so that T7 was able to encourage S7 by telling her that he knew what she wanted to hear and what she did not want to hear ("I know that you don't want to hear that but—")—that she needed to provide more support in the paragraph they had just read.

To sum up, tutors used motivational scaffolding to encourage student writers by building their interest in the task (for example, through humor), bolstering their confidence (for example, through praise), and promoting their self-regulation (for example, through demonstrations of concern).

Motivational Scaffolding Strategies in the Closing Stage

In contrast to the diversity of motivational scaffolding strategies that the experienced tutors in our study used in the opening stage, in conference closings, tutors often used a single strategy of demonstrating concern—usually via yes/no questions geared toward getting students to confirm that they had met their goals for the conference and to see whether they had any other issues that they wanted to address:

T1: But so you feel O.K. to go back and make a few changes?
T2: Any other questions?
T3: O.K. Well, what do you think? Is that enough to get you started?
T5: O.K. So, um, does this kind of help you? Did you have any more questions or anything like that?
T7: Now before you answer, just think about it. Do you have any other questions? Doubts? Concerns?
T9: Is there anything else I can help you with?
T10: Do you have any questions?

Besides demonstrating concern that the student writer's needs had been met, such questions signaled that the tutor was bringing the conference to a close.

In one conference closing, the tutor was able to combine reinforcing the student writer's ownership and control with praise. After asking questions that showed concern both for S5's satisfaction that his conference goals were met and that she had answered his questions, T5 used motivational scaffolding to bolster S5's confidence as he prepared to work on the assignment on his own:

T5: O.K. So, um, does this kind of help you? Did you have any more questions or anything like that?
S5: It does. That definitely helped me. At least, I have something to go with now. [Laughs.]
T5: Yeah, yeah. And I think, um, you—you actually came up with the idea all by [yourself too, um, which is good. Uh, and it—it kind of stuck out from
S5:   [Uh-huh.
T5: everything else. And I think you—you have a more narrow argument now.
S5: O.K.

T5 reinforced S5's ownership of the paper by pointing out that S5 was the one who had come up with what eventually became the working thesis of the paper: smoking should not be allowed in films, especially films aimed at children. Then, she praised his effort and contribution: "which is good." T5's strategy of reinforcing ownership and control seems particularly effective because it was, first of all, true: S5 *did* come up with the idea of Hollywood's implicit endorsement of smoking. T5 acknowledged as much in her postconference interview:

> What I am reading is that smoking is already banned in dorms and places like that. But his teacher wanted him to go further. His teacher said the topic wasn't anything new. So what I was trying to aim him toward was a place that was new. Later we will focus on smoking in the movies and how that is a bad influence. So I am trying to prod him, ask him questions about what he knows about smoking in the media. That was actually his idea.

Throughout the conference, T5 helped narrow S5's choices for a thesis, but her motivational scaffolding strategy of reinforcing ownership made salient S5's agency in the process of homing in on an arguable and interesting thesis statement. Second, T5's reinforcing-ownership strategy backed up with praise implied that S5 could have some confidence in his ability to draft the paper, potentially increasing S5's self-efficacy.

Tutors' motivational scaffolds in conference closings showed less diversity than those in conference openings; they mainly used demonstrations of concern to check student writers' understanding and level of satisfaction with the extent to which the conference had met their needs.

Conclusions and Implications for Tutor Training

Much of the time, tutors' motivational scaffolding strategies followed semantic and syntactic formulae; tutors used formulae to show concern for student writers' understanding and state of mind and also to praise student writers. Tutors used far more of these two strategies than they did the other three types of motivational scaffold, likely because the formulae were less cognitively taxing to produce than nonformulaic strategies. Tutors peppered their interactions with formulaic versions of these two strategies, and demonstrations of concern were particularly salient in the conference closings, where tutors used them to signal that they must soon finish up the conference.

Tutors' use of formulaic demonstrations of concern and formulaic praise carried out important functions. Formulaic praise such as "good job," for example, could bolster a student writer's confidence, and formulaic demonstrations of concern could prod student writers to assess their own learning. However, this study revealed that nonformulaic strategies do even more work. Nonformulaic demonstrations of concern—because they were so individualized—conveyed close attention to the individual student writer's state of mind and comprehension. Also, because it tended to be more specific, nonformulaic praise seemed more instructive than formulaic praise. Thus, writing center directors and others who work with and train tutors should differentiate between formulaic and nonformulaic language in general and strategies in particular to help tutors formulate effective shows of concern and praise.

Tutors also reinforced student writers' ownership and control, used optimism and humor, and showed sympathy or empathy. These three strategies occurred less often than the other two but still had an impact. We saw in particular how a tutor (T2) used optimism and other motivational scaffolds throughout two topic episodes to help a discouraged student writer (S2) to see that revising her paper would not be as bad as she seemed to think and to encourage her to continue her work on the paper after the conference. With all five types of motivational scaffolding strategies, tutors worked to increase student writers' interest in the writing task, their self-efficacy, and their ability to self-regulate. Tutors' motivational scaffolding strategies likely helped student writers see the value of the writing task, their abilities as writers, and their control over their writing process and their work.

The tutors did not supply many statements of sympathy or empathy. Tutors might use this strategy when students express vulnerability—either in terms of the content of their writing or in terms of their current state of mind—and such situations may occur infrequently. Even so, writing center directors should supply tutors with guidelines for working with student writers who warrant sympathy or empathy, as S2 certainly did. We recommend that writing center directors train tutors to differentiate between helping students with their writing process (including time management) and helping student writers with social and other problems outside the realm of writing pedagogy (Murphy 1989; Welsh 1993). Although writing centers should provide environments where student writers feel comfortable and able to speak freely, tutor training should cover strategies for dealing with requests for personal advice and resources for those who need professional help with such problems. Tutors should not become amateur psychologists.

Tutors used explicit optimism infrequently, but, when they did, they tempered their optimism with a dose of reality. Optimism tempered by reality seemed to be the best course of action for tutors who wanted to encourage student writers and promote their self-efficacy. Of course, tutors deal with cases every day that make optimism unrealistic. When student writers visit the writing center just a few hours (or minutes) before their assignments are due, tutors may find little to be optimistic about and little they can do to help. Tutor training should make clear that optimism should be warranted; if it is not, tutors might simply advise student writers to work as hard as they can and devote as much time as they can.

We coded statements of optimism and humor together, grouping them because they both conveyed positivity. When tutors used humor, they risked offending students and, more likely, annoying students whose attitude closed them off to attempts to lighten the mood. Discussing the risks of using humor during writing center conferences, Sherwood (1993) writes, "Tutors who resort to humor risk much. Our attempts at wit, however well-intended, may fall flat or backfire resulting in confused, wounded, impatient, or angry student writers" (4). The tutors in our study did not always use related humor or self-deprecating humor—two types that can facilitate learning (Wanzer, Frymier, and Irwin 2010). Even so, their humor appeared to build rapport or, as Sherwood (1993) puts it, to "build a bridge between tutor and student" and help to create a place where "collaboration can thrive" (4). The tutors in our study used appropriate, if at times unrelated, humor. Based on our analysis, we recommend that writing center directors encourage tutors to employ humor—if the tutors feel comfortable about doing so. The writing process need not be joyless.

With their motivational scaffolding strategies, tutors carried out a variety of motivational work, some of which could be easy to overlook during tutor training. When tutors encourage students, they move them along toward increased interest, self-efficacy, and self-regulation and thus move them along toward becoming better writers.

8

CASE STUDY

A Writing Center Tutor Becomes a Writing Fellow

- Quantitative Analysis: Frequencies of Tutoring Strategies in Four Conferences
- Close Analysis: Conferencing as a Writing Center Tutor versus Conferencing as a Writing Fellow
- Qualitative Results: Close Analysis of Conferencing with Unfamiliar versus Familiar Students
- Conclusions and Implications for Tutor (and Fellow) Training

In this chapter, we present a case study of T9 as she works with three different students in four conferences. Two of these conferences took place in the writing center, where T9 worked as an undergraduate. The conference between T9 and S9 was a first-time meeting. The other writing center conference was a third meeting between T9 and S11 about one essay assignment. The other two conferences occurred a few years later, when T9 was a graduate student enrolled in the Master of Technical and Professional Communication program at Auburn University and working as a writing fellow in the BWP of the COB. One of T9's BWP conferences was the first out of three conferences required for S12's purchasing course. The other conference was the third meeting between T9 and S12. In this chapter, we examine the differences in the frequencies of T9's tutoring strategies in the writing center conferences and the BWP conferences. We also examine differences in T9's conferences with unfamiliar students and familiar students. Unlike Thonus (2002) in her study of discourse features of conference success (125), we found some differences in the tutoring strategies that T9 used in conferences with the unfamiliar and the familiar student writers. Finally, we also examine differences in the make-up of the topic episodes within those conferences.

As we described in Chapter 3 and discussed elsewhere, in the meeting between T9 and S9, the two brainstormed ideas for a WL paper on a creation myth other than the Bible story of Genesis. In contrast, T9 had met before with S11 about a paper on presidential candidates' policies on cultural diversity issues such as immigration and same-sex marriage. In the T9–S11 conference, the agenda was revising the paper. According to T9 in a postconference interview, in her first conference with S11 about this paper, the two brainstormed ideas. In a subsequent conference such as this one, T9 said in her interview, she thought focusing on sentence structure as opposed to global-level issues to be pedagogically sound. In addition to their prior conferences that semester, T9 and S11 had met several times the previous semester—S11's first semester in college. In a postconference interview, T9 said the two had, in those conferences during the previous semester, focused mainly on developing clear and sophisticated sentences. In particular, she said, they worked on revising passive voice sentences into active ones.

The role of a writing fellow, or writing associate (WA) as Cairns and Anderson (2008) term the position, differs substantially from the role of a writing center tutor. Cairns and Anderson (2008) describe the main differences this way: "Unlike a writing-center peer tutor, a WA typically works with students in only one course, interacts closely with the course instructor, and assists students outside the student writing center" (para. 5). T9's two semesters of work as a graduate writing fellow in Dr. Page's purchasing class did indeed differ substantially from her previous work in the writing center. As an undergraduate tutor in the writing center—a writing center that limited its services to WL and FYC students—T9 worked often with inexperienced student writers. However, as a writing fellow, as we discussed in Chapter 3, she took on an intermediary role between the instructor and the students in the purchasing class, even to the extent of helping the instructor develop the writing assignment. Because writing fellows work closely with single instructors as well as a single class of students, they have a twofold role in a way that writing center tutors do not: they help "students improve their writing while also assisting faculty in teaching effectively with writing" (Zawacki 2008, para. 1). Gladstein (2008) argues that, in this twofold role, writing fellows operate in a "gray space":

> [They] may feel stuck in the middle as they need to navigate the expectations of the professor they are assigned to work with, the expectations of the writing program director and program, the expectations of the students enrolled in the course, and their own expectations for what defines their work as successful. (Gladstein 2008, para. 3)

The contextual differences seemed to have an effect on T9's use of some strategies. In addition, the conference agenda—brainstorming/planning, revising, or editing—made a difference. In the next sections, we examine some of these differences more closely. Table 8.1 summarizes the four conferences conducted by T9 and discussed in this chapter.

TABLE 8.1 Overview of T9's Four Conferences

Conference					
Code Used in this Chapter	*Participants*	*Duration (Minutes)*	*Course*	*Agenda*	*Topic of the Student's Paper*
WC-U	T9–S9	24	WL 1	Brainstorming	Analysis of a creation myth other than Genesis
WC-F	T9–S11	27	FYC II	Revising	Persuasive essay about presidential candidates' views on cultural diversity
BWP-U	T9–S12	24	Purchasing	Planning	White paper analyzing the merits of Coca Cola's supply chain
BWP-F	T9–S12	26	Purchasing	Editing	White paper analyzing the merits of Coca Cola's supply chain

Note: WC-U = writing center, unfamiliar student; WC-F = writing center, familiar student; BWP-U = Business Writing Prototype, unfamiliar student; BWP-F = Business Writing Prototype, familiar student; FYC = first-year composition; WL = world literature

Quantitative Analysis: Frequencies of Tutoring Strategies in Four Conferences

In this section, we look at the frequency with which T9 used instruction, cognitive scaffolding, and motivational scaffolding strategies across the four conferences. To provide a deeper analysis of T9's tutoring in writing center conferences versus BWP conferences and in conferences with unfamiliar versus familiar student writers, we also examine and discuss the four conferences at the macrolevel. We examine the volubility that T9 and each student writer contributed to their interactions. We also examine the frequencies with which T9 and the student writers took control by beginning topic episodes. With these frequency counts, we gain a better understanding of the relationship between tutoring strategies and student writers' active participation.

Table 8.2 shows the distribution of the three categories of strategies across the four conferences and points to one main finding: T9 used about the same frequency of strategies—30–35 per 10 minutes of conference talk in all four conferences. Regardless of whether she worked on brainstorming, planning, revising, or editing, or whether she worked in the writing center or in her office in the COB, she consistently peppered her talk with tutoring strategies at the rate of over one per minute (see Table 8.2). This finding indicates the pedagogical richness of one-to-one tutoring.

The frequency and diversity of T9's tutoring strategies also suggest an underlying reason that one-to-one tutoring, in comparison with classroom discourse, appears to provide students with more opportunities to talk, greater interactivity, and more individualized feedback (Graesser and Person 1994; Graesser et al. 2001; Maheady 1998): tutors' instruction can provide targeted feedback, and, in various ways and degrees, tutors' cognitive and motivational scaffolding strategies enjoin student writers to participate actively.

Indeed, volubility in T9's four conferences supports the benefits of one-to-one tutoring over classroom teaching for increasing students' active participation, especially in conferences with familiar students (see Table 8.3). As Chick (1996) points out, commenting on in-service teacher education in apartheid South Africa, "Teacher volubility and student taciturnity is the asymmetrical distribution of social power and knowledge between teachers and students evident in

TABLE 8.2 Frequency and Percentage of T9's Tutoring Strategies per 10 Minutes

| Category | Frequency per 10 Minutes (% Conference Total) | | | | | | | |
	WC-U		WC-F		BWP-U		BWP-F	
Instruction	14.58	(42)	24.07	(74)	26.25	(83)	20.77	(69)
Cognitive scaffolding	14.58	(42)	4.44	(13)	1.25	(4)	6.15	(21)
Motivational scaffolding	5.42	(16)	4.44	(13)	4.17	(13)	3.08	(10)
Total	34.58	(100)	32.95	(100)	31.67	(100)	30.00	(100)

Note: WC-U = writing center, unfamiliar student; WC-F = writing center, familiar student; BWP-U = Business Writing Prototype, unfamiliar student; BWP-F = Business Writing Prototype, familiar student

TABLE 8.3 Volubility in T9's Four Conferences

| | Number of Words (% Total) | | | | | | | |
	WC-U		WC-F		BWP-U		BWP-F	
T9	2,465	(74)	2,263	(65)	3,373	(83)	2,286	(62)
Student writer	875	(26)	1,192	(35)	704	(17)	1,401	(36)
Total	3,340	(100)	3,455	(100)	4,077	(100)	3,687	(100)

Note: WC-U = writing center, unfamiliar student; WC-F = writing center, familiar student; BWP-U = Business Writing Prototype, unfamiliar student; BWP-F = Business Writing Prototype, familiar student

educational institutions throughout the world" (27). The teacher–student relationship ubiquitously generates imbalances of contributions to classroom discourse.

Even T9's highest volubility—83% of the talk in her first conference with S12—compares favorably with the amount of talk an individual student can possibly contribute in a classroom setting. Some research suggests that instructor volubility increases as instructor expertise in the subject matter decreases: "When addressing unfamiliar topics, teachers will . . . limit the topic of classroom conversation to areas where their special status as subject-matter authorities can be maintained" (Carlsen 1993, 471). Carlsen (1993) studied the effects of instructor knowledge on volubility during a variety of activities in high school biology classes (for example, lecture and group work). These activities related to topics about which the instructor had either high or low subject-matter knowledge. He found that instructors contributed between 41.1% and 88.5% of the talk, talking more when their subject-matter knowledge was low. Students jointly contributed the remainder of the talk during the activities.

In contrast to classroom discourse and the distribution of talk between an instructor and his or her students, in one-to-one tutoring, a single student contributes the remainder of the talk. Thus, even when a writing center tutor (such as T9) contributes 83% of the talk in a one-to-one conference, the student writer contributes the entirety of the other 17%. Even though she talked far more than the student writers, T9's volubility reflects the way that one-to-one conferencing opens up opportunities for individual student writers to contribute to the conversation and to get more out of the time they spend focused on learning how to write.

In addition, as Table 8.3 shows, familiarity made a difference in tutors' and student writers' volubility. In both the writing center and the BWP, T9's volubility was higher in her conferences with unfamiliar student writers. T9's lower percentage of volubility with familiar student writers attests to the strong effect that a prior relationship and the rapport that can stem from it can have on a tutor's ability to generate opportunities for a student writer's participation and also for a student writer's level of comfort in contributing to the conversation.

Besides counts of volubility, the frequency with which T9 launched and initiated and student writers introduced topic episodes in the teaching stage also supports the idea that student writers can become more comfortable in contributing to the conference talk as familiarity increases. As Table 8.4 shows, T9 launched and initiated 82% of the topic episodes in WC-U and 67% in BWP-U; however, in WC-F, T9 launched and initiated just 38%, and, in BWP-F, she launched and initiated just 47%.

In fact, in WC-F and BWP-F, S11 and S12 each introduced the very first topic episode of the teaching stage in their respective conferences. In WC-F, S11 and T9 engaged in an extremely short opening stage before S11 introduced TE1:

S11: But it's so bad. Like, normally, I like read—read the um, like, the introduction, and it sounds good but it's just, like, boring. Like, I don't even know if I'm doing this right, like ah, ok, cause I keep like questioning myself, like what I'm supposed to be saying.

In BWP-F, S12 and T9 jumped right into the teaching stage, skipping an opening stage completely, and, like S11, S12 introduced the first topic (about formatting): "Alright. Well, the first things I did—I got rid of those goofy borders. And you told me to change the fonts of—Like, make these two the same."

In contrast, both WC-U and BWP-U manifested more substantial opening stages. Rather than diving right into a topic episode, in the opening stages of both WC-U and BWP-U, T9 asked questions (discussed in more detail below) to determine S9's and S12's level of preparation for their conferences ("Do you have a copy of your deliverable one with you, like, a printed out version?") and their understanding of their assignments ("When's it due?"). The willingness of S11 and S12 to move quickly to topic episodes and to introduce topic episodes suggests that familiarity can play a role in the comfort student writers feel in participating actively in their conferences.

T9's Instruction Strategies

As shown in Table 8.2, T9 used instruction less frequently in WC-U than in the other three conferences. In WC-U, T9 used instruction and cognitive scaffolding with equal frequency as she helped S9 brainstorm content for her paper. However, among the three instruction strategies, T9 used the highest percentage of telling in WC-U (see Table 8.5). In that conference, she supplied S9 with unmitigated advice, usually about how to begin writing the paper: "O.K. So, first of all, you have to write with the—with the term 'philosophical exile' in mind." Often, as

TABLE 8.4 Topic-Episode Launches, Initiations, and Introductions in T9's Four Conferences

	Number of Topic-Episode Launches, Initiations, and Introductions (% Total)							
	WC-U		*WC-F*		*BWP-U*		*BWP-F*	
T9	23	(82)	13	(38)	23	(67)	20	(47)
Student writer	5	(18)	21	(62)	11	(33)	23	(53)
Total	28	(100)	34	(100)	34	(100)	43	(100)

Note: WC-U = writing center, unfamiliar student; WC-F = writing center, familiar student; BWP-U = Business Writing Prototype, unfamiliar student; BWP-F = Business Writing Prototype, familiar student

in the previous example, T9 wrote notes for S9 while she was instructing her in how to compose the literary analysis. She used the highest percentage of suggesting in WC-F, the conference in which she worked with S11 for the third time that semester. In WC-F, T9 read through the paper, supplying mitigated advice as she proceeded, as was the case when she suggested that S11 omit an irrelevant, subjective phrase from her paper: "So like, the part about the 'dangerous to the citizens of the United States'—I don't think that's really the goal of your paper. So, uh, maybe, leave that, uh, out." She used the highest percentage of explaining in BWP-U. As we discuss later, in this conference T9 had to explain the multi-component white paper assignment as well as the white paper genre to S12: "Because it is like we are approaching it more like a magazine article. And even in a magazine article, you have some sort of an introduction that tells you what is coming, what is coming up." In these four conferences, T9's directiveness likely has as much to do with the agenda, for example, brainstorming versus revising, and the opportunities for certain strategies that those agendas afford, as it does with her familiarity with the student writer.

T9's Cognitive Scaffolding Strategies

T9 used far more cognitive scaffolding in WC-U than she did in the other three conferences. In fact, she used almost no cognitive scaffolding in BWP-U: just 1.25 occurrences per 10 minutes of talk (see Table 8.2). In that conference, T9 helped S12 plan his white paper. She spent much of her time in that conference explaining the assignment and the unfamiliar white paper genre, as opposed to probing S12's thinking about the topic. At the time of that meeting, S12 had just begun researching the topic—Coca Cola's supply chain—and thus had not yet formed much of an opinion about the topic.

T9 used slightly more cognitive scaffolding in WC-F and BWP-F (4.44 and 6.16 strategies per 10 minutes, respectively). In those conferences, T9 read aloud

TABLE 8.5 Frequency and Percentage of Instruction per 10 Minutes

Instruction Strategy	Frequency per 10 Minutes (% Conference Total)							
	WC-U		WC-F		BWP-U		BWP-F	
Telling	7.92	(54)	7.04	(29)	9.58	(36)	10.00	(48)
Suggesting	3.75	(26)	12.22	(51)	1.67	(6)	4.62	(22)
Explaining	2.92	(20)	4.81	(20)	15.00	(57)	6.15	(30)
Total	14.59	(100)	24.07	(100)	26.25	(100)	20.77	(100)

Note: WC-U = writing center, unfamiliar student; WC-F = writing center, familiar student; BWP-U = Business Writing Prototype, unfamiliar student; BWP-F = Business Writing Prototype, familiar student

from student writers' (draft) papers. Her use of the reading-aloud strategy substantially increased the overall frequency of cognitive scaffolds in those two conferences: in WC-F, 2.59 of 4.44 cognitive scaffolding strategies (per 10 minutes of talk) were reading aloud, and, in BWP-F, 3.08 of 6.16 were reading aloud (see Table 8.6). Without her use of the reading-aloud strategy, her overall frequency of cognitive scaffolding in those conferences would be cut by half.

As we discussed in Chapter 6, T9's brainstorming conference with S9 (WC-U) generated opportunities for her to use pumping questions in order to prod S9 to think about her topic and likely, in the process, to provide details about the myth for T9, as she had not read it. In contrast, T9's use of pumping questions fell away in BWP-U and BWP-F. In those two conferences, she used no pumps at all. This result might have stemmed from her need to give more instruction as she explained (especially in BWP-U) what a white paper is and what the white paper assignment should accomplish. As Table 8.4 shows, her use of explaining was far more frequent in BWP-U than in the other conferences: 15 explanations per 10 minutes. That amount of explaining is over twice that of BWP-F—the conference with the second-highest frequency of explanations.

To better describe and compare T9's conferences—particularly cognitive scaffolding in those conferences—we also coded and counted T9's and student writers' question types (cognitive-scaffolding questions plus four other types). We used the coding scheme that we developed for writing center conferences from Graesser, Person, and Huber's (1992) research on questions in tutoring interactions related to closed-world domains. As discussed in Chapter 2, in that study, we examined the questions that writing center tutors and student writers generated in 11 first-meeting writing center conferences (Thompson and Mackiewicz

TABLE 8.6 Frequency and Percentage of Cognitive Scaffolding per 10 Minutes

Cognitive Scaffolding Strategy	Frequency per 10 Minutes (% Conference Total)							
	WC-U		WC-F		BWP-U		BWP-F	
Pumping	7.08	(48)	0.37	(8)	0	(0)	0	(0)
Reading aloud	1.25	(9)	2.59	(59)	0	(0)	3.08	(50)
Responding as reader	3.33	(22)	1.11	(25)	0	(0)	0.77	(13)
Referring to a previous topic	1.25	(9)	0	(0)	0	(0)	0	(0)
Forcing a choice	1.25	(9)	0	(0)	0	(0)	0	(0)
Demonstrating	0	(0)	0	(0)	1.25	(100)	2.31	(37)
Hinting	0.42	(3)	0	(0)	0	(0)	0	(0)
Prompting	0	(0)	0.37	(8)	0	(0)	0	(0)
Total	14.58	(100)	4.44	(100)	1.25	(100)	6.16	(100)

Note: WC-U = writing center, unfamiliar student; WC-F = writing center, familiar student; BWP-U = Business Writing Prototype, unfamiliar student; BWP-F = Business Writing Prototype, familiar student

2014); one of the 11 conferences that we studied was T9's WC–U conference. We coded five types of questions (see Appendix D for more detail):

- *Knowledge deficit*: "Do I need to put another period after that at the end of the sentence or a comma?" (S12)
- *Common ground*: "At this point, do you have any questions about the assignment?" (T9)
- *Social coordination*: "Can you help me understand this thing?" (S11)
- *Conversation control*: "What did I say? Her pol—Her—Her—policies?" (S11)
- *Cognitive scaffolding*: "What kind of effects did that have on the reader?" (T9)

In that earlier study, we found that tutors asked most of the questions: 81% (562) of the total 690 questions, whereas student writers asked 19% (128). Tutors overwhelmingly used two question types: (1) common-ground questions, a category that included questions to determine student writers' conference goals and to ensure their understanding, and (2) cognitive-scaffolding questions to move student writers' along in their brainstorming and revising. Of tutors' 562 questions, 41% (232) sought common ground ("And then, do you see that would be a little bit easier to relate back to the thesis statement?"), and another 41% (231) provided scaffolds ("What do you think the main point is here that you're making?"). Of student writers' 128 questions, 94% (120) were knowledge-deficit questions, questions aimed at obtaining information that the questioner genuinely does not know or requesting clarification ("Should I group all the pros together or organize by pro, con, pro, con?").

Comparing our prior findings—the frequencies of tutors' and student writers' questions and the types of their questions—with T9's conference with S11 and her BWP conferences with S12, we found substantial differences (see Table 8.7). In T9's conference with S11 and in her BWP conferences, the student writers asked questions more frequently, but their questions did not differ in type from those we found in the prior study: they asked knowledge-deficit questions to find out topic and assignment information that they did not know.

In WC–F, S11 asked 14.8 knowledge-deficit questions per 10 minutes—over 10 times as many as S9 in WC–U. S11's questions—like her volubility—suggested that she was comfortable making her needs for information known. The same is true of S12 in BWP–F. S12's familiarity with T9 was likely a main reason behind the frequency of his knowledge-deficit questions—even more frequent than in BWP–U, where S12 asked knowledge-deficit questions about the white paper assignment.

In contrast, T9's questions differed substantially in both frequency and type from our previous findings. T9 asked far fewer questions than the tutors in our previous study; the student writers asked far more, suggesting they had some measure of self-efficacy and self-regulation. T9 used common-ground questions to check student writers' understanding, particularly in first meetings—in WC–U and

TABLE 8.7 Frequency and Percentage of Tutors' and Student Writers' Questions per 10 Minutes

Frequency (%) Questions

Question Type	WC-U				WC-F				BWP-U				BWP-F			
	T		S		T		S		T		S		T		S	
Knowledge deficit	1.66	(11)	1.25	(75)	1.48	(40)	14.81	(89)	1.66	(31)	8.33	(100)	2.69	(47)	11.15	(100)
Common ground	4.16	(27)	0	(0)	1.11	(30)	0	(0)	3.33	(62)	0	(0)	1.15	(20)	0	(0)
Social coordination	0.83	(5)	0	(0)	0.37	(10)	0.74	(4)	0.41	(7)	0	(0)	0	(0)	0	(0)
Conversation control	0.83	(5)	0.41	(25)	0.37	(10)	1.11	(7)	0	(0)	0	(0)	0.38	(7)	0	(0)
Cognitive scaffolding	7.91	(52)	0	(0)	0.37	(10)	0	(0)	0	(0)	0	(0)	1.53	(26)	0	(0)
Total	15.41	(100)	1.66	(100)	3.7	(100)	16.66	(100)	5.41	(100)	8.33	(100)	5.76	(100)	11.15	(100)

Note: T= tutor; S = student writer; WC-U = writing center, unfamiliar student; WC-F = writing center, familiar student; BWP-U = Business Writing Prototype, unfamiliar student; BWP-F = Business Writing Prototype, familiar student

BWP-U. However, she did not use cognitive-scaffolding questions as frequently as the tutors in our earlier research. One explanation stands out: T9 did not need to pump student writers with cognitive-scaffolding questions, because the student writers themselves asked questions.

Two other main differences between T9's use of cognitive scaffolding in writing center versus BWP conferences were the frequency with which she used the responding-as-a-reader-or-a-listener and demonstrating strategies. T9 used a higher percentage of the responding-as-a-reader-or-a-listener strategy in her writing center conferences. In WC-U she used the strategy 3.33 times per 10 minutes, a frequency that comprised 22% of her cognitive scaffolding in that conference. In WC-F, she used it just 1.11 times per 10 minutes, but the strategy still constituted 25% of the cognitive scaffolding in that conference. In WC-U and WC-F, she responded as a reader or listener to address S9's and S11's composing processes, their instructors' assignment sheets, and the source material for their papers with comments such as, "This story explains, and like you said, talked about the need for super superior being" (to S9) and "Basically they're saying here that he's standing up for the rights of immigrants" (to S11).

T9 did not use this strategy at all in BWP-U. Not only was T9 already familiar with the white paper as an assignment and thus did not need to read and respond to it, but also S12 did not have at that point a draft paper to which T9 could respond as a reader. Besides the difference in T9's knowledge about the assignment in her BWP conferences versus her writing center conferences, it might also have been the case that T9 tended to use this strategy with less experienced writers—those who came to the writing center. She paraphrased their meaning to ensure her understanding and to show student writers how others interpret them, and she paraphrased source material and assignment sheets to ensure student writers understood them. Her paraphrases gave them other language to access the meaning of those texts.

The final main difference between T9's use of cognitive scaffolding in writing center versus BWP conferences was the frequency with which she used demonstrating strategies. When T9 worked as a writing fellow in the BWP, she used demonstrating, a strategy we encountered just once in our examination of all 10 experienced tutors' writing center conferences (in the T2–S2 conference). However, T9's BWP conferences reveal that, under the right conditions, tutoring the open-world domain of writing can indeed generate demonstrating, just as closed-world domains do (see, for example, Chi 1996; Lepper, Drake, and O'Donnell-Johnson 1997). T9's use of this strategy was particularly frequent and salient in BWP-F, the conference that focused on editing the white paper. In BWP-F, demonstrating comprised 37% of T9's cognitive scaffolding, 7.8% of the total tutoring strategies in the conference. In BWP-U, T9's use of demonstrating (1.25 per 10 minutes) comprised 100% of the cognitive scaffolding that she used, but only 4% of the total number of tutoring strategies in the conference. We discuss some possible reasons behind these findings below.

T9's Motivational Scaffolding Strategies

Although instruction and cognitive scaffolding varied across the four conferences, the frequency of T9's motivational scaffolding remained fairly consistent. However, the specific motivational scaffolding strategies that she used across the conferences varied substantially. In WC-U, T9 used the two most common motivational scaffolding strategies appearing in the 10 conferences discussed previously: showing concern and praising (see Table 8.8).

Each of these two strategies comprised 31% of the motivational scaffolding in WC-U. However, T9's percentage of showing concern, if not the frequency, in BWP-U—her first conference with S12—surpassed her use of it in WC-U. In BWP-U, 40% of T9's motivational scaffolding strategies consisted of shows of concern, such as asking the formulaic question "Do you see what I'm saying?" at the end of an instruction-heavy episode.

We counted the number of formulaic and nonformulaic demonstrations of concern and praise strategies in T9's conferences to determine whether the formulaicity in those conferences—particularly the BWP conferences—compared with the formulaicity in the 10 writing center conferences. T9 used these two strategies fairly infrequently, and so we should not make too much of the calculated percentages of formulaic strategies; however, we found the percentages to be comparable with those of the other conferences. In the 10 writing center conferences, 83% of tutors' demonstrations of concern and 66% of their praise were formulaic. Table 8.9 shows the percentages of formulaic and nonformulaic expressions of concern and praise in T9's conferences. In general, she used more formulaic strategies than nonformulaic ones, as the other tutors did.

The one exception to T9's use of formulaicity was her use of nonformulaic praise in the BWP-F conference ("Well, I like, um, the fact that the heading has what Coke does best because kind of . . ."). However, these (few) nonformulaic

TABLE 8.8 Frequency and Percentage of Motivational Scaffolding per 10 Minutes

Motivational Scaffolding Strategy	Frequency per 10 Minutes (%)							
	WC-U		WC-F		BWP-U		BWP-F	
Showing concern	1.67	(31)	0.37	(8)	1.67	(40)	0.38	(12)
Praising	1.67	(31)	1.11	(25)	0	(0)	1.92	(64)
Reinforcing ownership/control	0	(0)	0	(0)	0	(0)	0	(0)
Being optimistic or using humor	1.25	(23)	2.59	(59)	2.08	(50)	0.38	(12)
Showing empathy or sympathy	0.83	(15)	0.37	(8)	0.42	(10)	0.38	(12)
Total	5.42	(100)	4.44	(100)	4.17	(100)	3.06	(100)

Note: WC-U = writing center, unfamiliar student; WC-F = writing center, familiar student; BWP-U = Business Writing Prototype, unfamiliar student; BWP-F = Business Writing Prototype, familiar student

TABLE 8.9 Frequency and Percentage of Formulaic and Nonformulaic Shows of Concern and Praise

	Frequency per 10 Minutes (%)							
	WC-U		WC-F		BWP-U		BWP-F	
Showing Concern								
Formulaic	1.25	(75)	0.37	(100)	1.25	(75)	0.38	(100)
Nonformulaic	0.41	(25)	0	(0)	0.41	(25)	0	(0)
Total	1.67	(100)	0.37	(100)	1.67	(100)	0.38	(100)
Praising								
Formulaic	1.25	(75)	1.11	(100)	0	(0)	0.76	(40)
Nonformulaic	0.41	(25)	0	(0)	0	(0)	1.15	(60)
Total	1.67	(100)	1.11	(100)	0	(0)	1.92	(100)

Note: WC-U = writing center, unfamiliar student; WC-F = writing center, familiar student; BWP-U = Business Writing Prototype, unfamiliar student; BWP-F = Business Writing Prototype, familiar student

occurrences bordered on formulaicity. For example, the praise "I like that you've expanded here" nearly fits the formula of "I" + ("really") "like" + noun phrase. In short, T9's formulaicity appeared comparable to the formulaicity in the 10 writing center conferences, and her formulaicity in her writing center conferences appeared comparable to that of her BWP conferences.

In addition, T9 used no praise in BWP-U—a marked difference from the WC-U conference, possibly because S9 had done more work on her paper than S12. S9 for the most part understood her assignment and had already done a lot of planning. In contrast, S12 did not understand the assignment; thus, as T9 spent a lot of time explaining the assignment and ways to proceed with research and organization, she had less cause or opportunity to praise. However, T9 clearly was not averse to using praise as a writing fellow. In fact, of the four T9 conferences we studied, she used the highest percentage of praise in BWP-F; it accounted for 64% of the motivational scaffolding that she used in that conference.

T9's familiarity with the student writer with whom she was working seemed to play a small role in her strategy use. In particular, she used demonstrations of concern more frequently with unfamiliar students, and she used reading aloud more frequently with familiar students. However, the conference agenda likely influenced T9's ability to read aloud. In her conferences with familiar students, the student writers had draft papers at the ready and available for comment (and reading aloud), whereas her conferences with unfamiliar students focused on brainstorming.

Whether the conference took place in the writing center or the BWP made some difference in the frequency with which T9 used some strategies. Most notably, she used more demonstrating in the BWP and more responding as a reader or listener and demonstrations of concern in the writing center. In the sections that follow, we more closely examine the strategies T9 used as she worked as a tutor and a writing fellow and as she worked with unfamiliar and familiar student writers.

Close Analysis: Conferencing as a Writing Center Tutor versus Conferencing as a Writing Fellow

In the following section, we compare the ways that T9 used tutoring strategies and the ways that she integrated strategies when she tutored in the writing center to the ways that she used and integrated the strategies as she tutored in the BWP. We try to point out patterns in T9's use of strategies across the three categories, recognizing that, in Chapters 5–7, we for the most part discussed the categories of strategies in isolation.

As we mentioned above, one of the main differences between the writing center and the BWP conferences was the extent to which T9 employed the instruction strategy of explaining during her conferencing work in the BWP. Explaining constituted 57% of T9's instruction in BWP-U and 30% in BWP-F. In BWP-U, T9 used 15 explaining strategies per 10 minutes—nearly 2.5 times as many as in BWP-F, the conference with the next highest frequency of explaining. In contrast, in both WC-U and WC-F, explaining constituted just 20% of her instruction. As we noted before in relation to this result, T9's frequent use of explaining likely reflects the nature of her role as an intermediary between the instructor and the students—one who interprets and conveys the concerns of one audience to the other—and that role's concomitant responsibility to ensure that the students understood both the genre that they were to write and the assignment itself.

The excerpt below exemplifies not only how T9 used explaining but also the way she indicated that, in addition to aligning herself with the purchasing students, she also aligned herself with Dr. Page, the course instructor, referring to a goal for student writers that she and Dr. Page shared. To contextualize her alignment with Dr. Page, it is important to recall that T9 had worked with him the previous semester as well. Throughout their work together in the BWP, Dr. Page listened to and carried out a variety of T9's suggestions for the white paper assignment and other writing assignments, particularly in the spring semester. He also trusted her to evaluate draft documents and used her rubric ratings and comments as components of the students' grades. In the exchange excerpted below, T9 responded to S12's question about an introduction by explaining the purpose of an executive summary, one component of the multicomponent white paper assignment. After her explanation, she closed with a motivational scaffolding strategy, humor, related to her use of the term "real world" in discussing the kind of writing that S12 would do after he graduates:

S12: Do I need, like, an introduction paragraph and then—[like the ideas in it
T9:   [That's what
S12: and then—
T9: your—Actually, yeah. That's what the executive summary is designed to do. And, um, executive summaries in like "real-world" documents. I hate to say that because this is real world too. You know, but like—[Laughs.]
S12: Yes. I know what you mean.
T9: Yeah. In a professional document can differ. The length can differ. We want you to have about a hundred words, which is essentially a paragraph.

T9 moved from explanation (about the purpose of an executive summary) to humor ("this is the real world too") back to explanation (about the length of the summary). In this excerpt, then, she kept on the task of explaining the advice about the executive summary that she had just offered, but she also lightened the mood by playing off of the notion that the (hard) work S12 did in college was not, in some sense, real.

Her integration of explanations and humor likely arose in part from her role as one who operates in the gray space, as Gladstein (2008) puts it, between instructor and peer. About writing fellows in this intermediary role, Gladstein writes, "[They] have insider knowledge on what the final product should resemble, yet they also understand what may be needed to accomplish that goal" (para. 13). As a writing fellow, T9 understood and could explain the assignment, but she also understood the challenge the purchasing students faced in meeting the assignment's requirements and thus successfully accomplishing the task that lay in front of them.

The white paper assignment did indeed warrant a substantial amount of explanation: students in the purchasing class had not even heard of a white paper, let alone written one. Indeed, as Willerton (2007) discusses in his study of current practices of technical communicators who develop and write white papers, the genre is heterogeneous in that it can address multiple audiences, for example, existing customers, internal colleagues, prospective customers (190), and focus on multiple purposes, for example, to persuade, to inform, and to provide reference material (191). This pedagogical situation—the students' lack of familiarity with an important disciplinary genre—is not at all uncommon. In contrast, the students who sought help in the writing center were likely familiar—via their high school English courses—with the academic essay genre assigned in the FYC and WL courses.

In addition to their having to develop a paper that conformed to an unfamiliar (and heterogeneous) genre, Dr. Page's white paper assignment required students to take up what was likely an unfamiliar tone, or register: the assignment asked them to write in engaging yet professional prose that would be suitable for a trade publication, as opposed to an academic one. Thus, students needed to familiarize themselves with articles in trade magazines to get a sense of the tone the authors employed and in order to avoid simply taking up the academic prose that they might use in a typical essay assignment.

T9's conferences with S12 in the BWP generated opportunities for T9 to use the demonstrating strategy—in part because the two worked together at T9's desk (and near her computer) in her shared office, as opposed to at a table in the writing center. In this setting, T9 had an office computer available to her, and she demonstrated by gesturing toward the screen and by using on-screen visuals. In addition to the BWP setting, the editing agenda of BWP-F also generated opportunities for demonstrating. With the planning and drafting work done, T9 and S12 had time in their third (and final) conference to discuss citation style and format, including the layout of the text and images on the page. These topics generated the demonstration strategy from T9 on several occasions. In comparison, the FYC and WL assignments that students brought to the writing center required minimal formatting (for example, one-inch margins and double spacing). They did, however, require correct documentation (MLA or APA) style, but in the WC-U conference, S9 was not yet far enough along in the composing process to focus on documentation style.

The value of demonstrating, coupling the visual input of pictures or gestures with the verbal input of talk, gains support from Paivio's (1986, 2007) dual coding theory (DCT). DCT posits that multisensory input improves comprehension and recall because it employs complementary (as opposed to conflicting) modes of information. The two most commonly studied modes of input are aural and visual, but recently other sensory input has received attention, including olfactory input in studies of advertising (for example, Lwin, Morrin, and Krishna 2010). DCT rests on the idea that people process verbal and visual information differently, through the two cognitive systems that operate independently. The verbal subsystem processes information sequentially, and the visual system processes information holistically. As Lwin, Morrin, and Krishna (2010) state in explaining the additivity hypothesis of DCT and the effect of two input modes on recall, "When incoming information is encoded via both verbal and imaginal codes, the verbal and imaginal memory traces are linked, so that, during attempts at retrieval, activation levels are pooled, enhancing the accessibility of the information" (318). Demonstrating—either by using pictures or gestures— provides additional cognitive pathways to stored information.

Many studies have supported the idea that two modes of input, specifically, verbal information and pictures (for example, Gersten and Baker 2000; Mayer 1999), as well as verbal information and gestures (Kelly, Özyürek, and Maris 2010; Macedonia, Müller, and Friederici 2011), enhance comprehension and recall. However, as studies of foreign language learning have shown, task complexity plays a role in the extent to which visuals facilitate learning. For example, McNeil, Alibali, and Evans (2000) found that redundant gestures improved comprehension of complex tasks but not simple ones. Rowe, Silverman, and Mullan (2013) found similar complexity in their study of visuals as additive, redundant information during language (first and foreign) learning. Gestures improved word learning for English language learners with low ability but not those with high ability. McNeil, Alibali, and Evans's (2000) complexity theory explains these results: redundant information helps novice learners—those for whom a task is complex—but impedes more advanced learners.

As the excerpts below illustrate, T9's use of pictures and gestures—her demonstrating—supplemented her verbal input and appeared to facilitate S12's learning. In the excerpt below, T9 demonstrated when she showed S12 how to wrap text around an image in Microsoft Word:

S12: For some reason, this wasn't on my computer. [Points to something on computer screen.] How do I get this back on there?
T9: Pull down here. [Shows him how on the screen.]
S12: Ah. Right there. [Smiles and shakes his head.]
T9: Yeah. Right. It's like these little tiny things. I could spend a lot of time talking about how Microsoft Word is not intuitive. But let's save that for another date. [Laughs.]
S12: [Laughs.]

This excerpt indicates how some writing conference topics—topics such as finding and using features of software—more readily lend themselves to a tutor or writing fellow walking a student step by step through a procedure for accomplishing some task, such as wrapping text around an image. As previously stated, in the step-by-step problem solving common to tutoring in many closed-world-domain disciplines, demonstrations are likely to be effective and thus frequent. Similarly, a student writer learning how to wrap text around an image in Word needs to follow discrete, objectively correct steps, and so demonstrating is likely effective in this context as well.

However, not all T9's demonstrating strategies occurred in occasions when she employed a visual (a picture of sorts) such as a shared computer screen. T9 also demonstrated by gesturing, such as when she pointed to words and punctuation in S12's paper:

T9: Oh, and any of these images. What we decided to do with this is paper is, um—an image from, like you have got here, or figure one or figure whatever from—and then do, essentially—
S12: Uh-huh. Uh-huh.
T9: You don't put this in parentheses. [Points to paper draft.] You would put that part in parentheses. So just like a regular—Just like this one right here. Like a regular citation.

Gestures such as the one T9 used when she pointed to S12's paper have been largely ignored in published writing center research, with the exception of

Thompson's (2009) microanalysis of one tutor's verbal and nonverbal (gestural) instruction, cognitive scaffolding, and motivational scaffolding. Thompson explains a main distinction in types of gesture: interactive and topic. Interactive gestures refer to the process of conversing. For example, a tutor might point to the student writer as he or she reiterates something the student writer said earlier, or might wave his or her hand when trying to find the "right" word. Topic gestures, on the other hand, represent information related to the discourse; they can be iconic, metaphoric, or deictic. Deictic gestures, according to Goodwin (2003), point to real or imaginary people and things and relate strongly to their environment, or gesture space. T9 repeatedly used the deictic type of topic gesture as she pointed to features of S12's paper and to the computer screen.

The other main difference between T9's use of strategies in her work as a writing fellow and her work as a tutor was her use of the responding-as-a-reader-or-a-listener strategy in her writing center conferences. She used far more cognitive scaffolding in WC-U than she did in any other conference, and 21% of that cognitive scaffolding was responding as a reader or listener (3.33 per 10 minutes). She used just 4.44 cognitive scaffolds per 10 minutes in WC-F, but 25% of them were responding as a reader or listener. In comparison, in BWP-U and BWP-F, she used 0% and 13%, respectively. However, examining the ways she used this strategy in WC-U and WC-F, we see a difference. In WC-U, T9 used the strategy mainly to respond to S9. She engaged with S9's description and analysis of the creation myth and tried to understand the meaning that S9 was trying to convey in what she had written and what she said. So she paraphrased S9's words, as in the excerpt here, to set up instruction and further cognitive scaffolding:

T9: So, yeah, I think it is easier to believe because—I don't know, I can't remember. I just blanked out. Um, but basically what you said. Easier to believe we came from a person than, say, from a tree. Because I think coming from a tree is more of a stretch of the imagination in a way than "I'm going to cut this person up and turn them into a human." [2 seconds] Um, do you think that—I wouldn't try and compare to evolution though because these are creation myths. It's like around long before evolution, so they wouldn't have had that to compare it to. But, um, do you think that it takes more faith or less faith to believe in something like this than something more commonplace?

S9: I think it takes more faith to step outside the box. Push your faith comfort zone.

When T9 responded as a listener, paraphrasing S9's analysis ("but basically what you said. Easier to believe we came from a person than, say, from a tree"), she constructed a base first for instruction, specifically, a telling strategy ("I wouldn't try and compare to evolution though") and an explanation of that telling strategy ("because these are creation myths. It's like around long before evolution, so they wouldn't have had that to compare it to"). After this instruction, she was able to move to cognitive scaffolding—a forced-choice question ("do you think that it takes more faith or less faith to believe in something like this than something more commonplace?")—that moved S9 ahead in her analysis of the creation myth, even as it constrained her possible responses.

In contrast, in WC-F, T9 used the responding-as-a-reader strategy mainly to paraphrase S11's source documents, in a sense, interpreting them for her:

T9: Basically they're saying here that he's standing up for the rights of immigrants. And in that article, they're like, "That's bad." But, in regard to cultural diversity, I think, it's a better thing.
S11:So he's standing up for the rights of immigrants.

Such interpretation was important in this case, as S11 had used a source with a clearly negative view about a presidential candidate's stance on immigration, even though the goal of her assignment was to objectively assess which candidates were more supportive of cultural diversity. When T9 used the responding-as-a-reader-or-a-listener strategy, she conveyed to these two students the meaning that she received from their writing, and she conveyed to them her own interpretation of their source texts. However, whatever the focus of her paraphrasing, when T9 used this strategy, she enacted another kind of intermediary role—an interpreter role.

Qualitative Results: Close Analysis of Conferencing with Unfamiliar versus Familiar Students

Even though writing center practitioners emphasize the importance of tutor–student writer rapport and say that tutors and students can build rapport in repeat conferences (for example, Mansfield 2013), writing center research has largely overlooked systematic study of the influence of repeat conferences. In looking at minor and sometimes only marginally relevant findings, we found some evidence to support the common-sense view that frequent writing center use has benefits. For example, as we discussed in Chapter 2, even though frequency of writing center visits did not correlate with increased satisfaction, Carino and Enders (2001) found that frequency of writing center use did correlate with student writers' increased confidence in their writing ability. In a longitudinal study, Williams a nd Takaku (2011) found that writing center use was a significant influence on grades in writing courses and even more important than L1 American English status. Porter (1991) and Waring (2005) report case studies of tutors and student writers who had been working together for some time. In both studies, the student writers appeared to be comfortable with the tutors, and they did not seem obligated to accept their tutors' advice—in fact, they freely disagreed with the tutors. Of the four conferences Davis et al. (1988) analyzed, one occurred between a tutor and student writer who had worked together frequently. This pair's working relationship was quite different than the other three. Although the tutor tightly controlled the conference—making twice as many structuring remarks as the other three tutors—the student writer made twice as many soliciting remarks and asked questions. However, in this conference, the tutor was an experienced high school teacher who was pursuing a doctorate in rhetoric and linguistics, and the student writer was a graduate student. Thus, as in Porter's (1991) and Waring's (2005) case studies, as well as the other studies described above, separating the influence of repeat visits from variables relating to age, experience, and education is not possible. These studies did not isolate the variable of tutor–student familiarity.

When T9 worked with unfamiliar students in WC-U and BWP-U, 31% and 40% of her motivational scaffolding strategies were demonstrations of concern. In contrast, in WC-F and BWP-F, showing concern constituted just 8% and 12% of the motivational scaffolding strategies. The difference in these percentages suggests that, as a tutor and a writing fellow, T9 especially concerned herself with the well-being of unfamiliar student writers, in particular through formulaic questions to check their comprehension (for example, "Do you see what I'm saying?", "You know?", and "Do you have any questions?"). The tutor and the writing fellow roles—despite their differences—shared a responsibility for encouraging student writers to continue their efforts and met this responsibility in large part through formulaic shows of concern that conveyed such encouragement.

The excerpt below shows how T9 employed the demonstrating-concern strategy in BWP-U, the planning conference for the white paper. She strung telling and explaining strategies together to help S12 understand the components of the assignment, and she ended with a demonstration of concern:

T9: What the basic, I think, argument of this whole assignment is, like, first you have to say that Coke is successful, which is like your company profile. You are saying they are successful.

S12: O.K.

T9: They are so big. They have locations everywhere. Blah, blah. And then the second part is and here's how they do what they do. And you sort of give a basic overview of their supply chain. How their logistics works. Whatever. And then, um, for that third section, best practices, you are kind of arguing, now this is what they do that puts them on that AMR top-25 list of suppliers. Not suppliers. Supply chains. Um, so this is why they are so successful. Because the main gist is like they are successful because of their supply chain. Um, and then your whole paper throughout those three sections, you are working to explain why. Um, so. Yeah. Does that make sense?

S12: Yeah. It makes a lot of sense.

T9 began with a telling strategy aimed at getting S12 on the right track as he started work on his assignment ("You have to say that Coke is successful"), as well as explaining ("Because the main gist is like they are successful because of their supply chain") to clarify reasons for her advice. Her advice was quite direct, but that directiveness is not surprising given her in-depth knowledge of the assignment, knowledge that shows through in her explanations. As we discussed in Chapter 4, T9 links motivational scaffolding to the end of a string of instruction—sequencing that allows tutors to supply advice and then check to make sure the student writer has comprehended it.

Another main difference between the two sets of conferences is manifested in T9's use of cognitive scaffolding, especially her use of the reading-aloud strategy. Both WC-F and BWP-F contained a higher percentage of cognitive scaffolding devoted to this strategy. In WC-F and BWP-F, respectively, 59% and 50% of T9's cognitive scaffolding consisted of reading aloud. In contrast, in WC-U and BWP-U, just 8% and 0% of T9's cognitive scaffolding consisted of reading aloud. Again, though, the difference likely stems from the absence of draft papers from which she could read in her conferences with unfamiliar student writers.

As we noted in Chapter 6, when tutors use the reading-aloud strategy, they provide another mode of input—the aural mode—and give student writers opportunities to hear their words and punctuation as a reader would understand them. Thus, this strategy appears to have real pedagogical benefits. However, if tutors repeatedly combine the reading-aloud strategy with telling or suggesting, they can run into the pedagogical problem of "fixing" the paper on a sentence-by-sentence basis, effectively taking ownership of the paper to make it "correct." The excerpt below ratifies concerns about tutors' use of such combinations:

T9: [Reading.] "Coca-Cola offers a variety of distribution channels, including, colon, vending machines, various supermarkets, and department stores." I don't know if I would say "various."

S12: O.K.

T9: But "supermarkets and department stores."

S12: O.K.

T9: And then you would start like a regular sentence. O.K. And I like this a lot. I like that you've expanded here. I think that's very good.

In this excerpt, T9 read S12's paper aloud; however, she moved from this reading-aloud strategy right to a suggestion about word choice (a suggestion to delete the word "various"). Thus, although she had focused S12's attention on the passage in question with her reading-aloud strategy, she bypassed S12's potential input on the problem she perceived.

However, as we pointed out in Chapter 6, tutors who use the reading-aloud strategy to focus student writers' attention on a particular passage and then refrain from telling or suggesting a solution—letting the student writer articulate a response—open up the possibility of scaffolding work to take place and take hold. In fact, one characteristic of T9's use of reading aloud was its ability to set off something akin to an elaborated IRF sequence (Mehan 1979). In such sequences, student writers responded in one of two ways: (1) with a question stemming from the passage just read—an inquiry aimed at determining the problem in the passage that led T9 to read it out loud or (2) with a correction to an element of the passage—its syntax, word choice, or some punctuation. The excerpt below with S11 shows these first two steps, initiation and response, and exemplifies a student writer's use of a question to respond to the passage read aloud:

T9: "John McCain has strong visions in securing US borders but is completely against same-sex marriages. Though Hillary Clinton and Barack Obama have nearly identical stances on immigration and same-sex marriage, Hillary is less welcome to im—welcoming to immigrants. The deciding factor between these two [Democratic candidates—"
S11:   [Should I put that in there?

In the third step, T9 expanded on S11's response. In the case of the sequence excerpted below, T9 responded to S11's question with an answer to S11's question and a (rather vague) suggestion to reword the sentence. To this advice, S11 responded again, acknowledging and accepting T9's advice. (Some of S11's brief response was lost in noise close to the microphone.)

T9: Yeah, I think. I don't know if less welcoming to immigrants, but that same idea. Maybe find a way to reword it. Um—
S11: O.K. I'm [unclear]
T9: But yeah, I think it sounds, sounds fine.

As in the last step, T9 evaluated the student writer's response about rewording the sentence. Sequences such as the one excerpted here appear to do some of the same work as the IRF sequence: they push student writers to think about their papers and to contribute (if only minimally) to the conference conversation.

In summary, what the WC-U and the BWP-U conferences had in common were T9's more frequent use of demonstrations of concern—a strategy that makes sense in relation to working with unfamiliar student writers. T9 did not know the habits of the unfamiliar student writers—how much they would advocate for themselves and speak up when they did not understand. Thus, she checked on their comprehension. WC-F and BWP-F had in common T9's use of the reading-aloud strategy. We found the reading-aloud strategy and the pattern described above in T9's conferences with familiar student writers, but these often appeared to have more to do with the agenda of the conference—revising an existing draft paper—than they did with the relationship between the tutor and the student writer. T9 could use the strategy or construct such a sequence when the student writer had an existing draft.

Conclusions and Implications for Tutor (and Fellow) Training

In this chapter, we compared the strategies that one tutor, T9, used in the writing center and in the BWP when she worked with familiar student writers and unfamiliar student writers. We found several differences in the frequencies and types of the strategies that she used. Based on our results and analysis, we offer some suggestions for writing center directors and WID administrators to consider as they plan and carry out their tutor and writing fellow training.

We found that T9 employed more shows of concern in conferences with unfamiliar student writers. Specifically, she followed up on her advice—her telling and suggesting—with questions aimed at checking the student writer's comprehension. Such attention to ensuring the student writer's well-being seems appropriate when a writing center tutor or writing fellow lacks familiarity with a student writer and, specifically, the extent of his or her willingness to interject comments or ask questions. However, showing concern, we think, is also appropriate in situations in which student writers are likely to feel anxiety about genres and writing tasks that are new to them. For this reason, we suggest that writing center directors and WID administrators encourage tutors and writing fellows to employ this strategy, even with student writers with whom they have worked previously.

Although this study of T9's conferences showed that she used the reading-aloud strategy more often in her conferences with familiar students, as we mentioned before, we think this result likely had more to do with the stage of the student writers' papers in the WC-F and BWP-F conferences, as opposed to the relationship that T9 had developed with the student writers in those conferences. To isolate and test the effects of familiarity, researchers might compare the talk of tutors and student writers who are familiar with each other as they work in conferences focused on brainstorming or planning with the talk of the same tutors and student writers working in conferences focused on revising and proofreading. Such an analysis would better indicate the extent of familiarity's role in a tutor's choice to read aloud, because it would keep familiarity constant but vary the stage of development of student writers' papers. It would also control for variables such as age and education. In addition, it may be the case that working together several times, gaining familiarity and building rapport, generates more (motivational) joking or more (instructional) directness. Further research might chart differences in the strategies that writing center tutors and writing fellows should employ as they construct relationships with student writers across the course of the semester or even the academic year.

As noted previously, the reading-aloud strategy can keep the conference talk focused on local-level issues as opposed to global-level ones such as organization, support, coherence, as well as other concerns that are not readily assessed when reading a paper sentence by sentence. However, this strategy allows the writing center tutor or writing fellow to focus the student writer's attention on particular sections of his or her draft. Such focus—particularly during proofreading—is both instructional and warranted. When writing center tutors or writing fellows notice an error while reading aloud, they should stop and follow up by sitting silently to allow the student writer to find the error or by asking a pumping question. If the student writer cannot find the error, then tutors can move to more constraining forms of cognitive scaffolding. When a paper is due very soon, and time for scaffolding is not available, writing center tutors or writing fellows may have to decide between providing answers (telling) or allowing the students to leave without having their questions answered.

Also in relation to the reading-aloud strategy, future research should investigate potential differences between student writers' ability to identify problems—local-level ones or not—when they read their own papers out loud versus when their writing center tutor or writing fellow does the reading. We encountered no research investigating these two methods, although many studies have investigated potential differences in comprehension between reading aloud and reading silently (for example, Prior et al. 2011). Results from such research would help writing center directors and WID program administrators to determine conference best practices for tutor and fellow training.

T9's heavy use of explaining in the BWP-U conference indicates that WID program directors should ensure writing fellows have sufficient time to explain the assignments and genres of the classes to which they have been assigned. Devoting class time to writing assignments is important, as is ensuring that writing fellows meet with each student for some sort of planning conference. Because T9 and S12 had a planning conference as one of three conferences during the semester, T9 had time to explain the white paper—a disciplinary writing assignment that challenged the students in the purchasing class.

T9's use of demonstrating in the BWP indicates that the strategy is more readily available to writing center tutors than our earlier analysis of the 10 conferences shows. T9's use of demonstrating strategies in the BWP conferences suggests that writing center directors and program administrators might encourage writing center tutors and writing fellows to use visuals, particularly pictures and gesturing, to supplement their verbal input. As previously stated, by adding on another input mode, demonstrating takes advantage of student writers' cognitive capacity for simultaneously processing visual information that accompanies verbal information (although other modes of information processing certainly are possible, including olfactory or tactile). Indeed, in her microanalysis of one writing center conference, Thompson (2009) goes so far as to say about gestures: "Referring to these physical expressions in terms of their relationship to verbal expressions—nonverbal—may inappropriately subordinate the influence they have on scaffolding in particular and on communication in general" (445). We might move away from the idea that other modes of information input, including from the visual mode, operate solely in relation to verbal input. As Thompson (2009) shows in far more detail, such modes contribute substantially to tutor–student communication in themselves. If writing center tutors and writing fellows overlook the potential of the demonstrating strategy to employ two modes of information input, they may be overlooking a good way to facilitate student writers' comprehension and recall. One way to facilitate tutors' and writing fellows' use of this strategy is to make computers available for all conferences. Doing so might allow writing center tutors to more readily incorporate more gestures and pictures in their work with students.

Another difference between T9's use of strategies in the writing center and in the BWP, particularly in terms of her use of cognitive scaffolding, was the greater frequency with which she used the responding-as-a-reader-or-a-listener strategy in the writing center conferences. In WC-U, T9 used the strategy mainly to paraphrase S9's oral summaries of the myth and the meager notes and outline. With such paraphrasing, T9 ensured that she understood what S9 was trying to convey about her topic. In WC-F, T9 paraphrased S11's source documents, helping her to interpret them. T9's more frequent use of the responding-as-a-reader-or-a-listener strategy in the writing center conferences likely had much to do with the difference in her conferencing responsibilities in the writing center versus in the BWP. At the beginning of writing center conferences, T9 needed to make sure that she understood the assignments and individual instructors' intentions for those assignments—even though she knew the genres required in FYC and WL courses. Indeed, she often was familiar with the texts that student writers analyzed. Reading the assignment handout aloud and responding as a reader or listener allowed T9 to ensure common ground. In contrast, as a writing fellow who participated in the assignment's design, T9 could from the outset be more certain that she shared that common ground with the student writer. Therefore, she did not need to use the responding-as-a-reader-or-a-listener strategy as often. Beyond its value as a method for ensuring common understanding, though, this strategy allows tutors and fellows to show that they are listening to—attending to—student writers. Thus, writing fellows, like writing center tutors, should employ this strategy, even if they are very familiar with the assignment content and genre.

The tutoring strategies that writing fellows use are likely to differ from those that writing center tutors use because writing fellows have more direct access to the student's instructor and are more familiar with the assignments. Indeed, as they work with a particular course, they become increasingly familiar with the course's subject matter—not just the genres and writing practices of the discipline. T9, for example, felt that she understood quite a lot about purchasing and supply chain management, and the other writing fellows who worked with business students made similar comments about their own course content. In fact, most of the BWP writing fellows mentioned that students sometimes asked them questions about course content other than that related to the writing assignments. Thus, a writing fellow's intermediary role—one in gray space between instructor and student writer—makes a difference. For this reason, the field needs far more research on the talk between writing fellows and student writers (and writing fellows and instructors, for that matter), particularly now that WID programs using writing fellows have become quite common.

9

TALK ABOUT WRITING

A Conclusion to Our Empirical Study

- Goal for *TAW* #1: Creating a Coding Scheme that Is Useful to Others
- Goal for *TAW* #2: Analyzing Tutor Talk in order to Facilitate Tutor Training
- Analysis at the Macrolevel: Conference Stages
- Analysis at the Microlevel: Tutoring Strategies
- Future Research on Talk about Writing
- The Last Words

In Chapter 1, we said that we have two main goals for *TAW*: (1) to present an analytical research and assessment tool that others outside our locality can use, and (2) to closely and empirically analyze experienced tutor talk for results that can facilitate tutor training. In this chapter, we discuss our findings in relation to these two goals. We conclude by discussing some ideas for future research on talk about writing.

Goal for *TAW* #1: Creating a Coding Scheme that Is Useful to Others

In relation to the first goal, we set out to develop and validate a framework for coding and classifying tutoring strategies that other writing researchers can modify and use in their own research on conferences between tutors and student writers or, really, any one-to-one pedagogical interaction about writing, such as the conferences between writing fellows and students writing in their disciplines, between tutors and writers in community writing centers and career centers, and even between editors and technical writers and subject-matter experts. Such researchers will not need to fall back on a coding scheme developed for tutoring in some other domain, such as algebra. They will have a sound starting point for their own studies of talk about writing.

However, writing researchers will likely want to and need to modify the scheme that we used in our study for their own work. We noted some possibilities in other chapters. For example, in chapter 3, we said that researchers particularly interested in tutors' (and perhaps student writers') humor would likely benefit from splitting our single code for humor and optimism into two codes. Similarly, we can easily see how researchers might want to separate explaining from exemplifying (very rare in our study). In addition, writing researchers who are particularly interested in hints (nonconventional indirectness, or vagueness) might attempt to break down this strategy type further in an attempt to identify hints with more ease. As we (and others) have found, hints are by definition difficult to identify because their expressed form (their locution) differs from their under-lying intended meaning (their illocution). Identifying them according to those with an unexpressed agent or patient or action might ameliorate this coding challenge. These are just a few potential changes that come to mind. As we sub-stantially modified Cromley and Azevedo's (2005) coding scheme to suit our research questions, so too might future writing researchers modify our scheme to suit their own.

Modifying an existing coding scheme rather than formulating one from scratch saves effort and time and provides a strong foundation in existing theory and research. Such modification, however, makes direct comparisons with prior work impossible. Because we modified Cromley and Azevedo's (2005) scheme sub-stantially, we cannot directly compare our results with results from their study of literacy tutoring or with results from prior work on math tutoring (Putnam 1987), physics tutoring (Chi 1996), and computer software tutoring (Lehman et al. 2008). Throughout *TAW*, we have tried instead simply to juxtapose our results with results from other studies when such an effort seemed useful.

However, in grappling with this issue, we have come to the conclusion that writing researchers, as well as researchers working in other domains, might reconsider the open- and closed-world domain bifurcation. Instead of thinking in terms of these two domain categories, they might think about the subject matter of tutoring on a spectrum of closed to open. Although we discussed writing as an open-world domain throughout *TAW*, we saw that, at times, the domain of writing took on characteristics commonly associated with closed-world domains, most notably when tutors and student writers discussed topics for which single, objective answers were indeed available (such as cases in which the topic episode focused on punctuation). Similarly, problem solving in closed-world domain disciplines—at least in their higher-order applications—does not necessarily lead down a path toward a single, objectively correct answer. We suggest, then, that it might be time to rethink open- and closed-world domains, perhaps applying those terms more specifically to topic episodes within the teaching stage, as opposed to entire conferences.

In addition to developing a coding scheme that facilitates future writing studies research, we wanted to develop a scheme that writing center directors could use for assessment. Directors who record and transcribe conferences can use our coding scheme (or a modified version of it) to analyze tutors' talk systematically. With the scheme, directors can assess the extent to which a tutor, across different conferences, employs strategies in ways that adhere to best (research-driven) practices and manifest the center's values. For example, they could determine whether tutors use instruction strategies with similar frequency when they converse with female as opposed to male student writers or when tutors converse with student writers whose cultural or ethnic backgrounds differ from their own. They could determine whether tutors use specific, nonformulaic praise as opposed to formulaic praise and whether they use that praise when it is truly deserved. They could determine whether tutors use sufficient cognitive scaffolding strategies to generate student writers' active participation—a possible way, according to Babcock and Thonus (2012), to operationalize "meaningful interaction" and measure conference "success" (154–56).

They could also determine whether tutors, as they gain experience, employ strategies more effectively. For example, they could see whether experienced tutors—countering the mandate against directiveness—move from cognitive scaffolding pump questions to instruction when student writers show confusion or frustration. A director analyzing the excerpt below might advise T6 (in future, similar situations) to move to instruction rather than pose additional pump questions:

T6: O.K. So what do we think about this here?
S6: Well, I just wanted that to be, really, one sentence. Like a list. So—
T6: O.K. All right. So, I mean, what is it that we have here right now?
S6: I guess these are—these could be separate things. Just separate sentences.
T6: Yeah, and—They could, right? Um, you do have this "and" here, which successfully combines those two. But what about this third one?
S6: Mm-hmm. I guess I could, well, could I omit that?
T6: Yeah, and that, that would make it correct. Yeah.

T6 began with a fairly vague pump question, "So what do we think about this here?" but realized that S6 did not understand what he had asked, and so he rephrased the question to home in on the problem: "What is it we have here right now?" But this pump question was just as vague, and S6 did not know how to respond. Nevertheless, she guessed at an answer, building on what the two had discussed previously. In his question's third iteration, T6 got more specific, providing feedback on S6's guess and zeroing in on what he had been trying to ask: "Um, you do have this 'and' here, which successfully combines the two, but what about the third one?" After this third question, S6 finally provided an acceptable answer. A director analyzing such an excerpt would likely advise the tutor to move to instruction when the time and effort involved in getting the student writer to conjure a correct or acceptable answer is no longer worthwhile or is generating frustration. Instruction might also have avoided the confusion generated by T6's unclear pumps.

We realize that writing center directors, particularly those deep in the task of carrying out assessment, do not have the time or resources to scrutinize conference transcript after conference transcript. However, they could periodically analyze tutors' talk to assess individual competency and improvement. Indeed, toward formative assessment, they might ask tutors to analyze their own use of tutoring strategies across the three conference stages and then compare the conclusions that they reach. Directors might also use the scheme to assess the performance of the writing center staff as a whole, particularly in conjunction with other assessment measures such as conference satisfaction surveys. In short, no writing center director wants to police her or his staff, but systematic discourse analysis can support fair assessment and tutoring practices.

Goal for *TAW* #2: Analyzing Tutor Talk in order to Facilitate Tutor Training

In relation to the latter goal, to closely and empirically analyze experienced tutor talk for results that can facilitate tutor training, we have carried out a variety of analyses at the macro- and the microlevel. Besides examining the three categories of tutoring strategies separately, we also examined the tutoring strategies that one tutor—working as a writing center tutor and working as a writing fellow—used with familiar and unfamiliar student writers.

Analysis at the Macrolevel: Conference Stages

In *TAW*, we analyzed tutoring strategies at the macrolevel within three distinct phases: the opening stage, the teaching stage, and the closing stage.

The opening stage presented tutors with their main opportunity to determine what student writers wanted to accomplish, what the final product should be, and where student writers were in the composing process. Equally important, tutors also worked to develop rapport with students. Therefore, in the opening stages of conferences, tutors sometimes used motivational scaffolding strategies, but instruction and cognitive scaffolding strategies did not occur and seem unlikely to occur in the opening stages of first-time meetings, such as in our 10 writing center conferences.

The main pedagogical work occurred during the teaching stage. During this stage, the tutor and the student writer linked topic episode to topic episode in a chain of pedagogical discourse. We found that tutors launched topic episodes, beginning with an instruction strategy or a motivational scaffolding strategy, and initiated topic episodes, beginning with a cognitive scaffolding strategy, five times as often as student writers—a ratio that indicates tutors' roles as experts in writing, as conference managers, and as conversation facilitators. It also shows that tutors typically determined the progression of the conference through controlling the topics discussed. We found diversity in the chains of topic episodes across the conferences' teaching stages. Some tutor–student pairs moved steadily and directly through topics; other chains were circular and less direct, moving from the global level to the sentence level and back.

During the closing stage, tutors helped student writers summarize what they had discussed during the conference and set goals for what the student writer should try to accomplish postconference. Along with occasional uses of instruction and cognitive scaffolding, tutors frequently used the motivational scaffolding strategy of demonstrating concern to confirm that student writers had met their goals and to check on whether student writers had other issues to discuss. Their demonstrations of concern usually took the form of yes/no questions, such as "Is there anything else I can help you with?"

Analysis at the Microlevel: Tutoring Strategies

In *TAW*, we analyzed three categories of tutoring strategies at the microlevel, using both quantitative and qualitative analysis.

Instruction Strategies

One of our most important findings about instruction strategies is that, even when they are direct, they can do positive-politeness work. When tutors used bald-on-record or other direct telling strategies to respond to student writers, they showed interest in and engagement with what student writers had said. Their direct instruction indicated excitement about and urgency in responding. This finding about telling's positive-politeness work supports what researchers in cross-cultural politeness have noted. Their findings have complicated Brown and Levinson's (1987) idea of universal politeness; specifically, their findings have called into question the useful though tenuous claim that a direct, linear relationship exists between politeness and indirectness and between clarity and directness. Discussing politeness and clarity and indirectness and directness in these terms can usefully simplify matters to be sure. However, cross-cultural research suggests that the story is far more complex.

As Yu (2011) points out, people perceive politeness quite differently across different cultures; for example, unmitigated directives can be polite in Turkish (Marti 2006), Japanese (Matsumoto 1988), and Korean (Yu 2004). Comparing request strategies in Korean, Hebrew, and English, Yu (2011) found that, in Korean, indirectness in requests did not correlate with politeness. More relevant to our finding that tutors' telling strategies showed attentiveness and thus did positive-politeness work, Yu (2011) found that, in Korean, people perceived direct strategies such as want statements (for example, "I want you to do X") as polite. We certainly agree with Yu (2011) and other researchers who examine politeness from a cross-cultural perspective that such contrastive analysis can increase "appropriate and effective communicative understanding by nonnative speakers in a second language teaching and learning context" (406), including the context of a writing center conference.

A second important finding about instruction was that only two tutors, T1 and T8, ensured that student writers had explicitly stated goals to follow when the conference ended. T8 used a combination of instruction and cognitive scaffolding in directing this goal setting, but T1 primarily used cognitive scaffolding to compel S1 to analyze what had been discussed and to prioritize future tasks. T1's use of a pump question ("What would you say is the main thing you're going to work on when you go home?") seemed particularly effective as a way to begin a conference closing. Such a pump question at the conference's closing requires student writers to review and prioritize the conference's topics, and tutors can help student writers through this process. This way, tutors not only help student writers to generate a list of tasks to carry out postconference, but also guide them through a meta-analysis task relating to self-regulation.

This finding about conference closings points to a need for further research to answer the question: To what extent do student writers revise in response to the conference talk, including the type and frequency of tutoring strategies that the tutor used? As Borg and Dean (2011) point out, "Teaching one-to-one is a costly approach and, in the current financial climate, it is crucial to evidence the benefits of this provision for managers and other stakeholders" (320). Besides administrative and political benefits, analyzing student writers' papers to determine the extent to which they implement tutors' advice and incorporate other conference talk would shed light on a potential component of one-to-one tutoring's efficacy and thus one potential component of conference success. As Williams (2004) points out, "Although one cannot directly extrapolate from short-term draft-to-draft change to long-term development, in the absence of demonstrated short-term revision, long-term improvement seems unlikely" (174). Short-term gains are likely necessary—but not sufficient—for long-term gains in writing ability.

Few researchers have attempted to analyze changes in student writers' papers from one version to another. Those who have studied revision have tended to use Faigley and Witte's (1981) method, which differentiates between meaning-preserving and meaning-changing revisions. Borg and Dean (2011) describe another method for assessing student writers' texts: a five-step analysis of the following: (1) fulfillment of the assignment, (2) effective information structure, or "flow," (3) effective thematic organization of sentences, (4) appropriate vocabulary, or register, and (5) lack of proofreading errors. Analyzing student writers' papers consumes substantial time, but efforts to quantify changes in student writers' papers will lend even more credibility to writing centers' work and, more important, will reveal gains (or, potentially, losses) in one component of conference success.

We also found that tutors explained just 16% of their telling and suggesting strategies. We posited in Chapter 5 that more tutor explanations might help student writers understand the "why" behind tutors' advice, as opposed to just the "how" of implementing that advice. However, in positing this view, we also recognized that explaining consumes time, and so tutors trying to explain a bit more would need to be judicious in choosing advice deserving of explanation. A further problem with explanations relates to student writers' resistance. Student writers often appear uninterested and even impatient with the "why," because they can make necessary revisions knowing only the "how." Our study does not supply solutions to these challenges, but further research on tutors' instruction might investigate a potential correlation between explanation length and student writers' satisfaction with those explanations, as well as their conferences as a whole.

More important, perhaps, is the need to train writing center tutors to help student writers generate explanations for themselves. Discussing what they call the S-hypothesis (the student-centered constructive hypothesis), Chi et al. (2001) note that the efficacy of certain tutor moves could stem from their ability to "promote constructive and effortful responses from the student" (477). Tutor discourse moves (such as tutoring strategies) gain efficacy from their capacity to get students to participate actively. As mentioned in Chapter 2, in one study, Chi et al. (2001), for example, asked tutors to suppress explanations as well as feedback in order to prompt student explanations instead. The students learned as much without tutor-provided explanations and feedback. The more interactive style of tutoring, they found, had three potential benefits: it appeared to motivate students more; it appeared to increase the accuracy with which tutors assessed students' comprehension, and it appeared to improve students' transfer of knowledge (517). So, it seems that, although more tutor explanations might facilitate students' understanding, pumping student writers for explanations is probably an even better strategy.

Cognitive Scaffolding Strategies

One of our main findings related to cognitive scaffolding strategies was that pumping strategies are especially critical to writing center tutoring, helping tutors guide student writers' thinking and soliciting responses (and thus more active participation) from them. This finding about the critical role that pumping strategies play corresponds with the previously mentioned S-hypothesis that Chi et al. (2001) explain when discussing their findings. They say that prompts that get students to "generate their own corrections" and leading questions, such as requests for explanations, are instances of "indirect tutoring" that "are consistent with the hypothesis that these tactics give students more opportunities to construct knowledge" (478). And, as we noted in Chapter 6, when student writers run into trouble coming up with an answer to a minimally constraining pump question, tutors could help end the impasse by switching to a more constraining pump or some other more constraining cognitive scaffold. Thus, during tutor training, writing center directors might show examples of experienced tutors starting with a minimally constraining pump question ("How might you limit the thesis claim?") and then shifting to another strategy (such as the forced-choice strategy) or a more constraining pump ("Do you want to argue that the library needs more quiet spaces?") to facilitate a response.

Writing center specialists might question the efficacy of sentence-by-sentence reading aloud. To the extent that tutors' reading aloud leads them to focus on sentence-level proofreading, especially when other, more global-level concerns need attention, directors have been wary of having tutors read student writers' papers, asking instead that tutors request that students read their own papers aloud. However, that method leaves open the possibility that student writers will devote their cognitive capacity to the task of reading aloud (focusing on correct pronunciation, for example) as opposed to analyzing their writing. We found, however, that tutors' use of the reading-aloud strategy has the potential to focus student writers' attention and make use of the aural mode, but we acknowledge that the field needs more research on this topic. Although Adams (2009) initiated research on reading aloud in writing center conferences, studying tutors' and student writers' preferences for who read aloud and when tutors made comments (throughout versus at the end), no study that we know has examined student writers' capacity to find errors or to evaluate and revise their own writing based on their own or tutors' reading of their paper aloud. Research in this area would be of great benefit.

In Chapter 6, we recommended that writing center directors might train tutors to employ the responding-as-a-reader-or-listener strategy so that tutors restate student writers' written and oral contributions. We also pointed out that honing this strategy would likely benefit tutors when they enter interviews and other professional discourse situations. Numerous business communication practitioners mention the benefits of paraphrasing to keep meetings on track and to show active listening during meetings and other workplace interactions (for example, The Meetings Expert 2013). Some tutoring strategies, then, benefit tutors as well as student writers.

Motivational Scaffolding Strategies

We found that tutors' motivational scaffolding, consisting mainly of demonstrations of concern and praise, followed semantic and syntactic formulae. In fact, these formulae—because they are less cognitively taxing to produce than nonformulaic strategies—are likely what allowed tutors to use these two motivational scaffolding strategies far more often than they did the other three types of motivational scaffolds. As we pointed out in Chapter 7, the distinction between formulaic and nonformulaic matters because people are more likely to interpret formulaic expressions holistically as opposed to as the sum of their parts. When people process formulae this way, the social function of the formulae dominates their meaning, and their referential meaning recedes (Kecskés 2000, 606). Tutors peppered their conferences with formulaic versions of demonstrations of concern and praise. Given these findings, we think future writing center research might examine the extent to which the formulaicity of tutors' motivational scaffolds influences student writers' motivation. Put another way, to what extent, if any, do motivational scaffolding strategies need to consist of novel language in order to generate and maintain student writers' motivation?

Working as a Tutor versus Working as a Fellow: A Case Study

In Chapter 8, we presented our findings from a case study of one person's (T9's) work as a writing center tutor and as a writing fellow in a business communication WID program, the BWP. Our goal was to compare her use of tutoring strategies in the two settings and also to compare her use of strategies in her conferences with unfamiliar student writers versus conferences with familiar student writers. In relation to the latter, we found that T9 employed more shows of concern in conferences with unfamiliar student writers. Specifically, she followed up on her advice—her telling and suggesting—with questions aimed at checking the student writer's comprehension. Future longitudinal research could test this finding to determine whether, with experienced tutors, such demonstrations of concern are typical.

We also found that T9 used the reading-aloud strategy more often in her conferences with familiar students, but we postulated that this result likely stemmed from the more advanced stage of the papers in T9's conferences with familiar students. As we mentioned in Chapter 8, future research might compare the talk of tutors and student writers who are familiar with each other as they work in conferences focused on brainstorming or planning with the talk of the same tutors and student writers working in conferences focused on revising and proofreading.

Indeed, we see this case study as a starting point for future research (beyond Bell, Arnold, and Haddock's [2009] study of two tutor–student writer duos over six months) on the effect an ongoing relationship between a tutor and a student writer plays in the talk that develops. Besides studies accounting for the critical variables of age, culture, subject-matter expertise, and writing ability, among others, future research should include longitudinal study of tutor–student writer pairs to see how tutoring strategies (and discourse in general, including student writers' talk) changes over time. Perhaps more important, we see it as a starting point for research on writing fellows' work with student writers as they develop writing in a variety of disciplines, including, but not limited to, the disciplines covered in the business course we studied.

Writing fellows—more so than writing center tutors—operate in what Gladstein (2008) calls a "gray space," as they work with an instructor and a program director yet build and maintain relationships with student writers (Gladstein 2008, para. 3). This intermediary role raises questions for future research: How do variables within writing fellows' tutoring situations affect the strategies that they use? For example, does the degree to which fellows work autonomously from the instructor or the extent to which fellows play a role in developing the course's writing assignments influence the frequency and types of strategies that they use? Does the size of the class, which impacts the amount of one-to-one time student writers get from fellows, play a role? Future research on writing fellows' use of tutoring strategies should certainly examine a larger data set (certainly more than one tutor) over a longer period of time (certainly more than one semester).

With each semester of WID work, writing fellows gain disciplinary subject-matter knowledge, and this growing expertise raises other questions for future research on writing fellows' talk: how does that increased knowledge about the subject affect tutors' choice of strategies? Does their additional expertise generate more telling as opposed to suggesting? Does it generate a higher percentage of cognitive scaffolding strategies, such as demonstrating or forced choice? Does it generate more (positive) evaluation via praise? Future research might address these and other questions about the relationship between writing fellows' knowledge of specific domains and the tutoring strategies that they use.

Future Research on Talk about Writing

Here in Chapter 9 and elsewhere in *TAW*, we have pointed to opportunities for future research that might extend the empirical research that we report here. In this section, we outline several other potential paths of research that we see as important, but that we have not yet addressed in *TAW*.

First, except in discussions of topic episodes and question types, we have not examined student writers' contributions to the conference talk. Future studies might examine, for example, the extent to which student writers introduce topic episodes, the ways that they ask and answer questions, and their volubility in response to tutors' strategies. In any case, future research on writing center talk should more carefully examine the reciprocal nature of tutoring interactions.

Also, we have not examined the quality of student writers' revisions. Measurement of outcomes in student writers' papers after conferencing with tutors is not only vastly complex but also theoretically questionable. North (1984) famously stated that the purpose of writing center tutoring is to "produce better writers, not better writing" (438). Leahy (1990) concurs, stating that the point of writing center tutoring is "not so much to produce a good single piece of writing as to give the writer confidence and strategies to keep growing and improving" (47). Resistance to the idea of measuring tangible outcomes in student writers' texts, then, has stemmed from a fundamental theoretical assumption about the purpose of writing center tutoring. In addition to pushback against writing-outcomes measurements is the problem of validly measuring gains through "the two most straightforward means" of study design: "comparison between 'experimental' and 'control' groups or pre-intervention/post-intervention" (Jones 2001, 8). Williams (2004) articulates some of the questions that arise in relation to these complexities:

> With the decision to analyze written products comes the vexing issue of measurement. What is the best way to express how and how much a text has been revised? How do we differentiate among the effects of revision? How can we measure the extent to which revision has resulted in improvement in the quality of the text? (175).

Despite the problems associated with measuring improvements in student writers' texts, such analysis is possible if researchers select and justify their criteria for evaluation and do what they can to control for instruction occurring outside the writing center. With a greater emphasis on program assessment and an increased need to justify funding, writing center directors may have little choice but to measure gains across student writers' papers.

Third, writing centers and writing fellows programs have spread far outside North America, but our study examines the tutor talk that occurred in one writing center and one writing fellows program situated in one university in the United States. We have not examined writing centers outside North America, as some other researchers have. Chang (2013), for example, describes the development of writing centers in Asia, focusing on Taiwan. Tan (2011) examines writing center developments in Hong Kong, Korea, Japan, and Singapore, as well as European efforts in Thessaloniki, Greece, and Paris, France. Cain (2011) describes her experience working in a writing center in Belfast, Northern Ireland, for a year before returning to the United States. Ronesi (2009), in an article describing her work training students to work as writing tutors and writing fellows at the American University of Sharjah in the United Arab Emirates, points out that, even as the move toward peer tutoring spreads overseas from North America, trainers of peer tutors face the challenge of developing training that suits "the unique local needs" of "contexts outside North America" (75–76). These researchers—in describing their own experiences in developing and working in writing centers in locales across the globe—have begun the much-needed broader analysis of the state of writing centers. However, their work is just a drop in the bucket. As the number of writing centers outside North America increases, so too does the need for writing center scholarship to keep pace.

The Last Words

Writing center scholars such as Pemberton (2010) and composition scholars such as Haswell (2005) have issued a call for more empirical, particularly quantitative, writing studies research that others can replicate and extend. Here, we have provided a single response to Pemberton's and Haswell's calls. In addition, and perhaps more important, *TAW* provides a framework—a coding scheme—that can facilitate the work of other writing researchers. We look forward to such research and the better understanding about talk about writing that it will bring.

APPENDIX A

Conducting a Conference with a Student

From the Auburn University English Department's (2008) "Reference Guide for English Center Consultants" (24–25)

These instructions are guidelines only. You should develop a conferencing procedure that feels comfortable to you.

1. Greet the student at the door and ask him to fill out the online "English Center Conference Report Form" at one of the computers. Pick up a copy of "Notes for Students." You may need to get up and meet him at the door and lead him to the computer and help him fill out the online form. Ask the student if he has an appointment.
2. Read the student's form. What does she want help with?
3. Set an agenda for the session. Write down the time you begin the session.
4. Ask the student what he wants help with. (This may or may not be the same as what the student has typed on his form.) If a referral form is sent, what does the teacher want you to help the student with? If there are several issues to be covered, prioritize them, especially if the English Center is busy. Use "Working the Writing Process" and "Hierarchy of Grammar and Usage Problems" on the following pages as guides for setting an agenda. Write down the session agenda on a "Notes for Students" form for you and the student to follow. Notify the student of the time constraints on sessions if the English Center is busy.
4a. If a student brings in a draft, ask, "Has your teacher read this paper?" If the teacher has read the paper, these are some possible follow-up questions. What you ask depends on what the student has requested and on your perception of the requirements of the student's assignment.
    - What did your teacher say?
    - What does the assignment sheet say?
    - What questions do you have?

- Where in your paper would you like to work today?
- What is your plan for completing the assignment?

If the teacher has not read the paper, these are some follow-up questions:

- What is your assignment? Look carefully at the assignment sheet together, identifying key words that establish the purpose and audience for the essay. Ask the student to underline or highlight the key words.
- What has your teacher told you in class about the essay?
- How does your teacher define "good" writing?
- What has your teacher told you about appropriate topics?
- What has your teacher told you about introductions and thesis statements? (Is the teacher really asking for a standard theme, or does she reward variation? Should the thesis be stated explicitly, or can it be implicit? Where should the thesis statement appear—the introduction?)
- Has your teacher given you any examples of well-written thesis statements?
- What has your teacher told you about style? (Can you use contractions? Can you use "I"? Can you use "you"?)
- What comments has your teacher given you on previous papers?
- What do you want your reader to get out of this paper?

4b. If a student does not have a draft, follow this procedure with variation that seems appropriate for the student and the situation.

- Read the assignment sheet with the student, identifying and defining key words. These words are usually verbs, for example, "compare," "contrast," "describe," and "analyze." (See "Frequently Used Key Words" for definitions. See "Guide to Understanding World Literature Terminology" when the student needs help in understanding assignments in world literature.)
- Ask the student questions about her understanding of the purpose of the assignment. Ask what the teacher may have said in addition to what is on the assignment sheet. (Are there any taboo topics? Are there any prerequisite readings?)
- Ask the student about her ideas for possible topics. If the student has more than one in mind, you can help her to decide which might be more appropriate by suggesting different brainstorming techniques, such as listing or clustering, after which the student will be better able to decide which topic would be better. (See the advice about topic development for ENGL 1100 and 1120 students and for ENGL 2200 and 2210 students in this section.)

5. Follow your plan for the conference, being sure to answer the student's questions before adding any other considerations to the agenda, though you might mention other things as you go along. For example, if a student asks for help with commas but, after reading a bit of the paper, you realize that the essay has no thesis statement, you might say something like, "I know

you want to work on comma usage, but I think we might also want to talk about your thesis statement."

6. End the conference.
    *   Help the student to sum up the progress made in the session. (You might simply recap your original agenda.)
    *   Answer any remaining questions about what the session covered.
    *   If appropriate, give the student a handout from the collection on the wall beside the transaction desk.
    *   Help the student set goals for the rest of his writing process on the particular assignment. Use "Notes for Students" to write down the short-range and long-range goals you and the student set collaboratively. Include target dates that fit within the teacher's due dates for each goal. Summarize what the student needs to do on his own using the front or the back of this form.
    *   Help the student make an appointment for her next session, or encourage her to come in again.
    *   Complete the online "Consultant Report Form." Make sure to be detailed in your account of the session.

APPENDIX B

"Notes for Students" Form and Instructions

From the Auburn University English Department's (2008) "Reference Guide for English Center Consultants" (14–15)

Notes for Students

Date and Time of Consulting Session: _____

Agenda for Session:

Topics Covered in this Conference: (Use the back if necessary.)

Schedule for Completing the Assignment

Remaining tasks for completing the assignment	Due date
FINAL READ THROUGH FOR GRAMMAR	

Goals for Next Appointment

Before your next appointment in the English Department, you should:

Date and Time for Next Appointment: _____

Instructions for Notes for Students

Purpose: to provide written advice for students based on the conference just completed. Although you may not need to use this form for every conference, it may be particularly important when you are discussing topic development and organization and helping students set goals at the beginning of the composing process.

Recipient: the student you have worked with.

Filling in the Form:

1. Record the date and time of the consulting session.
2. Write down the agenda for the session that indicates what you and the student plan to cover in order of importance.
3. At the end of the conference, fill in "Topics Covered in this Conference." This list will provide a summary of the conference for the student.
4. At the end of the conference, fill in both "Goals For Next Appointment" and "Schedule for Completing the Assignment."
   - Beginning with "Schedule for Completing the Assignment," outline the tasks remaining to finish the assignment and assign a date by which each task should be completed.
   - When you have completed the outline of tasks required to finish the assignment, set goals that the student should accomplish before the next English Center appointment. Be sure that these goals are reasonable in light of the remaining tasks and due dates and in light of the student's abilities and past performance as a writer.
5. End the conference by having the student use a computer to sign up for another appointment and write down the date and time for that conference on the line at the bottom of the form.

APPENDIX C

The T5–S5 Conference Coded for Stages, Topic Episodes, and Strategies

TABLE C.1 Codes for Conference Stages, Topic Episodes in Teaching Stages, and Tutoring Strategies

Stages	Code
	OPENING
	TEACHING
	CLOSING

Topic Episode	Code
	TE1, TE2 . . .

Tutoring Strategy	Code
Instruction	
Telling	I3
Suggesting	I1
Explaining and exemplifying	I2
Cognitive Scaffolding	
Pumping	C5
Reading aloud	C7
Responding as a reader or a listener	C8
Referring to a previous topic	C6
Forcing a choice	C2
Prompting	C4
Hinting	C3
Demonstrating	C1
Motivational Scaffolding	
Showing concern	M3
Praising	M1
Reinforcing student writers' ownership and control	M5
Using humor or being optimistic	M2
Giving sympathy or empathy	M4

T5: <OPENING STAGE> O.K. Um, my name is [T5].

S5: [S5].

T5: Good to meet you. O.K. Are we working on brainstorming today?

S5: Uh-huh.

T5: O.K. And this is your assignment sheet?

S5: Yes ma'am.

T5: O.K. I'll just read over this real quick.

S5: O.K.

T5: [20 seconds, reading the assignment sheet silently.] O.K. So today are we working on part one or part two?

S5: Part one, brainstorming of—

T5: O.K. O. K. So you haven't made your video yet [or anything like that?

S5:   [I have not. I have started it, but I haven't.

T5: O.K. All right. [3 seconds]

S5: And then the essay is about the [video so.

T5:   [Yeah. O.K. Alright. And, let's see. This is due—O.K. So you, so you still have some [time to work on this, right?

S5:   [Uh-huh. Uh-huh. Yes.

T5: O.K. [3 seconds] O.K. All right. Um. Oh, that's right. O.K. And um, have you talked to your teacher, um, [at all about what you wanted to do?

S5:   [A little bit. A little. I kind of had a, uh, topic.

T5: Uh-huh.

S5: That I just picked. But he gave me some advice. [That's the topic.

T5:   [Uh-huh.

S5: [Pointing to the paper.] And he said it needed to be more specific that, he really said it wasn't that good.

T5: O.K. So, um, you know, he agreed on the overall thing, he just wanted it more specific?

S5: He did approve it. But maybe more specific of an idea.

T5: O.K. O.K. O.K. Let's see. So right now you're working on, you know, the health issues caused by smoking.

S5: That—those are just some of the first things that popped in my head.

T5: Uh-huh. O.K. [5 seconds] O.K. So you're going to be arguing, you know, that smoking shouldn't be legal now? Is that what you're going to be doing? [O.K.

S5: [Yes. Uh-huh. And the reason he said that, that it wasn't that good, was because in a lot of places smoking is banned, so he said it really didn't apply.

T5: Uh-huh. O.K. O.K. So, um, maybe your argument should be something that could be applied?

S5: Uh-huh.

T5: O.K. That's not already—right?

S5: Yeah.

T5: O.K. O.K. Let's see. O.K. Well, um, I'll just get some of your ideas on it. <OPENING STAGE/><TEACHING STAGE><TE1><C5> Um. Have you really thought about maybe another way, um, we could kind of curb cancer, curb smoking, um other than, you know, banning the smoking? <C5/>

S5: Um, not really. I hadn't thought about that. So you're talking about, there's other ways of getting around?

T5: Uh-huh.

T5: <I1> Well maybe—and you know that that's what we're brainstorming through um. <I1/><TE1/><TE2><I3> So O.K. Um, like, let's talk about where it's being banned. <I3/> You know, um, like, <C5> what are some places that you— <C5/>

S5: There's um, most restaurants. [Sometimes, the band and, [um, I guess at bars

T5:   [Uh-huh.   [Yeah.

S5: but—Just really in public. They can't ban private, so.

T5: <C5>O.K. Is it, um, all over the United States or do you know, is it just [in—

S5: [It's—I <C5/> think it depends on the local—the local, um, government. I don't think there's like a national law that has banned smoking.

T5: O.K. O.K. <M3> Um, so, you know this is mostly local, right? <M3/>

S5: Yeah.

T5: O.K. All right. <TE2/><TE3><C5> Um, are there maybe some places where it's not banned that, you know, it should be? <C5/>

S5: Um, like, family-friendly restaurants, I don't know. Because some restaurants I go to, there is a smoking section and then suddenly there's not a section

T5: Uh-huh.

S5: or maybe just [unclear]. <TE3/><TE4>

T5: Yeah, and those are based on your own observations?

S5: Uh-huh.

T5: O.K. Um, now, this thing. Is this supposed to be, you know, research-based or is it from your own observations?

S5: Um, I think it—I think it's a little bit of both.

T5: Uh-huh.

S5: I'm not sure.

T5: <I1> O.K. O.K. Yeah. Because you're going to be drawing from outside sources [to create images. <I1/>

S5:   [Uh-huh. Like internet stuff, he said, wouldn't [unclear].

T5: Uh-huh. O.K. O.K. <I1>So, um, you know, it seems like you're already on, you know, you said that he approved, <TE4/><TE5> but, um, we just need to make it a little more narrow. So, O.K. so we're on the right track, <I1/><C8> [that, you know, we should stop smoking because it causes

S5:   [Yeah.

T5: cancer. Um, causes emphysema, and passes on the human lungs. <C8/> <TE5/><TE6><I1> O.K. Um, here the mainstream and the Hollywood endorsement of smoking, that—that's kind of different than [you know the

S5:   [Uh-huh.

T5: medical aspects of it. <I1/><C5> Um, did you still want to talk about that? <C5/>

S5: I'm not—I'm not sure [if that's that important with—I see how it doesn't

T5:   [Uh-huh. <I1>Uh-huh. Yeah, it—it doesn't quite

S5: fit in.

T5: fit in. But um, as far as being more narrow, <I1/><C5> um, you know, since um, smoking is already banned in you know, some restaurants, or um, whatever, uh, would you say anything that Hollywood should do as far as smoking? <C5/>

S5: Maybe like in movies that are kid oriented, there shouldn't be any smoking.

T5: O.K. O.K. <I1> Yeah. So. Um, those are good ideas that if you want to, you know, write some of these things down, I would—That's great. Um. O.K. So, um, yeah. Because if uh, smoking is in Hollywood movies then that's going to be like an advertisement [for them too. O.K. So um, was that

S5:   [Yeah.

T5: something, um, <I1/><TE6/><TE7><I1> there's two possible directions we could go here. One is, you know, the medical direction, [where you

S5:   [Uh-huh.

T5: have, you know, causes cancer, emphysema, we have all the side effects. Um, and then here, this is more like a cause. Um, the mainstream and Hollywood endorsement of smoking, you know, that—that's another direction you can take it. <I1/>

S5: Uh-huh.

T5: <C5> So um, which one were you interested more in? <C5/>

S5: That's what I'm having a hard decision with. Like. Picking.

T5: Uh-huh. Uh-huh. <TE7/><TE8><I1> Yeah. Because, um, as far as why is smoking still legal, um, you know, we—we don't really have a, not that I know of anyway, um, any laws that you should have, [um, smoking as a

S5:   [Uh-huh.

T5: [base or whatever. <I1/>

S5: [Yeah. I don't think there are.

T5: <C2> Uh-huh. So, um, do you think that should change or do you think it should stay the way it is? <C2/>

S5: Um, probably since it is such a big advertising thing, that could have a big effect—

T5: Uh-huh. O.K. <TE8/><TE9><I3> So do you think, um, if maybe none of the actors smoked in movies we would kind of lower the [um,

S5:   [Uh-huh.
Probably.

T5: Uh-huh. O.K. O.K. Yeah. And um, especially since this is a visual thing that you are going to be making like a visual movie on this, right? <I3/>

S5: Uh-huh.

T5: <I1> O.K. And especially if we have Hollywood, you can find tons and tons of stuff. <I1/><I2> So, you know, especially, you know, the gangster movies [or um, you know, people in power that could be smoking, or um,

S5:   [Uh-huh.

T5: and you could kind of look at what messages is this giving, you know, is smoking good for you, is it bad? <I2/>

S5: Uh-huh.

T5: <C5> Um, especially if it's an advertisement. What would you think they're really going to say about their product? <C5/>

S5: They want you to buy it, so [unclear]—

T5: Exactly. Uh-huh. Yeah. <I1> So, I mean, we could kind of look at um, what messages Hollywood is telling us [about smoking and whether that should

S5:   [Uh-huh.

T5: change. So, um, if you wanted to kind of, go on this—

S5: I think I like that.

T5: Uh-huh. Uh-huh. Yeah. And I think you could find a lot of [visuals here

S5:   [Uh-huh.

T5: and, um, for your argument rather than "Why is smoking still legal?" you know, you could kind of explore, you know, should this be allowed in Hollywood? Especially with kid-oriented films. So. Because that's when a lot of people start smoking, in their teens. <I1/>

S5: Uh-huh.

T5: Or something kind of—

S5: So [unclear] [Reaches for paper.]

T5: Uh-huh. Yeah. Definitely.

S5: <TE9/><TE10>[Writing and speaking.] [3 seconds] Should smoking be allowed in, um, kid-oriented movies, or just movies?

T5: <M5> That is up to you. Um, what you want to argue. <M5/><I1> You could maybe say movies, especially kid-oriented movies, [or something like that

S5:   [Uh-huh.

T5: just to be more specific. <I1/>

S5: [8 seconds] [S5 writing.] All right.

T5: <TE10/><TE11><I1> Uh-huh. Yeah. Yeah. And um, since you have this in a question, um, you want to make sure to answer that question [in your

S5: [Uh-huh.

T5: paper. You know, yes, it should be allowed or no it should not be allowed. And that should be very clear, especially if this could be your thesis that you're going to argue. <I1/> So, O.K. Um, that seems like, we definitely narrowed it down there. <TE11/><TE12><I3> [Um, what you might want to do,

S5: [Uh-huh.

T5: um, especially since you still have some time to work on this, is maybe run this by your teacher and um, see if it's narrow enough. If you're going along the right track. And kind of just keep your eye out. <TE12/><TE13>Um, maybe do an internet search or Google images or something. <I3/><I1> [Um, like cigarettes in movies you know, who is holding the cigarettes and

S5: [Uh-huh.

T5: what—what kind of message is it giving out to people? Is it good, or is it bad? And um, kind of think about that, and you know, what you might want to talk about in your paper. <I1/>

S5: I'm actually going to him in just a little bit, so he'll be able to tell me if it's better.

T5: Um, now? <TE13/><TEACHING STAGE/><CLOSING><M3> O.K. O.K. O.K. So, um, does this kind of help you? Did you have any more questions or anything like that? <M3/>

S5: It does. That definitely helped me. At least I have something to go with now. [Laughs.]

T5: Yeah, yeah. <M1> And I think, um, you—you actually came up with the idea all by [yourself too, um, which is good. Uh, and it—it kind of stuck

S5: [Uh-huh.

T5: out from everything else. And I think you—you have a more narrow argument now. <M1/>

S5: O.K.

T5: So.

S5: Thank you so much.

T5: Yeah. You're welcome.

S5: O.K.

T5: <I3> Um, and if you uh, if your teacher [O.K.s it and everything, if you

S5: [Uh-huh.

T5: want to kind of come back once you have some images. Or, um, even once you start your paper—

S5: Yeah. I'll probably be back definitely for the paper.

T5: Yeah. Yeah so we kind of look at the organization, make sure we're going on the right track and things like that. <I3/><M3> O.K.? <M3/>

S5: Yeah. Thanks.

<CLOSING STAGE/>

APPENDIX D

Questions Coding Scheme

Taken from Thompson and Mackiewicz (2014)

TABLE D.1 Coding Scheme for Question Types

Question Type	Definition and Examples (T = Tutor; S = Student Writer)
Knowledge deficit (T and S)	Questions **obtaining information that they genuinely do not know**. These questions aim to gain information or request clarification about a topic. • S asks a question to obtain a crucial piece of information and to ensure S's knowledge is correct: "What is a scholarly journal?"; "Is this answer correct?"; "Should I group all the pros together or organize by pro, con, pro, con?" • T asks a question to gain information T does not already know about the topic and to ensure T's knowledge is correct: "What is the name of the company you worked for?"
Common ground (T and S)	T questions **ascertaining what S needs, wants, knows, and understands about an assignment**: • To assess what S knows about writing: "Do you know what a noun is?" • To assess what S knows about the topic of S's writing: "What is the bubonic plague?" • To assess what S knows about the assignment and/or S's stage in the composing process: "Do the articles you've chosen support your position?"; "Has your teacher commented on this draft?" • To understand the assignment: "What did your teacher say are out-of-bounds topics for this paper?" • To understand what S wants to do in the conference (agenda setting): "And your goal is to have a thesis that is making sense, right?"; "So, do you want to go through this end part now?" • To gauge whether S is understanding—nonformulaic: "Do you see where we are going with this argument?"

TABLE D.1 *continued*

Question Type	Definition and Examples (T = Tutor; S = Student Writer)
	• To gauge whether S is understanding—formulaic: "So, you would put a comma here. You know?"; "Do you understand?" S (occasionally) asks common-ground questions to gauge whether T understands.
Social coordination (T and S)	Questions **relating to the actions** of S and T during the conference: • Indirect requests: "Would you read this sentence aloud?" • Indirect advice about improving the composing process: "Why don't you go home, have lunch, and come back later?"; "Why don't you put a check mark next to words you want to change?" • Permission: "Can I come back tomorrow?" • Negotiations: "If I come back tomorrow, will you work with me again?"
Conversation control (T and S)	Questions **relating to the flow of the T–S dialogue and to their attention**: • Greetings and closings: T says, "Hello, how's it going?"; "Have I answered all your questions?" • Gripes: S says, "How am I ever going to get this work done by tomorrow?" • Questions intended to change the flow of the conversation: S says, "My teacher doesn't like me." T replies, "Now how about looking at your thesis statement? Where is it?" • Replies to summons: T says, "Hello, Alice."; S says, "How long can we work together today?" • Rhetorical questions: T says, "What's appropriate business dress? Well, it involves meeting the expectations of colleagues."
Scaffolding and leading (T only)[a]	Questions **leading S to an answer, one that T seems to have already in mind. Often the answer is "yes" or "no."** S is writing a spatial description of the library, starting from the top floor and including each floor. T reads the description and finds that S stops at the second floor. T says, "Do you think you should write about going downstairs?" S answers, "Yes." Questions **pushing S forward in revising or brainstorming. The answer is not "yes" or "no," but T is able to evaluate the appropriateness of S's response**. "What do you think?"; "How might you incorporate examples into this paragraph?"; "How do you argue that people should be informed?" Scaffolding occurs through pumping, prompting, referring to a previous discussion, providing alternatives, responding as a reader or listener, paraphrasing.

a Since the publication of Thompson and Mackiewicz (2014), we have decided to call these questions simply "cognitive-scaffolding questions"

REFERENCES

Adams, Joyce. 2009. "Engaging Students in Writing Labs: An Empirical Study of Reading and Commenting on Student Papers." *International Journal of Education* 1 (1): 1–9.

Agar, Michael. 1985. "Institutional Discourse." *Text* 5 (3): 147–68.

Altenberg, Bengt. 1990. "Recurrent Verb–Complement Constructions in the London-Lund Corpus." In *English Language Corpora: Design, Analysis, and Exploitation*, edited by Jan Aarts, Pieter de Haan, and Nelleke Oostdijk, 227–45. Amsterdam: Rodopi.

Applebee, Arthur N., and Judith A. Langer. 1983. "Instructional Scaffolding: Reading and Writing as Natural Language Activities." *Language Arts* 60 (2): 168–75.

Auburn University English Department. 2008. "Reference Guide for English Center Consultants."

Auerbach, Carl F., and Louise B. Silverstein. 2003. *Qualitative Data: An Introduction to Coding and Analysis*. New York: New York University Press.

Babcock, Rebecca Day, Kellye Manning, and Travis Rogers. 2012. *A Synthesis of Qualitative Studies of Writing Center Tutoring, 1983–2006*. New York: Peter Lang.

———, and Terese Thonus. 2012. *Researching the Writing Center: Towards an Evidence-Based Practice*. New York: Peter Lang.

Baker, Wendy, and Rachel Hansen Bricker. 2010. "The Effects of Direct and Indirect Speech Acts on Native English and ESL Speakers' Perceptions of Teacher Written Feedback." *System* 38 (1): 74–84.

Bandura, Albert. 1986. *Social Foundations of Thought and Action: A Social Cognitive Theory*. Englewood Cliffs, NJ: Prentice-Hall.

———. 1997. *Self-Efficacy: The Exercise of Control*. New York: W. H. Freeman and Company.

Bell, Diana Calhoun, Holly Arnold, and Rebecca Haddock. 2009. "Linguistic Politeness and Peer Tutoring." *Learning Assistance Review* 14 (1): 37–54.

———, and Madeleine Youmans. 2006. "Politeness and Praise: Rhetorical Issues in ESL (L2) Writing Center Conferences." *The Writing Center Journal* 26 (2): 31–47.

Blau, Susan R., John Hall, and Tracy Strauss. 1998. "Exploring the Tutor/Client Conversation: A Linguistic Analysis." *The Writing Center Journal* 19 (1): 19–48.

Block, Rebecca R. 2010. "Reading Aloud in the Writing Center: A Comparative Analysis of Three Tutoring Methods." PhD diss., University of Louisville. ProQuest (3415200).

Blum-Kulka, Shoshana, Juliane House, and Gabriele Kasper. 1989. *Cross-Cultural Pragmatics: Requests and Apologies*. Norwood, NJ: Ablex.

Boquet, Elizabeth H. 1999. "'Our Little Secret': A History of Writing Centers, Pre- to Post-Open Admissions." *College Composition and Communication* 50 (3): 463–82.

Borg, Erik, and Mary Deane. 2011. "Measuring the Outcomes of Individualised Writing Instruction: A Multilayered Approach to Capturing Changes in Students' Texts." *Teaching in Higher Education* 16 (3): 319–31.

Boscolo, Pietro, and Suzanne Hidi. 2007. "The Multiple Meanings of Motivation to Write." In *Writing and Motivation*, edited by Suzanne Hidi and Pietro Boscolo, 1–14. Boston: Elsevier.

Botelho da Silva, Teresa, and Anne Cutler. 1993. "Ill-Formedness and Transformability in Portuguese Idioms." In *Idioms: Processing, Structure, and Interpretation*, edited by Cristina Cacciari and Patrizia Tabossi, 129–43. Hillsdale, NJ: Lawrence Erlbaum.

Bowers, Mary Y., and Marcia A. Metcalf. 2008. "What Employers Want and What Students Need: Integrating Business Communication into Undergraduate and Graduate Business Courses." *Proceedings from the 73rd Annual ABC Convention*. Available: www.business communication.org/CMS/Resources/proceedings/2008annual/02abc2008.pdf.

Boyer, Kristy Elizabeth, Robert Phillips, Michael Wallis, Mladen Vouk, and James Lester. 2008. "Balancing Cognitive and Motivational Scaffolding in Tutorial Dialogue." In *Proceedings of the 9th International Conference on Intelligent Tutoring Systems*, edited by Beverly Woolf, Esma Aimeur, Roger Nkambou, and Susanne Lajoie, 239–49. Berlin: Springer.

Bransford, John D., Ann L. Brown, and Rodney R. Cocking. 2003. *How People Learn: Brain, Mind, Experience, and School*, 2nd ed. Washington, DC: National Academy Press.

Brooks, Jeff. 1991. "Minimalist Tutoring: Making the Student Do All the Work." *Writing Lab Newsletter* 15 (6): 1–4.

Brown, Penelope, and Stephen C. Levinson. 1987. *Politeness: Some Universals in Language Usage*. Cambridge: Cambridge University Press.

Bruffee, Kenneth A. 1978. "Training and Using Peer Tutors." *College English* 40 (4) 432–49.

———. 1984. "Peer Tutoring and the 'Conversation of Mankind.'" *Writing Centers: Theory and Administration*, edited by Gary A. Olson, 3–15. Urbana, IL: National Council of Teachers of English.

Bruner, Jerome. 1962. Introduction to *Thought and Language*, by Lev S. Vygotsky, v–x. Translated and edited by Eugenia Hanfmann, Gertrude Vakar, and Norris Minick. Cambridge: MIT Press.

———. 1963. *The Process of Education*. New York: Vintage.

———. 1986. *Actual Minds: Possible Worlds*. Cambridge, MA: Harvard University Press.

———. 1996. *The Culture of Education*. Cambridge, MA: Harvard University Press.

Bruning, Roger, and Christy Horn. 2000. "Developing Motivation to Write." *Educational Psychologist* 35 (1): 25–37.

Budd, Richard W., Robert K. Thorp, and Lewis Donohew. 1967. *Content Analysis of Communications*. New York: Macmillan.

Butler, Christopher S. 1997. "Repeated Word Combinations in Spoken and Written Text: Some Implications for Functional Grammar." In *A Fund of Ideas: Recent Developments in Functional Grammar*, edited by Christopher S. Butler, John H. Connolly, Richard A. Gatward, and Roel M. Vismans, 60–77. Amsterdam: IFOTT, University of Amsterdam.

Bye, Dorothea, Dolores Pushkar, and Michael Conway. 2007. "Motivation, Interest, and Positive Affect in Traditional and Nontraditional Undergraduate Students." *Adult Education Quarterly* 57 (2): 141–58.

Cain, Kathleen Shine. 2011. "From Comfort Zone to Contact Zone: Lessons from a Belfast Writing Centre." *Arts and Humanities in Higher Education* 10 (1): 67–83.

Cairns, Rhoda, and Paul V. Anderson. 2008. "The Protean Shape of the Writing Associate's Role: An Empirical Study and Conceptual Model." *Across the Disciplines* 5. Available: http://wac.colostate.edu/atd/fellows/cairns.cfm.

Capossela, Toni-Lee. 1998. *The Harcourt Brace Guide to Peer Tutoring.* Fort Worth, TX: Harcourt Brace.

Carino, Peter. 1996. "Open Admissions and the Construction of Writing Center History: A Tale of Three Models." *The Writing Center Journal* 17 (1): 30–49.

——, and Doug Enders. 2001. "Does Frequency of Visits to the Writing Center Increase Student Satisfaction? A Statistical Correlation Study—or Story." *The Writing Center Journal* 22 (1): 83–103.

Carlsen, William S. 1993. "Teacher Knowledge and Discourse Control: Quantitative Evidence from Novice Biology Teachers' Classrooms." *Journal of Research in Science Teaching* 30 (5): 471–81.

Cazden, Courtney B. 2001. *Classroom Discourse: The Language of Teaching and Learning,* 2nd ed. Portsmouth, NH: Heinemann.

Chafe, Wallace. 1994. *Discourse, Consciousness, and Time: The Flow and Displacement of Conscious Experience in Speaking and Writing.* Chicago: University of Chicago Press.

——. 2001. "The Analysis of Discourse Flow." In *Handbook of Discourse Analysis*, edited by Deborah Schiffrin, Deborah Tannen, and Heidi E. Hamilton, 673–87. Malden, MA: Blackwell.

Chang, Tzu-Shan. 2013. "The Idea of a Writing Center in Asian Countries: The Preliminary Search of a Model in Taiwan." *Praxis: A Writing Center Journal* 10 (2). Available: http://praxis.uwc.utexas.edu/index.php/praxis/article/view/102.

Chi, Michelene T. H., Miriam Bassok, Matthew W. Lewis, Peter Reimann, and Robert Glase. 1989. "Self–Explanations: How Students Study and Use Examples in Learning to Solve Problems." *Cognitive Science* 13 (2): 145–82.

——, Nicholas De Leeuw, Mei-Hung Chiu, and Christian Lavancher. 1994. "Eliciting Self–Explanations Improves Understanding." *Cognitive Science* 18 (3): 439–77.

——. 1996. "Constructing Self-Explanations and Scaffolded Explanations in Tutoring." *Applied Cognitive Psychology* 10 (7): 33–49.

——, Stephanie A. Siler, Heisawn Jeong, Takashi Yamauchi, and Robert G. Hausmann. 2001. "Learning from Human Tutoring." *Cognitive Science* 25 (4): 471–533.

Chi, Min, Kurt VanLehn, and Diane Litman. 2010. "Do Micro-Level Tutorial Decisions Matter: Applying Reinforcement Learning To Induce Pedagogical Tutorial Tactics." *Intelligent Tutoring Systems* 6094: 224–34.

Chick, J. Keith. 1996. "Safe-Talk: Collusion in Apartheid Education." *Society and the Language Classroom*, edited by Hywel Coleman, 21–39. Cambridge: Cambridge University Press.

Clark, Irene Lurkis. 1988. "Collaboration and Ethics in Writing Center Pedagogy." *The Writing Center Journal* 9 (1): 3–12.

——. 1990. "Maintaining Chaos in the Writing Center: A Critical Perspective on Writing Center Dogma." *The Writing Center Journal* 11 (1): 81–93.

——. 2001. "Perspectives on the Directive/Non-Directive Continuum in the Writing Center." *The Writing Center Journal* 22 (1): 33–58.

Clark, Kathleen F., and Michael F. Graves. 2005. "Scaffolding Students' Comprehension of Text: Classroom Teachers Looking to Improve Students' Comprehension Should Consider Three General Types of Scaffolding." *The Reading Teacher* 58 (6): 570–81.

Conklin, Kathy, and Norbert Schmitt. 2008. "Formulaic Sequences: Are They Processed More Quickly than Nonformulaic Language by Native and Nonnative Speakers?" *Applied Linguistics* 29 (1): 72–89.

Conroy, Thomas Michael, Neal Lerner, and Pamela J. Siska. 1998. "Graduate Students as Writing Tutors: Role Conflict and the Nature of Professionalization." In *Weaving Knowledge Together: Writing Centers and Collaboration*, edited by Carol Peterson Haviland, Maria Notarangelo, Lene Whitley-Putz, and Thia Wolf, 128–51. New York: Taylor & Francis.

Cooper, Bridget. 2003. "Care-Making the Affective Leap: More Than a Concerned Interest in a Learner's Cognitive Abilities." *Journal of Artificial Intelligence in Education* 13 (1): 3–9.

Coulmas, Florian. 1981. *Conversational Routine: Explorations in Standardized Communicative Situations and Prepatterned Speech*. The Hague: Mouton.

Cromley, Jennifer G., and Roger Azevedo. 2005. "What Do Reading Tutors Do? A Naturalistic Study of More and Less Experienced Tutors in Reading." *Discourse Processes* 40 (2): 83–113.

Cyphert, Dale. 2002. "Integrating Communication across the MBA Curriculum." *Business Communication Quarterly* 65 (3): 81–86.

Daniels, Harry. 2001. *Vygotsky and Pedagogy*. New York: Routledge Falmer.

Davies, Ann P., and Michael J. Apter. 1980. "Humour and Its Effect on Learning in Children." In *Children's Humour*, edited by Paul E. McGhee and Antony J. Chapman, 237–53. Chichester, England: John Wiley & Sons.

Davis, Kevin M., Nancy Hayward, Kathleen R. Hunter, and David L. Wallace. 1988. "The Function of Talk in the Writing Conference: A Study of Tutorial Conversation." *The Writing Center Journal* 9 (1): 45–51.

DeCheck, Natalie. 2012. "The Power of Common Interest for Motivating Writers: A Case Study." *The Writing Center Journal* 32 (1): 28–38.

Decuyper, Stefan, Filip Dochy, and Piet Van den Bossche. 2010. "Grasping the Dynamic Complexity of Team Learning: An Integrative Model for Effective Team Learning in Organisations." *Educational Research Review* 5 (2): 111–33.

Dinitz, Sue, and Susanmarie Harrington. 2014. "The Role of Disciplinary Expertise in Shaping Writing Tutorials." *The Writing Center Journal* 33 (2): 73–98.

Dweck, Carol S. 2007. "The Perils and Promises of Praise." *Educational Leadership* 65 (2): 34–39.

Ede, Lisa, and Andrea Lunsford. 1990. *Singular Texts/Plural Authors: Perspectives on Collaborative Writing*. Carbondale, IL: Southern Illinois University Press.

Faigley, Lester, and Stephen Witte. 1981. "Analyzing Revision." *College Composition and Communication* 32 (4): 400–414.

Fónagy, Ivan. 1961. "Communication in Poetry." *Word* 17 (2): 194–212.

Fox, Barbara. 1993. *The Human Tutorial Dialogue Project: Issues in the Design of Instructional Systems*. Hillsdale, NJ: Lawrence Erlbaum.

Franklin, Michael S., Benjamin W. Mooneyham, Benjamin Baird, and Jonathan W. Schooler. 2013. "Thinking One Thing, Saying Another: The Behavioral Correlates of Mind-Wandering While Reading Aloud." *Psychonomic Bulletin & Review* 21 (1): 205–10.

Gaskins, Irene W., Sharon Rauch, Eleanor Gensemer, Elizabeth Cunicelli, Colleen O'Hara, Linda Six, and Theresa Scott. 1997. "Scaffolding the Development of Intelligence among Children Who Are Delayed in Learning to Read." In *Scaffolding Student Learning: Instructional Approaches and Issues*, edited by Kathleen Hogan and Michael Pressley, 43–73. Albany, NY: State University of New York.

Gass, Susan M., and Alison Mackey. 2000. *Stimulated Recall Methodology in Second Language Research*. Mahwah, NJ: Lawrence Erlbaum.

Gersten, Russell, and Scott Baker. 2000. "What We Know about Effective Instructional Practices for English-Language Learners." *Exceptional Children* 66 (4): 454–70.

Gillespie, Paula. 2002. *Writing Center Research: Extending the Conversation.* Mahwah, NJ: Lawrence Erlbaum.

———, and Neal Lerner. 2008. *The Longman Guide to Peer Tutoring*, 2nd ed. New York: Pearson/Longman.

Gladstein, Jill. 2008. "Conducting Research in the Gray Space: How Writing Associates Negotiate between WAC and WID in an Introductory Biology Course." *Across the Disciplines* 5. Available: http://wac.colostate.edu/atd/fellows/gladstein.cfm.

Goffman, Erving. 1955. "On Face-Work: An Analysis of Ritual Elements in Social Interaction." *Psychiatry* 18 (3): 213–31.

———. 1959. *The Presentation of Self in Everyday Life.* New York: Doubleday.

———. 1967. *Interaction Ritual: Essays on Face-to-Face Behavior.* Garden City, NY: Aldine.

Goodwin, Charles. 2003. "Pointing as Situated Practice." In *Pointing: Where Language, Culture, and Cognition Meet*, edited by Sotaro Kita, 217–41. Mahwah, NJ: Lawrence Erlbaum.

Graesser, Arthur C., Kurt VanLehn, Carolyn P. Rosé, Pamela W. Jordan, and Derek Harter. 2001. "Intelligent Tutoring Systems with Conversational Dialogue." *AI Magazine* 22 (4): 39–51.

———, and Natalie K. Person. 1994. "Question Asking During Tutoring." *American Educational Research Journal* 31 (1): 104–37.

———, Natalie K. Person, and John Huber. 1992. "Mechanisms that Generate Questions." In *Questions and Information Systems*, edited by Thomas W. Lauer, Eileen Peacock, and Arthur C. Graesser, 167–87. Hillsdale, NJ: Lawrence Erlbaum.

———, Natalie K. Person, and Joseph P. Magliano. 1995. "Collaborative Dialogue Patterns in Naturalistic One-to-One Tutoring." *Applied Cognitive Psychology* 9 (6): 495–522.

———, William Baggett, and Kent Williams. 1996. "Question-Driven Explanatory Reasoning." *Applied Cognitive Psychology* 10 (7): 17–31.

Harris, Muriel. 1992. "Collaboration Is Not Collaboration Is Not Collaboration: Writing Center Tutorials vs. Peer-Response Groups." *College Composition and Communication* 43 (3): 369–83.

———. (1988) 2006. "The Concept of the Writing Center." Available: http://writingcenters. org/resources/starting-a-writing-cente/writing-center-concept.

Haswell, Richard H. 2005. "NCTE/CCCC's Recent War on Scholarship." *Written Communication* 22 (2): 198–223.

Hawthorne, Joan. 1999. "'We Don't Proofread Here': Re-Visioning the Writing Center to Better Meet Students' Needs." *The Writing Lab Newsletter* 23 (8): 1–6.

Henning, Teresa. 2001. "Theoretical Models of Tutor Talk: How Practical Are They?" Paper presented at the Annual Meeting of the Conference on Composition and Communication, Denver, CO. ERIC Document (ED 451569).

———. 2005. "The Tutoring Style Decision Tree: A Useful Heuristic for Tutors." *The Writing Lab Newsletter* 30 (1): 5–7.

Hidi, Suzanne, and Judith M. Harackiewicz. 2000. "Motivating the Academically Unmotivated: A Critical Issue for the 21st Century." *Review of Educational Research* 70 (2): 151–79.

———, and Pietro Boscolo. 2006. "Motivation and Writing." In *Handbook of Writing Research*, edited by Charles A. MacArthur, Steve Graham, and Jill Fitzgerald, 144–57. New York: Guilford Press.

Ho, Robert, and Sandra Mitchell. 1982. "Students' Nonverbal Reaction to Tutors' Warm/Cold Nonverbal Behavior." *The Journal of Social Psychology* 118 (1): 121–30.

Hoffman, Robert, and Susan Kemper. 1987. "What Could Reaction-Time Studies Be Telling Us about Metaphor Comprehension?" *Metaphor and Symbolic Activity* 2 (3): 149–86.

Hogan, Kathleen, and Michael Pressley. 1997. "Scaffolding Scientific Competencies with Classroom Communities of Inquiry." In *Scaffolding Student Learning: Instructional Approaches and Issues*, edited by Kathleen Hogan and Michael Pressley, 74–107. Albany, NY: State University of New York.

Holton, Derek, and David Clark. 2006. "Scaffolding and Metacognition." *International Journal of Mathematical Education in Science and Technology* 37 (2): 127–43.

Hubbuch, Susan M. 1988. "A Tutor Needs to Know the Subject Matter to Help a Student with a Paper: _Agree _Disagree _Not Sure." *The Writing Center Journal* 8 (2): 23–30.

Hunt, Kellogg W. 1965. *Grammatical Structures Written at Three Grade Levels. NCTE Research Report No. 3*. Champaign, IL: National Council of Teachers of English.

Hurlow, Marcia. 1993. "Experts with Life, Novices with Writing." In *Dynamics of the Writing Conference: Social and Cognitive Interaction*, edited by Thomas Flynn and Mary King, 62–68. Urbana, IL: National Council of Teachers of English.

Johnson, W. Lewis, Sander Kole, Erin Shaw, and Helen Pain. 2003. "Socially Intelligent Learner–Agent Interaction Tactics." In *Artificial Intelligence in Education*. Amsterdam: IOS Press.

Jones, Casey. 2001. "The Relationship between Writing Centers and Improvement in Writing Ability: An Assessment of the Literature." *Education* 122 (1): 3–20.

Juel, Connie. 1996. "What Makes Literacy Tutoring Effective?" *Reading Research Quarterly* 31 (3): 268–89.

Karpov, Yuriy V., and H. Carl Haywood. 1998. "Two Ways to Elaborate Vygotsky's Concept of Mediation." *American Psychologist* 53 (1): 27–36.

Kecskés, Istvan. 2000. "A Cognitive–Pragmatic Approach to Situation-Bound Utterances," *Journal of Pragmatics* 32 (5): 605–25.

Kelly, Spencer D., Asli Özyürek, and Eric Maris. 2010. "Two Sides of the Same Coin: Speech and Gesture Mutually Interact to Enhance Comprehension." *Psychological Science* 21 (2): 260–67.

Kiedaisch, Jean, and Sue Dinitz. 1993. "Look Back and Say 'So What': The Limitations of the Generalist Tutor." *The Writing Center Journal* 14 (1): 63–74.

Knapp, Mark L., Roderick P. Hart, and Harry S. Dennis. 1974. "An Exploration of Deception as a Communication Construct." *Human Communication Research* 1 (1): 15–29.

Korolija, Natascha, and Per Linell. 1996. "Episodes: Coding and Analyzing Coherence in Multiparty Conversation." *Linguistics* 34 (4): 799–831.

Koshik, Irene. 2010. "Questions that Convey Information in Teacher–Student Conferences." In *"Why Do You Ask?": The Function of Questions in Institutional Discourse*, edited by Alice F. Freed, and Susan Ehrlich, 159–86. Oxford: Oxford University Press.

Lafuente-Millán, Enrique. 2014. "Reader Engagement across Cultures, Languages and Contexts of Publication in Business Research Articles." *International Journal of Applied Linguistics* 24 (2): 201–23.

Lajoie, Susanne P. 2005. "Extending the Scaffolding Metaphor." *Instructional Science* 33 (5/6): 541–57.

Landis, J. Richard, and Gary G. Koch. 1977. "The Measurement of Observer Agreement for Categorical Data." *Biometrics* 33 (1): 159–74.

Langer, Judith A., and Arthur N. Applebee. 1986. "Reading and Writing Instruction: Toward a Theory of Teaching and Learning." In *Review of Research in Education, Volume 13*, edited by Ernst Z. Rothkopf, 171–94. Washington, DC: American Educational Research Association.

Latterell, Catherine G. 2000. "Decentering Student-Centeredness: Rethinking Tutor Authority in Writing Centers." In *Stories from the Center: Connecting Narrative and Theory in the Writing Center*, edited by Lynn Craigue Briggs and Meg Woolbright, 17–30. Urbana, IL: National Council of Teachers of English.

Leahy, Richard. 1990. "What the College Writing Center Is—and Isn't." *College Teaching* 38 (2): 43–48.

Lee, Lina. 2008. "Focus-on-Form through Collaborative Scaffolding in Expert-to-Novice Online Interaction." *Language Learning & Technology* 12 (3): 53–72.

Lehman, Blair, Melanie Matthews, Sidney D'Mello, and Natalie K. Person. 2008. "What Are You Feeling? Investigating Student Affective States during Expert Human Tutoring Sessions." In *Proceedings of the 9th International Conference on Intelligent Tutoring Systems*, edited by Beverly Woolf, Esma Aimeur, Roger Nkambou, and Susanne Lajoie, 50–59. Berlin: Springer.

Lepper, Mark R. 1988. "Motivational Considerations in the Study of Instruction." *Cognition and Instruction* 5 (4): 289–309.

———, Lisa G. Aspinwall, Donna L. Mumme, and Ruth W. Chabay. 1990. "Self-Perceptions and Social-Perception Processes in Tutoring: Subtle Social Control Strategies of Expert Tutors." In *Self-Inference Processes: The Ontario Symposium, Volume 6*, edited by James M. Olson and Mark P. Zanna, 217–37, Hillsdale, NJ: Lawrence Erlbaum.

———, Maria Woolverton, Donna L. Mumme, and Jean-Luc Gurtner. 1993. "Motivational Techniques of Expert Human Tutors: Lessons for the Design of Computer-Based Tutors." In *Computers as Cognitive Tools: Technology in Education*, edited by Susanne P. Lajoie and Sharon J. Derry, 75–105. Hillsdale, NJ: Lawrence Erlbaum.

———, Michael F. Drake, and Teresa O'Donnell-Johnson. 1997. "Scaffolding Techniques of Expert Human Tutors." In *Scaffolding Student Learning: Instructional Approaches and Issues*, edited by Kathleen Hogan and Michael Pressley, 108–44. Albany, NY: State University of New York.

Limaye, Mohan R. 1988. "Buffers in Bad News Messages and Recipient Perceptions." *Management Communication Quarterly* 2 (1): 90–101.

———. 1997. "Further Conceptualization of Explanation in Negative Messages." *Business Communication Quarterly* 60 (2): 38–50.

Litowitz, Bonnie E. 1993. "Deconstruction in the Zone of Proximal Development." In *Contexts for Learning: Sociocultural Dynamics in Children's Development*, edited by Ellice A. Forman, Norris Minick, and C. Addison Stone, 184–96. New York: Oxford University Press.

Locker, Kitty O. 1999. "Factors in Reader Responses to Negative Letters: Experimental Evidence for Changing What We Teach." *Journal of Business and Technical Communication* 13 (1): 5–48.

Louwerse, Max M., and Heather Hite Mitchell. 2003. "Toward a Taxonomy of a Set of Discourse Markers in Dialog: A Theoretical and Computational Linguistic Account." *Discourse Processes* 35 (3): 199–239.

Lunsford, Andrea. 1991. "Collaboration, Control and the Idea of a Writing Center." *The Writing Center Journal* 12 (1): 3–10.

Lwin, May O., Maureen Morrin, and Aradhna Krishna. 2010. "Exploring the Superadditive Effects of Scent and Pictures on Verbal Recall: An Extension of Dual Coding Theory." *Journal of Consumer Psychology* 20 (3): 317–26.

Macedonia, Manuela, Karsten Müller, and Angela D. Friederici. 2011. "The Impact of Iconic Gestures on Foreign Language Word Learning and Its Neural Substrate." *Human Brain Mapping* 32 (6): 982–98.

Mackiewicz, Jo. 2004. "The Effects of Tutor Expertise in Engineering Writing: A Linguistic Analysis of Writing Tutors' Comments." *IEEE Transactions on Professional Communication* 47 (4): 316–28.

———. 2005. "Hinting at What They Mean: Indirect Suggestions in Writing Tutors' Interactions with Engineering Students." *IEEE Transactions on Professional Communication* 48 (4): 365–76.

———. 2006. "Functions of Formulaic and Nonformulaic Compliments on Interactions About Technical Writing." *IEEE Transactions on Professional Communication* 49 (1): 12–25.

———. 2007. "Compliments and Criticisms in Book Reviews about Business Communication." *Journal of Business and Technical Communication* 21 (2): 188–215.

———, and Isabelle Thompson. 2013. "Motivational Scaffolding, Politeness, and Writing Center Tutoring." *The Writing Center Journal* 33 (1): 38–73.

———, and Kathryn Riley. 2003. "The Technical Editor as Diplomat: Linguistic Strategies for Balancing Clarity and Politeness." *Technical Communication* 50 (1): 83–94.

Maclellan, Effie. 2005. "Academic Achievement: The Role of Praise in Motivating Students." *Active Learning in Higher Education: The Journal of the Institute for Learning and Teaching* 6 (3): 194–206.

Maheady, Larry. 1998. "Advantages and Disadvantages of Peer-Assisted Learning Strategies." In *Peer-Assisted Learning*, edited by Keith J. Topping and Stewart W. Ehly, 45–65, Mahwah, NJ: Lawrence Erlbaum.

Malouff, John M., Alexsandra Calic, Catherine M. McGrory, Rebecca L. Murrell, and Nicola S. Schutte. 2012. "Evidence for a Needs-Based Model of Organizational-Meeting Leadership." *Current Psychology* 31 (1): 35–48.

Mansfield, Scott. 2013. "Making the Most of Drop-in Tutoring." In *The Tutoring Book: Fall 2013 Edition*, edited by CSUS (California State University Sacramento) University Reading and Writing Center Tutors. Available: www.csus.edu/writingcenter/writingcenter/Tutoring_Book_Fall_2013.pdf.

Margolis, Howard. 2005. "Increasing Struggling Learners' Self-Efficacy: What Tutors Can Do and Say." *Mentoring & Tutoring: Partnership in Learning* 13 (2): 221–38.

Marti, Leyla. 2006. "Indirectness and Politeness in Turkish–German Bilingual and Turkish Monolingual Requests." *Journal of Pragmatics* 38 (11): 1836–69.

Matsumoto, Yoshiko. 1988. "Reexamination of the Universality of Face: Politeness Phenomena in Japanese." *Journal of Pragmatics* 12 (4): 403–26.

Mayer, Richard E. 1999. "Multimedia Aids to Problem-Solving Transfer." *International Journal of Educational Research* 31 (7): 611–23.

McNeil, Nicole M., Martha W. Alibali, and Julia L. Evans. 2000. "The Role of Gesture in Children's Comprehension of Spoken Language: Now They Need It, Now They Don't." *Journal of Nonverbal Behavior* 24 (2): 131–50.

Meetings Expert, The. 2013. Available: www.themeetingsexpert.com.

Mehan, Hugh. 1979. *Learning Lessons: Social Organization in the Classroom*. Cambridge, MA: Harvard University Press.

Mercer, Neil. 2010. "The Analysis of Classroom Talk: Methods and Methodologies." *British Journal of Educational Psychology* 80 (1): 1–14.

Merrill, Douglas C., Brian J. Reiser, Michael Ranney, and J. Gregory Trafton. 1992. "Effective Tutoring Techniques: A Comparison of Human Tutors and Intelligent Tutoring Systems." *Journal of the Learning Sciences* 2 (3): 277–305.

——, Brian J. Reiser, Shannon K. Merrill, and Shari Landes. 1995. "Tutoring: Guided Learning by Doing." *Cognition and Instruction* 13 (3): 315–72.

Meyer, Debra K., and Julianne C. Turner. 2002. "Discovering Emotion in Classroom Motivation Research." *Educational Psychologist* 37 (2): 107–14.

Moon, Rosamund. 1998. *Fixed Expressions and Idioms in English.* Oxford: Clarendon Press.

Murphy, Christina. 1989. "Freud in the Writing Center: The Psychoanalytics of Tutoring Well." *The Writing Center Journal* 10 (1): 13–18.

——, and Steve Sherwood. 2011. *The St. Martin's Sourcebook for Writing Tutors*, 4th ed. Boston, MA: Bedford/St. Martin's.

Murphy, Susan Wolff. 2006. "'Just Chuck It: I Mean, Don't Get Fixed on It': Self Presentation in Writing Center Discourse." *The Writing Center Journal* 26 (1): 62–82.

Myers, Greg. 1989. "The Pragmatics of Politeness in Scientific Articles." *Applied Linguistics* 10 (1): 1–35.

Nassaji, Hossein, and Gordon Wells. 2000. "What's the Use of 'Triadic Dialogue'?: An Investigation of Teacher–Student Interaction." *Applied Linguistics* 21 (3): 376–406.

North, Stephen M. 1984. "The Idea of a Writing Center." *College English* 46 (5): 433–46.

Novick, David G., Oscar D. Andrade, and Nathaniel Bean. 2009. "The Micro-Structure of Use of Help." In *Proceedings of the 27th ACM International Conference on Design of Communication*, 97–104. New York: ACM.

Nystrand, Martin, Jeffrey Wielmelt, and Stuart Greene. 1993. "Where Did Composition Studies Come From?" *Written Communication* 10 (3): 267–333.

Paivio, Allan. 1986. *Mental Representations: A Dual Coding Approach.* New York: Oxford University Press.

——. 2007. *Mind and Its Evolution: A Dual Coding Theoretical Approach.* Mahwah, NJ: Lawrence Erlbaum.

Pajares, Frank. 2003. "Self-Efficacy Beliefs, Motivation, and Achievement in Writing: A Review of the Literature." *Reading and Writing Quarterly* 19 (2): 139–58.

——, and Gio Valiante. 2006. "Self-Efficacy Beliefs and Motivation in Writing Development." In *Handbook of Writing Research*, edited by Charles A. MacArthur, Steve Graham, and Jill Fitzgerald, 158–70. New York: Guilford.

Papagno, Costanza, and Giuseppe Vallar. 2001. "Understanding Metaphors and Idioms: A Single-Case Neuropsychological Study in a Person with Down Syndrome," *Journal of the International Neuropsychological Society* 7 (4): 516–28.

Patton, Michael. 2001. *Qualitative Research and Evaluation Methods*, 3rd ed. Thousand Oaks, CA: Sage.

Pea, Roy D. 2004. "The Social and Technological Dimensions of Scaffolding and Related Theoretical Concepts for Learning, Education, and Human Activity." *The Journal of the Learning Sciences* 13 (3): 423–51.

Pemberton, Michael. 2010. Introduction to "The Function of Talk in the Writing Center Conference: A Study of Tutorial Conversation." *The Writing Center Journal* 30 (1): 23–26.

Person, Natalie K., Arthur C. Graesser, Joseph P. Magliano, and Roger J. Kreuz. 1994. "Inferring What the Student Knows in One-to-One Tutoring: The Role of Student Questions and Answers." *Learning and Individual Differences* 6 (2): 205–29.

——, Roger J. Kreuz, Rolf A. Zwaan, and Arthur C. Graesser. 1995. "Pragmatics and Pedagogy: Conversational Rules and Politeness Strategies May Inhibit Effective Tutoring." *Cognition and Instruction* 13 (2): 161–88.

Piazza, Roberta. 2002. "The Pragmatics of Conducive Questions in Academic Discourse." *Journal of Pragmatics* 34 (5): 509–27.

Pinnell, Gay Su, Carol A. Lyons, Diane E. DeFord, Anthony S. Bryk, and Michael Seltzer. 1994. "Comparing Instructional Models for the Literacy Education of High-Risk First Graders." *Reading Research Quarterly* 29 (1): 8–39.

Porter, Felicia Lincoln. 1991. "An Examination of Consultant–Student Discourse in a Writing Center Conference." *Penn Working Papers* 7 (2): 93–108. ERIC Document (ED 341250).

Prior, Suzanne M., Kimberley D. Fenwick, Katie S. Saunders, Rachel Ouellette, Chantell O'Quinn, and Shannon Harvey. 2011. "Comprehension after Oral and Silent Reading: Does Grade Level Matter?" *Literacy Research and Instruction* 50 (3): 183–94.

Pryor, Susie, Avinash Malshe, and Kyle Paradise. 2013. "Salesperson Listening in the Extended Sales Relationship: An Exploration of Cognitive, Affective, and Temporal Dimension." *Journal of Personal Selling and Sales Management* 33 (2): 185–96.

Puntambekar, Sadhana, and Roland Hübscher. 2005. "Tools for Scaffolding Students in a Complex Learning Environment: What Have We Gained and What Have We Missed?" *Educational Psychologist* 40 (1): 1–12.

Putnam, Ralph T. 1987. "Structuring and Adjusting Content for Students: A Live and Simulated Tutoring of Addition." *American Educational Research Journal* 24 (1): 13–48.

Roehler, Laura R., and Danise J. Cantlon. 1997. "Scaffolding: A Powerful Tool in Social Constructivist Classrooms." In *Scaffolding Student Learning: Instructional Approaches and Issues*, edited by Kathleen Hogan and Michael Pressley, 6–42. Albany, NY: State University of New York.

Ronesi, Lynne. 2009. "Theory In/To Practice: Multilingual Tutors Supporting Multilingual Peers: A Peer-Tutor Training Course in the Arabian Gulf." *The Writing Center Journal* 29 (2): 75–94.

Rosé, Carolyn, Dumisizwe Bhembe, Stephanie Siler, Ramesh Srivastava, and Kurt VanLehn. 2003. "The Role of Why Questions in Effective Human Tutoring." In *Proceedings of Artificial Intelligence in Education* 13: 55–62.

Rourke, Liam, Terry Anderson, D. R. Garrison, and Walter Archer. 2000. "Methodological Issues in the Content Analysis of Computer Conference Transcripts." *International Journal of Artificial Intelligence in Education* 11. Available: http://iaied.org/pub/951.

Rowe, Meredith L., Rebecca D. Silverman, and Bridget E. Mullan. 2013. "The Role of Pictures and Gestures as Nonverbal Aids in Preschoolers' Word Learning in a Novel Language." *Contemporary Educational Psychology* 38 (2): 109–17.

Ryan, Leigh, and Lisa Zimmerelli. 2010. *The Bedford Guide of Writing Tutors*, 5th ed. Boston, MA: Bedford/St. Martin's.

Saldaña, Johnny. 2013. *The Coding Manual for Qualitative Researchers*, 2nd ed. Thousand Oaks, CA: Sage.

Schiffrin, Deborah. 1987. *Discourse Markers*. Cambridge: Cambridge University Press.

Scholfield, Phil. 1995. *Quantifying Language: A Researcher's and Teacher's Guide to Gathering Language Data and Reducing It to Figures*. Clevedon, England: Multilingual Matters.

Schulz, Marion, and Daniela Schmidt. 1993. "Yes/No Questions with Negation: Towards Integrating Semantics and Pragmatics." In *Proceedings of the 16th German Conference on Artificial Intelligence*, edited by Hans Jürgen Ohlbac, 247–54. Berlin: Springer.

Scollon, Ron, Suzanne Wong Scollon, and Rodney H. Jones. 2012. *Intercultural Communication: A Discourse Approach*, 3rd ed. Malden, MA: Wiley–Blackwell.

Severino, Carol. 1992. "Rhetorically Analyzing Collaboration(s)." *The Writing Center Journal* 13 (1): 53–64.

Shamoon, Linda K., and Deborah H. Burns. 1995. "A Critique of Pure Tutoring." *The Writing Center Journal* 15 (2): 134–52.

Sherwood, Steve. 1993. "Humor and the Serious Tutor." *The Writing Center Journal* 13 (2): 3–12.

Sloan, Phillip J. 2013. "Are We Really Student-Centered? Reconsidering the Nature of Student 'Need.'" *Praxis: A Writing Center Journal* 10 (2). Available: http://praxis.uwc.utexas.edu/index.php/praxis/rt/printerFriendly/133/html.

Smith, Heather, and Steve Higgins. 2006. "Opening Classroom Interaction: The Importance of Feedback." *Cambridge Journal of Education* 36 (4): 485–502.

Smith, Sara W., and Andreas H. Jucker. 2000. "*Actually* and Other Markers of an Apparent Discrepancy between Propositional Attitudes of Conversational Partners." In *Pragmatic Markers and Propositional Attitudes*, edited by Gisle Andersen and Thorstein Fretheim, 207–38. Philadelphia, PA: John Benjamins.

Stadler, Stefanie Alexa. 2011. "Coding Speech Acts for Their Degree of Explicitness." *Journal of Pragmatics* 43 (1): 36–50.

Stone, C. Addison. 1993. "What Is Missing in the Metaphor of Scaffolding." In *Contexts for Learning: Sociocultural Dynamics in Children's Development*, edited by Ellice A. Forman, Norris Minick, and C. Addison Stone, 169–83. New York: Oxford University Press.

———. 1998. "The Metaphor of Scaffolding: Its Utility for the Field of Learning Disabilities." *Journal of Learning Disabilities* 31 (4): 344–64.

Tan, Bee-Hoon. 2011. "Innovating Writing Centers and Online Writing Labs Outside North America." *Asian EFL Journal* 13 (2): 391–418. Available: www.asian-efl-journal.com/PDF/Volume-13-Issue-2-Tan.pdf.

Thompson, Isabelle. 2009. "Scaffolding in the Writing Center: A Microanalysis of an Experienced Tutor's Verbal and Nonverbal Tutoring Strategies." *Written Communication* 26 (4): 417–53.

———, Alyson Whyte, David Shannon, Amanda Muse, Kristen Miller, Milla Chappell, and Abby Whigham. 2009. "Examining Our Lore: A Survey of Students' and Tutors' Satisfaction with Writing Center Conferences." *The Writing Center Journal* 29 (1): 78–106.

———, and Jo Mackiewicz. 2014. "Questions in Writing Center Tutoring." *The Writing Center Journal* 33 (2): 37–70.

Thonus, Terese. 1999a. "Dominance in Academic Writing Tutorials: Gender, Language Proficiency, and the Offering of Suggestions." *Discourse & Society* 10 (2): 225–48.

———. 1999b. "How to Communicate Politely and Be a Tutor, Too: NS-NNS Interaction and Writing Center Practice." *Text* 19 (2): 253–79.

———. 2001. "Triangulation in the Writing Center: Tutor, Tutee, and Instructor Perceptions of the Tutor's Role." *The Writing Center Journal* 22 (1): 59–82.

———. 2002. "Tutor and Student Assessments of Academic Writing Tutorials: What Is 'Success'?" *Assessing Writing* 8 (2): 110–34.

Tienken, Christopher, Stephanie Goldberg, and Dominic DiRocco. 2010. "Questioning the Questions." *Education Digest: Essential Readings Condensed for Quick Review* 75 (9): 28–32.

Trimbur, John. 1987. "Peer Tutoring: A Contradiction in Terms." *The Writing Center Journal* 7 (2): 21–28.

Tuleja, Elizabeth A., and Anne M. Greenhalgh. 2008. "Communicating across the Curriculum in an Undergraduate Business Program: Management 100–Leadership and Communication in Groups." *Business Communication Quarterly* 71 (1): 27–43.

Turner, Keri Martha. 2002. "An Analysis of *You Know* in Face-to-Face Interaction." PhD diss., University of Louisiana at Lafayette. ProQuest (3057549).

Van Lancker, Diana. 2001. "Is Your Syntactic Component Really Necessary?" *Aphasiology* 15 (4): 343–406.

Van Lancker-Sidtis, Diana, and Gail Rallon. 2004. "Tracking the Incidence of Formulaic Expressions in Everyday Speech: Methods for Classification and Verification." *Language & Communication* 24 (3): 207–40.

VanLehn, Kurt, Arthur C. Graesser, G. Tanner Jackson, Pamela Jordan, Andrew Olney, and Carolyn P. Rosé. 2007. "When Are Tutorial Dialogues More Effective Than Reading?" *Cognitive Science* 31 (1): 3–62.

———, Stephanie Siler, Charles Murray, Takashi Yamauchi, and William B., Baggett. 2003. "Why Do Only Some Events Cause Learning during Human Tutoring?" *Cognition and Instruction* 21 (3): 209–49.

Vygotsky, Lev S. 1978. *Mind in Society: The Development of Higher Psychological Processes.* Cambridge, MA: Harvard University Press.

———. 1987. *Thinking and Speech.* In *L. S. Vygotsky, Collected Works, Volume 1,* edited by Robert W. Rieber and Aaron S. Carton, 239–85. Translated by Norris Minick. New York: Plenum Press.

Walton, Douglas N. 1988. "Question-Asking Fallacies." In *Questions and Questioning,* edited by Michael Meyer, 195–221. Berlin: De Gruyter.

Wanzer, Melissa Bekelja, Ann Bainbridge Frymier, Ann M. Wojtaszczyk, and Tony Smith. 2006. Appropriate and Inappropriate Uses of Humor by Teachers. *Communication Education* 55 (2): 178–96.

———, Ann B. Frymier, and Jeffrey Irwin. 2010. "An Explanation of the Relationship between Instructor Humor and Student Learning: Instructional Humor Processing Theory." *Communication Education* 59 (1): 1–18.

Waring, Hansun Zhang. 2005. "Peer Tutoring in a Graduate Writing Centre: Identity, Expertise, and Advice Resisting." *Applied Linguistics* 26 (2): 141–68.

Wells, Gordon. 1999. *Dialogic Inquiry: Toward a Sociocultural Practice and Theory of Education.* Cambridge: Cambridge University Press.

Welsh, Nancy. 1993. "From Silence to Noise: The Writing Center as Critical Exile." *The Writing Center Journal* 14 (1): 3–15.

Wilcox, Brad. 1994. "Conferencing Tips." *The Writing Lab Newsletter* 18 (8): 13.

Willerton, Russell. 2007. "Writing White Papers in High-Tech Industries: Perspectives from the Field." *Technical Communication* 54 (2): 187–200.

Williams, James D., and Seiji Takaku. 2011. "Help Seeking, Self-Efficacy, and Writing Performance among College Students." *Journal of Writing Research* 3 (1): 1–18.

Williams, Jessica. 2004. "Tutoring and Revision: Second Language Writers in the Writing Center." *Journal of Second Language Writing* 13 (3): 173–201.

Wittwer, Jörg, and Alexander Renkl. 2008. "Why Instructional Explanations Often Do Not Work: A Framework for Understanding the Effectiveness of Instructional Explanations." *Educational Psychologist* 43 (1): 49–64.

Wolcott, Willa. 1989. "Talking It Over: A Qualitative Study of Writing Center Conferencing." *The Writing Center Journal* 9 (2): 15–29.

Wood, David, and David Middleton. 1975. "A Study of Assisted Problem-Solving." *British Journal of Psychology* 66 (2): 181–91.

———, and Heather Wood. 1996. "Vygotsky, Tutoring, and Learning." *Oxford Review of Education* 22 (1): 5–17.

———, Heather Wood, and David Middleton. 1978. "An Experimental Evaluation of Four Face-to-Face Teaching Strategies." *International Journal of Behavioral Development* 1 (2): 131–47.

———, Jerome S. Bruner, and Gail Ross. 1976. "The Role of Tutoring in Problem Solving." *Journal of Child Psychiatry and Psychology* 17 (2): 89–100.

Wray, Alison. 2002. *Formulaic Language and the Lexicon.* Cambridge: Cambridge University Press.

———, and Michael R. Perkins. 2000. "The Functions of Formulaic Language: An Integrated Model." *Language & Communication* 20 (1): 1–28.

Yelland, Nicola, and Jennifer Masters. 2007. "Rethinking Scaffolding in the Information Age." *Computers & Education* 48 (3): 362–82.

Yu, Kyong-Ae. 2004. "Explicitness for Requests Is a Politer Strategy than Implicitness in Korean." *Discourse and Cognition* 11 (1): 173–94.

———. 2011. "Culture-Specific Concepts of Politeness: Indirectness and Politeness in English, Hebrew, and Korean Requests." *Intercultural Pragmatics* 8 (3): 385–409.

Zawacki, Terry Myers. 2008. "Writing Fellows as WAC Change Agents: Changing What? Changing Whom? Changing How?" *Across the Disciplines* 5. Available: http://wac.colostate.edu/atd/fellows/zawacki.cfm.

Zimmerman, Barry J. 1998. "Academic Studying and the Development of Personal Skill: A Self-Regulatory Perspective." *Educational Psychologist* 33 (2/3): 73–86.

———. 2001. "Theories of Self–Regulated Learning and Academic Achievement: An Overview and Analysis." In *Self-Regulated Learning and Academic Achievement: Theoretical Perspectives*, 2nd ed., edited by Barry J. Zimmerman and Dale H. Schunk, 1–37. Mahwah, NJ: Lawrence Erlbaum.

———. 2008. "Investigating Self-Regulation and Motivation: Historical Background, Methodological Developments, and Future Prospects." *American Educational Research Journal* 45 (1): 166–83.

———, and Anastasia Kitsantas. 1999. "Acquiring Writing Revision Skill: Shifting from Process to Outcome Self-Regulatory Goals." *Journal of Educational Psychology* 91 (2): 241–50.

———, and Anastasia Kitsantas. 2007. "A Writer's Discipline: The Development of Self-Regulatory Skill." *Writing and Motivation*, edited by Suzanne Hidi and Pietro Boscolo, 51–69. Boston, MA: Elsevier.

Ziv, Anver. 1979. *L'Humour en Education: Approche Psychologique.* Paris: Éditions Sociales Françaises.

INDEX

Printed by PGSTL